RUNNING
MICROSOFT. WORKS

RUNNING
MICROSOFT WORKS

CHARLES RUBIN

Microsoft PRESS

PUBLISHED BY
Microsoft Press
A Division of Microsoft Corporation
One Microsoft Way
Redmond, Washington 98052-6399

Library of Congress Cataloging-in-Publication Data

Rubin, Charles, 1953–
    Running Microsoft Works / Charles Rubin.
        p.   cm.
    ISBN 1-55615-246-9 : $19.95
    1. Integrated software.   2. Microsoft Works (Computer program)
  I. Title.
  QA76.76.I57R83   1990
  005.369--dc20   89-14406
                                    CIP

Printed and bound in the United States of America.

1 2 3 4 5 6 7 8 9 MLML 4 3 2 1 0

Distributed to the book trade in Canada by General Publishing Company, Ltd.

Distributed to the book trade outside the United States and Canada by Penguin Books Ltd.

Penguin Books Ltd., Harmondsworth, Middlesex, England
Penguin Books Australia Ltd., Ringwood, Victoria, Australia
Penguin Books N.Z. Ltd., 182-190 Wairau Road, Auckland 10, New Zealand

British Cataloging in Publication Data available

Project Editor: Barbara Olsen Browne   **Manuscript Editor:** Wally Parker
Technical Editor: Roger Shanafelt   **Acquisitions Editor:** Marjorie Schlaikjer

Contents

Introduction

This book is for people who want to learn to get the most out of Microsoft Works for MS-DOS, version 2.0. You can learn how to use Works from the program's printed and on-line documentation, but by reading this book you'll master many techniques, tips, and shortcuts that will help you use Works to its best advantage. As you learn, you'll also discover how to apply the Works Word Processor, Spreadsheet, Database, and Communications tools to data-handling tasks in your daily life.

Most computer manuals do a good job of explaining which keys to press to operate a program. The manuals and on-line documentation provided with Works are no exception. For most of us, though, knowing how a program works doesn't help much unless we also know how to apply that knowledge. Everybody knows how to use a hammer, for example, but few people know how to build a table. This book will show you not only how to use Works but also what to do with it.

Why Works Works

The original version of Works for MS-DOS quickly became a best-selling program because it was both easy to use and powerful. Many software programs sacrifice ease of use for power, but Microsoft Works 2.0 offers most of the power that most people need for most of the things they do, and it does so in a way that's easy to learn and understand.

There are, of course, a lot of fancy features that Works doesn't have, but if you're a typical computer user you'll rarely miss them. And if, after a while, you find that one of the Works tools just doesn't have the power you need, you can always buy a more sophisticated word processor, spreadsheet, database, or communications program for that particular application and continue to use Works for your other tasks. Particularly if you're new to computers, Works is a good choice because it provides an easy and useful introduction to the four most-common computer applications in one low-cost program.

One of the major reasons people choose Works is that it combines, or integrates, four different applications. Rather than having to buy separate programs for word processing, spreadsheet and chart creation, database management, and communications, and then learn to use each of those programs, with Works you get all these tools in one program. This integration of four distinct capabilities in one program means that many of the commands in Works are the same for each tool, so you only have to learn them once. All the Works tools have the same basic interface—the way you choose commands and view or manage data on the screen is the same in every situation.

Another benefit of having four integrated application tools is that you can easily move data from one tool to another. You can work with the data using the tool that you need at the time. If you calculate a lot of numbers with the spreadsheet tool, for example, and you then want to apply some fancy formatting to them, you can easily copy the numbers to a word processor document and use that tool's formatting features.

Finally, Works is popular because the program is easy to learn. Works comes with an extensive on-line help file and the Learning Works tutorial program that you can use either to look up instructions for specific procedures or to practice procedures using simulated Works screens. You can access these facilities while you use the program. For example, you can pause and learn about word processor formatting while you work on a word processor document. By following the lessons in the Learning Works tutorial, you can learn all the basic operations of the program in just a few hours. Later, when you need help with a particular command or procedure, Works' on-line Help file is like having a Works expert beside you.

What's New About 2.0

Version 2.0 of Works responds to feedback from Works owners about extra capabilities they want in the program. When adding new features, Microsoft was careful to avoid making the program harder to use. The following are some of the new features that have been added in Works version 2.0. You'll discover other enhancements as you explore this new version of Works. In every case, Works' power has been improved without diminishing its ease of use.

General features

- You can now display up to eight overlapping windows on the screen at once.

- Works lets you preview the appearance of printed documents on the screen.

- A pop-up calculator, an appointment manager, and an alarm clock have been added to the Options menu.

- You can run other programs from inside Works and then return to the Works session as you left it.

- You can perform common MS-DOS commands from inside Works.

- Works allows you to see character styles such as boldface, italic, and underlining on the screen.

- You can save a Formatting Template for each Works tool so that all new files you open with that tool will have the custom format settings and boilerplate text (text that you can reuse) that you specify.

- Works now offers better support for color display cards, including VGA.

- Works now supports LIM 4.0 Extended Memory beyond the 640-KB limit.

Word processor features

- You can add footnotes to documents, and Works will keep track of the footnotes.

- Works allows you to format paragraphs so that they are surrounded by borders.

- You can insert invisible bookmarks in documents and then quickly jump to them later.

- Works now includes an on-line thesaurus.
- You can convert files from PC Word, Microsoft RTF, and IBM DCA formats to Works-formatted files and from Works Word Processor files to any of those formats.

Spreadsheet features

- You can fill a group of cells in the spreadsheet with a series of dates or numbers.
- Works now lets you sort spreadsheet rows on up to three columns (or sort keys).

Database features

- You can print the Form view of a database file.
- Form screens can be up to 256 lines long and can be scrolled.
- You can copy report summaries to other Works documents using the Copy command.

Communications features

- Incoming data is stored in a memory buffer so that you can scroll up through the document window to view data that is off the screen.

How to Use This Book

As mentioned, Works comes with an excellent disk-based tutorial and a large on-line help file. This book is intended to supplement these learning aids. Although many parts of the book provide step-by-step instructions for completing a procedure, you'll also find references to a section of the Help or the tutorial files to learn more on your own. Rather than reiterating the contents of the printed manual and the Help and tutorial files, this book focuses on explaining Works' concepts and techniques in a way that might make more sense to you, on anticipating questions you might have that Works' own documentation doesn't answer, and on showing you how to use Works in practical ways.

Organization of this book

The first chapter of this book is devoted to installing Works and running it. To get the program installed and running, you can follow the instructions in the pamphlet *Ten Minutes to Productivity,* which comes with Works. But Chapter 1 shows you some special ways in which to start up Works automatically when you turn on your computer. A quick primer covers the basic MS-DOS concepts and commands you'll need in order to create and use files and directories in Works.

Chapter 2 discusses basic Works techniques. You'll learn how to move around in the Works screen, choose commands, create and manage files, use the Help and tutorial files, change Works' hardware settings, use the Works Accessories (the Calculator, the Alarm Clock, and the Dial This Number accessory), and use Works' built-in macro feature. These Works techniques are explained in overview fashion; the goal is to help you understand how each one fits in with the Works program in general and with your daily use of Works. When a tutorial lesson or Help explanation would be beneficial, this book directs you to it.

The rest of the chapters deal with using the individual Works tools. You'll find several chapters each on the Word Processor, Spreadsheet, and Database. The first chapter about each tool is an overview in which you'll follow a quick series of exercises to learn the basics of using the tool. Unlike the Learning Works tutorial, these exercises emphasize a broader understanding of each tool's capabilities and how the tools relate to the rest of the program. The exercises also help you learn and practice the most efficient ways to issue commands. The second chapter in each group contains general tips for using the tool to its best advantage. The final chapter in each group is a series of business and personal projects that show you how to use Works' power to simplify your life. These projects include a form letter, a budget, an amortization table, an appointment calendar, and an expense and income tracking system.

Finally, individual chapters cover creating spreadsheet charts, using the Communications tool, and using all the Works tools together. Chapter 8, "Charting Tips," contains an overview and general tips for creating charts. Charting projects are also included in Chapter 9, "Spreadsheet and Charting Projects." Each of the other two chapters contains an overview, tips, and practical projects you can complete.

Conventions

Although you can use either the mouse or the keyboard to issue Works commands, this book assumes you will use the keyboard most of the time. In some cases, alternative methods of controlling the program with a mouse are also suggested.

Many keyboard commands in Works require that you press two keys at the same time. You must hold down either the Ctrl key or the Alt key and then press a letter key to complete the command. In the book, these keystrokes are indicated together, with a hyphen between them. For example, if you're supposed to hold down the Alt key and then press the F key, you'll be told to press Alt-F; if you're supposed to hold down the Ctrl key and then press the B key, you'll be told to press Ctrl-B.

As you use the commands on the Works menus, you must take one action to display the menu and then press a letter key to choose the command itself. To choose the Create New File command from the File menu, for example, you must first display the File menu by pressing Alt-F and then press the N key by itself to choose the Create New File command. In the book, these keystrokes are all indicated together, with hyphens between them. If you're supposed to press Alt-F and then press the C key, therefore, you'll be asked to press Alt-F-C.

Often, a section of the book will discuss how a command works without asking you to actually issue the command. Often the keys you would press to issue the command are included in parentheses for your reference. A section that explains the Copy command, for example, might include the following: "the Copy command (Alt-E-C)."

Where to go from here

To use this book, you'll need an IBM PC, PC/XT, PC/AT, PS/2, or 100% compatible computer, a copy of PC-DOS or MS-DOS version 2.0 or later, and a copy of the Microsoft Works 2.0 program. If you have never used Works before, read Chapters 1 and 2. Then focus on the chapters that describe the tool you want to learn about first.

If you have used Works before, you might want to skim Chapters 1 and 2 to pick up some new techniques for running Works, loading files, or performing other basic tasks. Then you can continue to the chapters that describe the individual tools. If you need help with a specific subject, check the index for related information.

Microsoft Works is an easy program to learn, but mastering any computer program requires some effort and concentration. You'll benefit most from this book if you can set aside an hour or so each time you want to learn something, and devote that hour exclusively to Works. Everybody makes mistakes when learning, so don't get frustrated when you do so. You cannot possibly press a key that will damage your computer while running Works, and if you're about to do something—such as erasing a file—that you might later regret, Works will alert you with clear warnings.

Although learning to use any computer program is difficult at times, it's also rewarding. Few experiences can match the satisfaction you'll get from learning something new and then using the knowledge to improve your life. You're at the beginning of such an experience now.

Installing and Running Works

Microsoft Works will run on any IBM PC, PC/XT, PC/AT, PS/2, or 100% compatible computer running PC-DOS or MS-DOS version 2.0 or later, and using either a fixed disk or one or two floppy-disk drives. It will also work with every widely used PC-compatible display adapter card, printer, and mouse. Before you can use Works on your machine, however, you must install it. Thanks to the Works Setup program and Setup disk, Works is easy to install. The procedure is explained in Appendix F of the *Microsoft Works Reference* manual. By following a few simple steps, you can have Works installed on your machine and running in a few minutes.

In this chapter, we'll take a thorough look at the installation process. You'll find out what happens during the installation so that you'll know how the Setup program and Works operate and what to do if something goes wrong. You'll also find out how to start Works and load one or more Works files at the same time and how to modify the AUTOEXEC.BAT file on your startup disk so that Works will load whenever you start your computer.

MS-DOS Basics

Before you can begin using Works properly, you need to understand some basics about MS-DOS, the operating system that manages files and programs on every IBM PC and PC-compatible computer. You're probably eager to dive into Works, but if you take a few minutes to learn some fundamental MS-DOS techniques and concepts now, you'll save yourself a lot of frustration and head-scratching later. This section will tell you enough to get Works installed and running, but you should also study the MS-DOS tutorial that most likely came with your computer. Trying to run a computer without knowing MS-DOS is like trying to drive a car without knowing the traffic laws: You can do it, but the situation can get sticky.

Your computer is only an inert hunk of hardware until you insert an MS-DOS disk and turn on the computer. When you turn on the computer, a built-in set of instructions (stored in one of the computer's memory chips) tells the computer to look for an MS-DOS disk in one of the disk drives. If your computer doesn't find MS-DOS, you'll see a message on the screen telling you so.

If you have only floppy-disk drives in your computer system, you'll need to insert an MS-DOS disk before you turn on the computer in order for MS-DOS to start up properly. If you have a hard disk, MS-DOS will load from the hard disk when you turn on the power, provided the floppy-disk drive is empty.

After your computer locates and loads MS-DOS, your screen displays a command prompt, like this:

A>

The letter in the prompt indicates the current disk drive, which is the drive from which the MS-DOS program was loaded. In most computers that are MS-DOS–compatible, the first (the left-most or upper-most) floppy-disk drive is designated as drive A. The second (the right-most or lower-most) floppy-disk drive is designated as drive B. The hard-disk drive is called drive C.

Along with disk drive names, you'll also find named subsections, called directories, on any disk. When you first prepare (or format) a floppy disk for use with MS-DOS, for example, the root directory represents all the space on the disk. If the disk is in the A drive, the root directory is designated as A:\. You can think of the backslash mark (\) as the name of the root directory. Exactly as you can subdivide the space in a file drawer with labeled folders, you can subdivide a disk directory into named subdirectories. A subdirectory name can be up to eight characters long, and it is always identified at the MS-DOS prompt with a backslash mark that separates it from other directories. A subdirectory called BUDGETS on the disk in drive A, therefore, would be referenced by the name *A:\BUDGETS*.

To run a program, format a disk, copy a file, erase a file, or perform any other system activity, you must type the correct command at the MS-DOS prompt and then press the Enter key on your keyboard. You usually need to type only the program's name to run a program. MS-DOS assumes that any command you type will refer to the current drive and directory showing at the prompt, so if you type the name of a program in drive B when the prompt reads *A>*, MS-DOS won't be able to find and load the program because MS-DOS will be looking for the program on drive A. Unless you know you want to work with a file located in the current directory, you must type the directory name along with the name of the program or command.

To change the current disk drive from the MS-DOS prompt, you simply type the new drive name followed by a colon. If you loaded MS-DOS from drive A and the current prompt is *A>*, for example, and you wanted to work with files on a disk in drive B, you would type *b:* and press the Enter key to change to drive B. If you were at the *C>* prompt and you wanted to change to the \DATA subdirectory on the hard disk, you would type *cd \data* (*cd* is the MS-DOS command to change the current directory). You can also tell MS-DOS to look on a different disk and run a certain program there at the same time. If you were at the *A>* prompt and you wanted to run the Start program from the root directory of a disk in drive B, you would type *b:\start*. MS-DOS would find the program on drive B and run it.

Navigating among directories to locate files and programs and creating new directories in which to store groups of files are fundamental MS-DOS activities. Other common tasks include formatting blank floppy disks, listing the files in a directory, copying files, renaming files, and erasing files. The following are some examples of basic MS-DOS commands and their functions. The command listings include the MS-DOS prompt so that you can see the current directory name.

BASIC MS-DOS COMMANDS

Command	*Description*
A>*b:\start*	Run the Start program from the root directory on the disk in drive B.
C>*cd \data*	Change the current directory to C:\DATA.

(continued)

BASIC MS-DOS COMMANDS *continued*

Command	Description
A>*dir*	List all the files in the current directory on drive A.
C>*mkdir \budget*	Make a new directory called BUDGET in the current directory of drive C.
C>*erase \budget\fall89*	Erase the file FALL89 from the subdirectory \BUDGET in the current directory of drive C.
B>*ren report q1rept*	Rename the file REPORT on drive B to Q1REPT
B>*copy report c:\data*	Copy the file REPORT from the current directory on drive B to the directory \DATA on drive C.

These examples give you an idea of how to structure MS-DOS commands. MS-DOS isn't sensitive to whether you use uppercase or lowercase letters in commands, but it is particular about spaces in commands. If you don't include the spaces between the parts of the commands shown above, you'll get an error message. For more information about MS-DOS commands, check the MS-DOS manual that came with your copy of MS-DOS, or see *Running MS-DOS* by Van Wolverton, also published by Microsoft Press.

Installing Works

Works comes on eight 5¼-inch or four 3½-inch floppy disks (depending on which package you buy) that contain the following:

- The Works program

- Dictionary and Thesaurus files

- Help files

- Printer, mouse, and display card drivers

- Other miscellaneous files

Microsoft has made the process of installing these files painless through the Setup program on the Works Setup disk. These are the steps you take:

1. Turn on your computer and boot MS-DOS. (If you don't have a hard disk, insert an MS-DOS disk in drive A and then turn on the computer.)

2. Insert the Works Setup disk in drive A.

3. Type *setup*, and then press the Enter key. Works starts the Setup program. (If you have a hard disk and the A drive is not the current drive, type *a:\setup* instead.)

4. Answer the questions displayed on your screen, and insert the appropriate Works disks as instructed. (Answer the questions by pressing the Up arrow key or Down arrow key to highlight the answer you want and then pressing the Enter key to select the highlighted answer.)

As you go through the Setup program, you'll answer questions and follow directions to perform the following tasks:

■ Choosing the hard-disk, directory, or floppy-disk drive on which you'll install a working copy of Works

■ Copying the Works program, Help, dictionary, thesaurus, and miscellaneous files either on your hard disk or on a set of floppy disks

■ Selecting and copying a video card driver onto your hard disk or working floppy disk so that Works can be displayed on your monitor using all the capabilities of the particular video display card installed in your computer

■ Selecting a printer driver and copying it onto your hard disk or working floppy disk so that Works can print documents using all of the capabilities of your printer (or printers)

■ Selecting a mouse driver and copying it onto your hard disk or working floppy disk so that you can control Works with your mouse if you have one

Although you can create a working copy of Works without using the Setup program by copying all the necessary files onto your working disk, it's simpler to use the Setup program. A working copy of Works includes many different files, and it's easy to overlook some of the necessary ones if you copy them yourself. Let's look at the setup tasks a little more closely to see what really goes on and why.

Choosing a disk and a directory

Before it presents you with any options, the Setup program scans your computer system and tries to determine your hardware setup. It checks to see how many disk drives your system has, what kind of video card is installed, and whether a printer is connected to a parallel printer port.

Your first Setup task is to select a disk drive for the new copy of Works that will be installed:

- If you have a floppy-disk system, select either drive A or drive B. The Setup program asks you to insert as needed formatted blank floppy disks on which to install a copy of Works.

- If you have a hard disk, select drive C. The Setup program copies the necessary Works files to a directory on drive C so that you can run the program from there.

The Works program is really several separate files that are loaded at various times as you use Works. When all the necessary files are stored on your hard disk, these program files will load much more quickly and you'll be able to get your work done faster. If you're running Works from floppy disks, the program asks you to insert a different floppy disk at times, such as when you check a document's spelling, so that the program can access the extra files it needs in order to continue.

When you copy Works onto a hard disk, the Setup program asks you to name a directory in which to store the program files. After you type a directory name, the Setup program creates the directory if it doesn't already exist and then stores all the Works files there. It's more convenient to store all the Works files in their own directory so that they're not mixed in with files from MS-DOS or with other programs on your hard disk.

Typically, you'll want to name your directory WORKS—the name the Setup program proposes. If you want to type a new name, delete the proposed directory name by pressing the Backspace key five times, and then type the new name. MS-DOS directory names can be up to eight characters long.

After you begin using Works, you'll want to create other directories in which to store your data files on your hard disk. It's better to separate data files from program files on your hard disk because separating them will make it easier to find and work with the data files later. You can use the Create Directory option in the File Management command's dialog box to create additional directories on your hard disk or floppy disk. (See Chapter 2 for more information.)

If you have only floppy-disk drives in your system, it's best to install a copy of Works on a new set of disks and then to store your original Works disks in a safe place because floppy disks can be damaged in a variety of ways. You can then use the copy of the program in your daily work. If your working copy becomes damaged, you can always make another copy from the originals.

When running Works from floppy disks, you'll want to store your data files separately from the program. It will be easier to find and select your data files if they're stored on their own floppy disks rather than jumbled together with Works program files on the same disk.

Choosing a video card

After you select a disk and (if necessary) name a directory, the Setup program copies the main Works program files into that directory. Next, you're asked to specify which video card is installed in your system. You'll see a list of video cards on the screen. Press the Down arrow key to highlight the card you want to select from this list, and then press the Enter key to select the card.

The Setup program attempts to determine which video card is installed when it initially examines your system. When it displays the list of video cards, the Setup program highlights the card you appear to have installed in your system. If you know that a different card is installed, select the correct card. If you aren't sure which card is installed, press the Enter key to select the card that the Setup program proposes.

After you choose a video card, Setup asks you to choose whether you would like Works to run in Text mode or in Graphics mode. In Text mode, Works runs faster. In Graphics mode, Works can display special formats on your screen (such as italics and boldface) exactly as they will appear when you print. Later, you can choose the Works Settings command from the Options menu to change this setting and see which mode you prefer.

Next, the screen displays four bars in different colors or shades (depending on which card you selected). The Setup program asks you to choose an option based on which colors or intensities you see on your screen. Choosing an option helps the Setup program fine-tune Works to display text and graphics as well as possible using your video card.

Choosing printers

To print a Works document on a printer, you must install the proper printer driver file on the same disk or in the same directory as your working copy of Works. The Works package comes with dozens of printer driver files for various brands and models of printers.

When running the Setup program, you can choose drivers for more than one brand and model of printer. No matter how many drivers you select, the Setup program copies them to your working copy of Works. When you have more than one printer driver installed in Works, you can use Works' Printer Setup command to select the driver you want to use. (See Chapter 2 for more information about the Printer Setup command.)

After you choose a printer, you're asked to indicate where the printer is connected. The Setup program highlights the first parallel printer port, LPT1, as the likely printer port because it's the most common. If you know your printer is using a different parallel port, however, or if your printer has a serial interface and is therefore using one of your computer's COM ports, you must choose the correct port here. For information about these printer issues, see the manuals that came with your computer and your printer. You will also find information about these topics in *Running MS-DOS* by Van Wolverton, also published by Microsoft Press.

If you make a mistake on this screen and choose the wrong port, you can always correct your error by using the Printer Setup command after you start running Works. (See the Printer Setup command in Chapter 2.) If the printer you use isn't listed as an option, choose the Can't Find My Printer option from the printer listbox. The Setup program lists a telephone number that you can call at Microsoft to order a driver for your printer.

Copying the Learning Works tutorial

Works comes with an excellent computer-based training program called Learning Works. The Setup program gives you the option of installing this tutorial on the Works Help menu so that you can access the tutorial lessons at any time while you're running Works. As you'll see in Chapter 2, Learning Works is a great way to learn the basics of every Works tool. It's handy to have these lessons available while you're running the Works program so that you can quickly learn new procedures or brush up on those you haven't used for awhile.

If you don't install the tutorial on your working copy of Works, you'll have to run it from floppy disks when you need it. On the other hand, the Learning Works tutorial takes up over a megabyte of disk space, and you might not want to use that much storage space if you feel you won't ever need the tutorial. The choice is yours.

Specifying the country

After you specify whether you want the Tutorial installed, Setup begins copying the appropriate files to the target drive and directory you specified earlier. You will need to insert several disks into drive A during this process. After several minutes, Setup asks what country you live in so that Works will use the right conventions and will understand what kind of keyboard you are using with your computer. If you choose USA, for example, Works will use the United States Currency symbol ($). Again, if you change your mind, you can use Works' Settings command on the Options menu to change this setting.

Copying the mouse driver

If you don't have a mouse for your computer, you don't need to install a mouse driver. If you want to use a mouse and your computer does not already have a mouse driver installed, you'll need to let the Setup program know by selecting Yes when prompted and then pressing the Enter key. Setup also modifies the CONFIG.SYS and AUTOEXEC.BAT files on your MS-DOS startup disk so that the new mouse driver can be accessed properly.

Modifying CONFIG.SYS

The Setup program might need to modify the line in the CONFIG.SYS file (found in the root directory of your MS-DOS startup disk) that specifies how many files can be open at the same time. Unless you are familiar with how the contents of the CONFIG.SYS file affect the performance of MS-DOS, select Yes, and press the Enter key.

Ending the installation

After you have made all the installation decisions, the Setup program quits and you're returned to the MS-DOS prompt. If you answered Yes to either the Mouse driver installation or Modifying the CONFIG.SYS file, you will need to reboot your machine by pressing Ctrl-Alt-D.

Next, if you have a hard disk, you need to make C:\WORKS (or the directory name you chose for it) your current MS-DOS directory. If you use floppy disks, the MS-DOS prompt will indicate drive A. In either case, do the following to start Works:

☐ Type *cd \works*, and press the Enter key. Then type *works*. The Works program loads. The Works opening screen is displayed, and you can begin working in the program.

This procedure is the one you'll follow if you want to run Works immediately after installing it using the Setup program. When you start Works in the future, you'll use a slightly different set of steps.

Starting Works Manually

Each time you start Works, you must either insert the floppy disk that contains the Works program or change the current MS-DOS directory on your hard disk to C:\WORKS (or whatever you named it) before typing *works* to start the program. If you type *works* with the wrong floppy disk inserted or if the current MS-DOS directory is not the one that contains the Works program, you'll get an error message saying that the file was not found. If you have a floppy-disk system, the complete startup procedure is this:

1. Insert an MS-DOS disk in drive A.

2. Turn on your computer. MS-DOS loads, and you see the MS-DOS prompt.

3. Remove the MS-DOS disk from drive A, and insert your Works program disk.

4. Make the WORKS directory the current directory by using the Change directory command, *cd \works*.

5. Type *works*, and press the Enter key. Works starts up.

If you have a hard disk, it's likely that the current MS-DOS directory from which you start up your computer is not the one that contains the Works program. To start Works from your hard disk each day, you'll probably need to change the current MS-DOS directory first and then start Works. These are the steps:

1. Turn on your computer. MS-DOS loads from your hard disk, and the MS-DOS prompt is displayed.

2. Type *cd \works* (or whatever you named the directory), and press the Enter key. The current directory changes, and the MS-DOS prompt now reads: C:\WORKS>.

3. Type *works*, and press the Enter key. The Works program starts up.

In some cases, you might want to load one or more files along with the Works program when you start it up. For example, if you've created an appointment calendar with the Works database, you might want to load the calendar file along with Works each time so that it will always be available as you work. You can load Works files along with the Works program by typing the filenames and locations after the Works program name. For example, suppose you want to load a database file called CALENDAR.WDB along with Works, and suppose that the file is located in the directory \DATA. Do the following after the Works directory is displayed at the MS-DOS prompt:

☐ Type *works \data\calendar.wdb*, and press the Enter key. Works and the CALENDAR.WDB file load into memory. (Again, MS-DOS doesn't care whether you use uppercase or lowercase letters in filenames and commands.)

In this case, you are telling MS-DOS to load Works from the current directory and then to load the file CALENDAR.WDB from the \DATA directory. If you start Works from a floppy-disk system, and you load MS-DOS from drive A (so the current drive shown at the MS-DOS prompt is drive A), follow these steps to load Works and the CALENDAR file:

1. Insert the Works program disk in drive A and the data disk in drive B.

2. Type *works b:\calendar.wdb*.

MS-DOS loads Works from drive A and then from drive B loads the CALENDAR.WDB file.

This technique for loading a data file isn't limited to only one file. You can load several files at one time by typing their locations and names one after the other at the MS-DOS prompt. For example, if you use a hard-disk system and want to load the files CALENDAR.WDB and REPORT.WPS from the \DATA directory, type the following, and Works loads both files:

```
works \data\calendar.wdb \data\report.wps
```

For many people, Works is the first and only program that they use throughout the day, or it's the program that they use the most. If you use a floppy-disk system, you'll want to start your computer with the MS-DOS disk in drive A and then replace the MS-DOS disk with the Works program disk. After that, you simply type *works* at the MS-DOS prompt to start the program.

If you have a hard disk, however, and if Works is the program you use first each day, you might want to change the default MS-DOS directory to \WORKS so that you can turn on your computer and type *works* to start the program. In fact, if you know you will always want to load Works from your hard disk as soon as you start up your computer, you can set up your computer to load Works when you turn it on. The next section explains how.

Starting Works Automatically from a Hard Disk

The procedure for automating the Works startup assumes that Works is installed on your hard disk. Whenever you load MS-DOS, it looks for a file on your startup disk called AUTOEXEC.BAT. This file contains instructions about how MS-DOS should display its command prompt, which directory should be made the current directory, and whether MS-DOS should load any programs for you. AUTOEXEC.BAT is stored as a text file, and it is always found in the root directory of your hard disk or MS-DOS floppy disk.

The current directory when you start your computer is normally the root directory of your hard disk, or C:\. To set up your system so that you can simply type *works* at the MS-DOS prompt (which appears when you turn on your computer) or to set up your system so that Works starts automatically when you turn on your computer, modify the AUTOEXEC.BAT file to tell MS-DOS to establish a different current directory. Instead of making C:\ the current directory on startup, you want MS-DOS to make C:\WORKS the current directory.

Opening AUTOEXEC.BAT

AUTOEXEC.BAT is stored on disk as a text file, so you can open it with the Microsoft Works word processor, make the changes you want, and then save it back to the same place on your disk. Then, the next time you start up your computer, the modified instructions will be read from the AUTOEXEC.BAT file. Here's the procedure, assuming the Works program file is located in a directory on your hard disk called \WORKS.

1. Start up your computer.

2. Type *cd \works* and press the Enter key. The current directory changes to C:\WORKS.

3. Type *works* to start the Works program. The opening Works screen is displayed, and the File menu is opened.

4. Press the O key to open an existing file. Works displays a dialog box in which you can select the location and name of the file you want to open, like this:

5. You want to open the AUTOEXEC.BAT file, so you must type the name of the directory in which the file is located, followed by the filename itself: Type *c:\autoexec.bat*, and press the Enter key.

   You can open text files with the Works word processor, spreadsheet, or database tool. When Works finds the text file you want to open, it displays a dialog box that asks whether you want to open the text file as a word processor, spreadsheet, or database document. The Word Processor option is selected.

6. Press the Enter key to open the file as a word processor document. Works opens the file and displays it in a new word processor document window, as shown in Figure 1-1 on the following page.

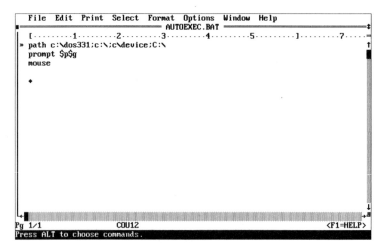

Figure 1-1.
New word processor document window.

Later in this book, you'll read more about using the word processor and its document window. For now, we'll follow some specific steps to modify the file.

Modifying AUTOEXEC.BAT

Modifying the AUTOEXEC.BAT file involves adding new instructions to it so that MS-DOS will know to change your current directory and, if you like, load Works when you start your computer.

Your AUTOEXEC.BAT file most likely contains different commands from those shown in Figure 1-1. For instance, if you do not have a mouse installed, the *mouse* command would not be displayed on the third line of the file. Also, the prompt command shown on the second line might be different. The *prompt pg* command makes the prompt appear in a specific and informative way. For instance, up until now, the default prompt was *C>* if you have a hard disk. The *pg* parameter tells MS-DOS to display not only the drive but also the current directory at the prompt. For example, if the current directory were the \WORKS directory on the C drive, the prompt would be *C:\WORKS>*. This book assumes that you have this prompt command in your AUTOEXEC.BAT file and also that you have a mouse installed.

Follow these steps to modify the AUTOEXEC.BAT file:

1. Hold down the Ctrl key and the End key at the same time. Doing so moves the cursor to the end of the text in the document.

2. Press the Enter key. Doing so moves the cursor down to the next line in the document.

You are now ready to type some new instructions in the file. If you want to add the commands shown in Figure 1-1, you can do that here by typing the command shown and then pressing the Enter key. If you want to change this file so that the current directory shown at the prompt after you boot MS-DOS is C:\WORKS, type *cd \works*. If changing the current directory shown at the MS-DOS prompt is all you wanted to do, you've finished typing new text. Skip the next two steps, and proceed to the next section, "Saving the changes."

If you want Works to start up whenever you turn on your computer, you'll have to add a command to start the program:

1. Press the Enter key to move the cursor to the line below your new *cd \works* command.

2. Type *works*. (Don't type the period.)

If you've typed the instructions for changing the current directory and starting Works, your screen now looks like this:

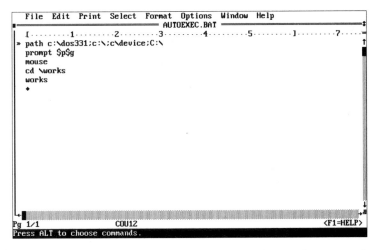

Now that you've typed the new instructions, you're ready to save the file onto your disk.

Saving the changes

Whenever you open a disk file, make changes to it, and then save the file with the same name in the same disk location, the old version of the file is replaced with the new version. This is what we want to do now.

◻ Press Alt-F-S to choose the Save command. Works saves the changed version of the file onto the same place on the disk.

Now you've replaced the old AUTOEXEC.BAT file with a new version that contains the extra instructions. When you start your computer, MS-DOS will read the instructions in the AUTOEXEC.BAT file and perform them one by one. Because you added new instructions at the end of the file to change the current directory to \WORKS and (if you chose this option) to start the Works program, these instructions will be carried out whenever you start your computer.

If you ever decide you don't want the \WORKS directory to be the current directory at startup or that you don't want MS-DOS to start Works for you, open the AUTOEXEC.BAT file, delete the two added lines of instructions, and save the file again.

Changing the Works Setup

As time goes by, you might acquire a new printer, mouse, or video card for your computer, and you'll want Works to take full advantage of it. Every time you change your hardware setup, you need to modify your working copy of Works to take advantage of the changes. Exactly as you used the Setup program to install a working copy of Works in the first place, you must use Setup to make any changes to that working copy.

To make changes using Setup:

1. Insert the Setup disk in drive A.

2. Type *a:\setup* to start the program. The screen displays a dialog box that asks whether you want to create a new Works installation or modify an existing one.

3. Select the option to modify an existing Works installation. You'll see a dialog box that asks you to identify the disk drive where you want to modify the installation.

4. Press the Down arrow key to select the disk drive in which your Works program is installed.

If you choose drive A or drive B, you'll be prompted to insert the appropriate program disk as needed, depending on which setup option you want to modify. If you choose drive C, you'll be prompted to enter the name of the directory that contains your installed copy of Works.

After you identify the copy of Works that you want to modify, the screen displays a list of the setup procedures, including selecting a video card, selecting a text printer or a chart printer, specifying the presence of a mouse (if not already installed), and copying the Works tutorial on your disk.

5. Press the Down arrow key to select Yes when Setup presents the option that you want to modify, and then press the Enter key. Works displays that setup option as it appeared during the initial installation.

6. Choose the new video card, printer, or other setup option, and then press the Enter key. The Setup program makes the selected modification to your installed copy of Works, and then redisplays the list of setup procedures on your screen.

7. Press the Down arrow key to select Yes when another setup option is presented to modify, or choose the last option on the list, Cancel Setup, which exits the Setup program without making the changes you requested.

If you modify the video card selection, Setup replaces the current video card driver with the new one. If you choose to modify the printer, you select another printer driver to add to the existing printer drivers you've already installed. After you exit the Setup program, you're again at the MS-DOS prompt. You can restart Works, and the new setup options you chose will be activated.

This concludes our look at installing and running Works. Let's move on to Chapter 2 and the basics of using Works.

Basic Works Techniques

Before you begin using each of the Works tools, you'll need to learn some basic techniques for using the program in general. In this chapter, we'll look at the fundamentals that are common to using every Works tool. These basics include:

- Using the Works interface
- Using on-line help
- Working with files
- Changing Works' hardware settings
- Using accessories
- Using macros

Each of these procedures is covered in detail in both the *Microsoft Works Reference* manual and in the on-line Help and tutorial files. In this chapter you'll practice using the procedures. You'll develop a broader understanding of how they work in the context of the entire Works program and of how to handle these tasks in the easiest or fastest ways.

Using the Works Interface

The appearance of the Works screen and the elements of the screen that let you control the program are called the Works interface. Whenever you're using Microsoft Works, several elements of the Works interface are displayed on the screen at all times. Let's open a new word processor document and look at a typical screen.

1. Press Alt-F-N to choose the Create New File command from the File menu. Works displays a dialog box in which you can choose the type of new document you want to create.

2. Press the W key to choose a new word processor document. Works displays a new word processor document on the screen, as in Figure 2-1.

3. Press Alt-F again to display the File menu.

This screen now includes the interface features that are common to every screen in Works.

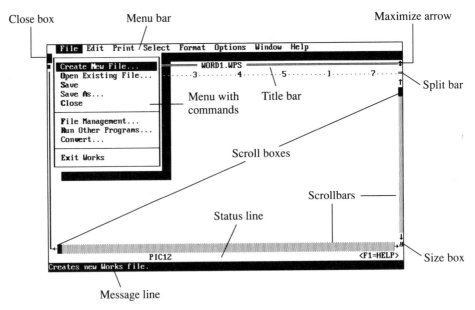

Figure 2-1.
A typical Works screen.

Every Works screen has a menu bar at the top, a message line at the bottom, and a status line above the message line.

- The menu names showing in the menu bar change, depending on whether you have a document open and, if so, whether it's a word processor, spreadsheet, database, or communications document.

- The commands showing on the displayed menu let you perform specific program functions.

- The message line at the bottom of the screen suggests which key you should press next to issue a command or provides a brief description of what the currently selected command does.

- The status line shows the cursor's current location in a document (which is the current page number of a word processor document, for example, or which is the active cell of a spreadsheet) and which function key to press to display the introduction to Works' Help facility. This line will also show other information specific to the Works document you're working on, such as the font size and style in a word processor document or how many records are contained in a database file.

These interface features let you issue program commands or get information about what you're doing in Works.

Works windows

Some interface elements shown in Figure 2-1 appear only when you have a word processor, spreadsheet, database, or communications document open. Each time you open a document, Works opens a window on the screen in the area between the menu bar and the status line. You can have up to eight different documents open at one time in Works. When you open each document, its window is stacked on top of the windows of any other open documents. To activate a particular document, you choose its name from the Window menu, and that document's window moves to the top of the stack of open windows so that you can work on it. (If part of the window you want to work with is showing behind the currently active one, you can also click on that part of the window with the mouse to activate it and bring it to the top of the stack.) Only one document window can be active at a time in Works.

A window always starts at a certain size and in a certain place, but you can move a window around on the screen and make it larger or smaller. You can control the size and location of a window by using either the keyboard or the mouse. Each window also has interface features that let you control which part of a document is displayed in it at any given time. Every window has the following:

- A title bar, which shows the name of the document

- A close box, which you can click using a mouse to close the window

- A maximize arrow, which you can click using the mouse to change the size of a window quickly

- A split bar that lets you split a window into two parts, each of which can be independently scrolled so that you can view two different parts of a document on the screen at one time

- Scroll bars and scroll boxes, which let you use the mouse to display different parts of a document

- A size box, which lets you use a mouse to change the size of a window

This window system was designed with a mouse in mind, but you can also control any window setting with the keyboard by using the commands on the Window menu. Let's use the keyboard now to resize the open word processor window:

1. Press Alt-W-S to choose the Size command from the Window menu. Works highlights the window border, and the SIZE indicator appears in the status line at the bottom of the screen.

2. Press the Up arrow key five times. Each time you press the Up arrow key, the highlighted window border becomes shorter.

3. Press the Left arrow key five times. The window border becomes narrower.

4. Press the Enter key to confirm the new window size.

We could return the window to its full size by choosing the Size command again and pressing the Down and Right arrow keys five times each. But the Window menu has another command that you can use to change the size of a window from full size to a smaller size you have set, and back again:

1. Press Alt-W-X to choose the Maximize command from the Window menu. The window immediately expands to full size.

2. Press Alt-W-X again. The window shrinks to the smaller size you just set.

3. Press Alt-W-X again to return the window to full size.

You can also move the window around on the screen by using the Move command. Again, the window border is selected, and you can move the whole window left, right, up, or down by pressing the arrow keys. When you have more than one window open, the Arrange command changes the sizes of all the open windows and arranges them so that you can see part of every window at the same time. Finally, the Split command lets you divide the window vertically or horizontally so that you can view two (or four) different parts of a document on the screen at the same time.

Often a document will contain more information than can be displayed in one screen window. To view other information in the file, scroll the window up, down, left, or right. Using the keyboard, you can press the Page Up or Page Down keys to scroll the screen up or down. (For a complete list of keyboard navigation keys, press Alt-H-K to choose the Keyboard topic from the Help menu.) If you have a mouse, you can click in the scroll bars to scroll up, down, left, or right, one screen at a time. You can click on the scroll arrows to scroll one line or one character at a time, or you can drag the scroll boxes to move greater distances in a document. (See ''Controlling Works'' later in this chapter for descriptions of mouse clicking and dragging.)

Menus, commands, and dialog boxes

You can initiate any operation you want to perform in Works with a menu command. If you have a mouse, Works lets you display any menu by pointing to its name in the menu bar and clicking the left mouse button. If you're using the keyboard, press the Alt key to activate the menu bar and then type the letter key from a menu name to display that menu. When you press the Alt key, the letter key for each menu is highlighted. After a menu is displayed, you select a command by pressing the letter key for the command (these are also highlighted on your screen), by pointing to the command with the mouse and clicking the left mouse button, or by using the Up or Down arrow keys and pressing the Enter key.

Some commands, such as Save, execute immediately when you choose them and require no further action from you. If a command requires several steps, the message line at the bottom of the screen prompts you with information about which step to take next. Other commands offer you more than one option for accomplishing a task. These command names are always followed by an ellipsis (...) on the menus, and choosing them always displays dialog boxes, such as the Format Indents & Spacing dialog box shown in Figure 2-2.

When a dialog box is displayed, you can select options using either the keyboard or the mouse. From the keyboard, press the Alt key and the key letter for the option you want to choose, or press the Tab key to advance the cursor to the next set of options. In a few cases in which only a handful of options are available in a dialog box (as in the dialog box that appears when you choose the Create New File command from the File menu), you can simply press the letter key alone without the Alt key. (If you're not supposed to press the Alt key, Works will beep at you.) If you have a mouse, you can simply click on the options you want to select.

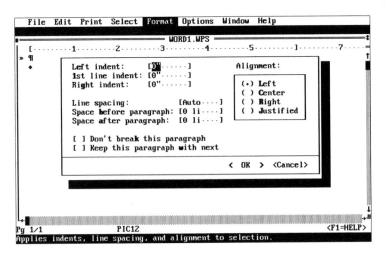

Figure 2-2.
Dialog boxes contain several options.

Most dialog boxes have a Cancel option that you press to tell Works to put the dialog box away without choosing any options and an OK button that you press to tell Works to accept the options you've chosen and put the dialog box away. Usually, the OK option in the dialog box is outlined with highlighted brackets. When a dialog box option is outlined with highlighted brackets, you can choose it simply by pressing the Enter key.

You might get into the habit of pressing the Enter key whenever you finish typing a line of text, but be careful with dialog boxes: Sometimes you will enter text, such as a filename, but you won't want to press the Enter key yet. You might want to choose other options in the dialog box, and pressing the Enter key will close the dialog box and accept the current options. Be sure you don't press the Enter key when you're in a dialog box until you've chosen all the options you want.

Controlling Works

You can manipulate windows, open or create documents, and issue Works commands using either the keyboard or the mouse. Each of these devices has its own strengths, weaknesses, and shortcuts.

Using the keyboard is the fastest way to choose commands from menus because most often your hands are already on the keys. To choose options from a dialog box using the keyboard, press either Alt and the highlighted letter key of the option you want, or, in some cases, only the highlighted letter key. For more information about using the keyboard to control Works, choose the Keyboard command from the Help menu (Alt-H-K).

Using the mouse is the fastest way to change the size of windows, move windows, or select multiple options in dialog boxes. Using the mouse is also a faster way to select text.

The mouse displays a pointer on the screen (either a highlighted rectangle or an arrow, depending on whether your screen is set for text or graphics mode), and the pointer moves as you move the mouse device on your desk. You'll use three basic mouse techniques:

- Clicking, which is moving the pointer to a specific place and then pressing and quickly releasing the mouse button. To try clicking, point to a menu name on the Works screen and click the mouse button: The menu appears, showing a list of commands. You use clicking primarily to select dialog box options and to move the cursor, cell, or field selection position on the screen. (If your mouse has two buttons, press the left-hand button. The left-hand button is what is meant by "mouse button." In this book, references to the right-hand button will always mean the "right mouse button"; it produces other effects, as we'll see.)

■ Dragging involves pointing to an object on the screen, holding down the mouse button, moving the pointer as you hold down the mouse button, and then releasing the button after you move the object to its new location. You use dragging to change the size or position of document windows. You also use dragging to select several characters, words, or lines of word processor text or to select several cells or fields in a spreadsheet or database.

■ Double-clicking is clicking two times, quickly. This maneuver is a shortcut that lets you select a dialog box option and exit the dialog box at the same time. For example, if you use the keyboard to select a filename in the Open Existing File dialog box, you must then press the Enter key to tell Works to open the file. If you're using the mouse, you can simply point to the filename in the list and double-click: Works opens the file.

Depending on the Works tool you're using, these mouse maneuvers let you select text or data in different ways. (In word processor documents, for example, clicking in the left margin next to a line of text selects that whole line.) As you read on in this book, you'll see explanations of several additional mouse shortcuts. As an alternative, try experimenting on your own with double-clicking. You can't hurt anything by trying it.

If you have a two-button mouse, you can use the right mouse button for additional Works functions. For example, clicking on a word in a word processor document with the left mouse button only moves the cursor to the pointer position, but clicking on a word with the right mouse button selects the whole word. And, although clicking to the left of a word in a word processor line with the regular mouse button selects that line of text, clicking with the right mouse button selects the whole paragraph. Again, try using the right mouse button as you do your work in Works—you might discover some selecting shortcuts, and you can't hurt anything by trying. For more information about using the mouse, choose the Mouse command from the Help menu (Alt-H-M).

Using On-Line Help

The extensive on-line Help and tutorial facilities in Works will be a great source of quick information as you work with this program. You've already been referred to specific topics in the on-line Help file for further information about some Works procedures. You can also use the Learning Works tutorial to learn more about the Works fundamentals explained in the preceding sections. Both of these help options are available from the Help menu in Works.

The Learning Works tutorial

The Learning Works tutorial is a series of lessons you can complete to learn about the basic Works functions and how to use each Works tool. You can use the Works tutorial before you install the Works program, or you can access it from inside Works as needed. Because you can use the tutorial at any time, you can easily learn about and practice a specific group of procedures if you're not familiar with them.

If you chose the option to copy the Learning Works tutorial to your installed copy of Works, the tutorial program automatically loads when you choose the Works Tutorial command from the Help menu (Alt-H-W). If you did not choose to copy the tutorial, you'll be asked to insert the LEARNING WORKS 1 disk in order to run the tutorial from there.

Let's start up the tutorial now and take a quick tour. We'll run the tutorial from inside Works for this tour, so this exercise assumes you've already completed the Works installation with the Setup program, as described in Chapter 1.

1. Start the Works program, following the appropriate instructions in the "Starting Works Manually" section of Chapter 1.

2. Press Alt-H-W to select the Works Tutorial command from the Help menu. Works displays a screen on which you're asked to enter your first name.

3. Type your first name and press the Enter key. Works displays the Learning Works menu, like this:

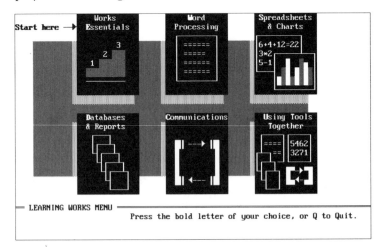

This screen shows the tutorial's six sections. You choose a section by pressing the letter key that is highlighted in the section's name:

☐ Press E to display the Works Essentials section.

After you select a tutorial section, you'll find a list of several lessons, each of which shows you how to perform a particular Works activity such as entering word processor text or entering spreadsheet formulas. The list of lessons for the Works Essentials section looks like this:

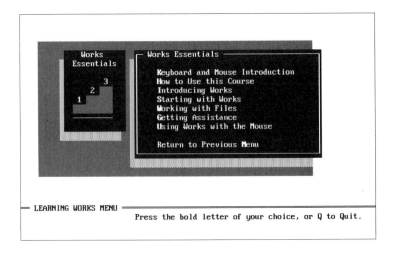

The name of each lesson contains one highlighted letter. To choose a lesson, press the letter key that matches the highlighted letter in the lesson's name:

□ Press H to choose How To Use This Course.

When you choose a lesson by pressing the key that matches the highlighted letter in the lesson's name, Works begins by describing what you'll learn in the lesson and about how long it will take to complete the lesson, like this:

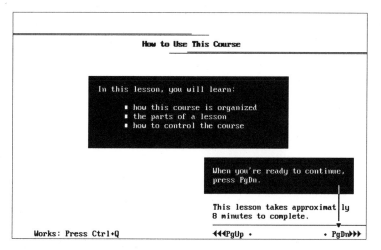

Each lesson begins with a list of concepts it will cover, followed by an overview of the lesson. Next, you'll read some descriptions of each concept and see an automated demonstration of the concept in action. Finally, you'll be asked to perform the task yourself for practice. Each lesson takes about 10 or 20 minutes to complete. After you complete a lesson, a check mark appears next to the lesson's name in the list for that section to remind you that you've completed that lesson.

If you haven't done the portion of the Works tutorial called Works Essentials, do it now. This section shows you how to use the keyboard and mouse, how to choose commands, how to work with files, and how to use the Help file as well as the Works tutorial itself. (If you've already read and worked through Chapter 1 of this book, you probably won't need to do the Starting With Works part of the tutorial.)

After you finish the tutorial's Works Essentials section, quit the tutorial. The opening Works screen returns.

The Help function

Even if you complete all the lessons in the Works tutorial, you probably won't know everything about every Works command. The Help function will help fill the gaps in your knowledge by explaining every menu command and procedure in Works. The Help function is an indexed list of topics in six different categories. These are the categories and what they cover:

WORKS HELP CATEGORIES AND CONTENTS

Category	Contents
Basic Skills	Fundamental Works techniques that are common to all the tools, including choosing commands, working with files, and changing Works settings.
Introducing The Tools	How to open new word processor, spreadsheet, database, and communications documents, and how to get more specific help about each tool.
Keyboard	The keyboard commands and navigation keys for each Works tool.
Mouse	How to use the Mouse.
Commands	An alphabetic reference to every menu command in Works. Each command name begins with the name of the menu on which the command is located.
Procedures	An alphabetic list of topics indexed by function rather than by command name. Although you would choose the Connect Connect command to read about calling another computer in the Commands category, you would select the Calling With A Modem option from the list of procedures.

You can choose from several ways to find information about a specific procedure or command with the Help function. Let's choose some topics now to see how this feature works.

□ Press either the F1 function key or Alt-H-H to select the Help Index. Works displays the Help Index dialog box, as shown in Figure 2-3.

In the Help Index dialog box you can see the six categories of information. The list at the right contains the topics in each category, and it changes, depending on which category you select. To select a category and a topic, perform the steps on the following page.

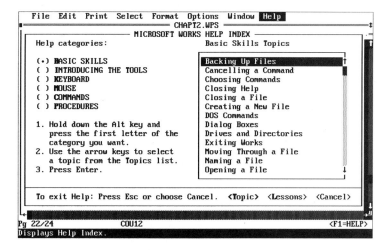

Figure 2-3.
Help Index dialog box.

1. Hold down the Alt key and press the first letter of the category name you want.

2. Press the Down arrow key to select the topic you want from the list.

3. Press the Enter key to display information about that topic.

If you have a mouse, you can click on the category name and then double-click on the topic name to display the category's information. Let's choose a topic now to see how you can move through the Help file:

1. Display the Help Index dialog box, if it isn't already showing, by pressing F1 or Alt-H-H.

2. Press the M key. The selection in the list of topics jumps to Moving Through a File. You can always jump to different places in a list of topics by pressing the first letter of the topic name. If more than one topic begins with that letter, Works selects the first topic name in alphabetic order. Then you can press the Down arrow key to select a topic name farther down the list.

3. Press the Enter key. Works displays the topic, like this:

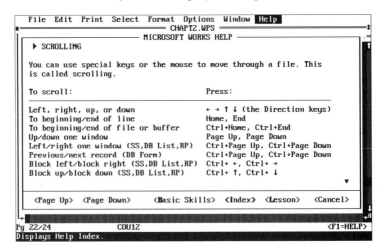

The topic name is shown at the top of the screen. To see the second page of this topic, press the Page Down key.

You can see that this topic name is Scrolling, rather than Moving Through A File, because the same screens of information are used to provide information for different topics in different categories in the Help file. For example, if you select the Creating A New File topic in the Basic Skills category, you'll see the same screen of information that you would see if you selected the File Create New File topic in the Commands category or the Creating A New File topic in the Procedures category.

The Help screens are all stored in one big file, with each screen for each topic placed one after the other. When you reach the end of a topic, you can continue to press the Page Down key to see the next topic in the Help file. In the same way, you can press the Page Up key to back up in the file and view the preceding topic.

Whenever you display topic information, different options appear at the bottom of the Help screen:

■ The Page Up and Page Down options let you move forward or backward in the Help file by clicking them with the mouse (instead of by pressing the Page Up and Page Down keys on the keyboard).

- The Basic Skills option (press Alt-B or click on it with the mouse) returns you to the Help Index dialog box and selects the Using Help topic in the Basic Skills category.

- The Index option (press Alt-I or click on it with the mouse) returns you to the Help Index screen, and the same topic that you selected earlier remains selected.

- The Lesson option (press Alt-L or click on it with the mouse) starts the Learning Works tutorial and opens a lesson that relates to the Help topic you've chosen.

- The Cancel option (press Escape or click on it with the mouse) returns you to the Works screen that was displayed before you first chose the Help Index from the Help menu.

Try choosing different categories and selecting different topics to see what kind of help is available.

Throughout this book, you'll be directed to certain topics in the Help file for further information. These references always include the name of the topic as well as the name of the category you must choose first to locate the topic name. In most cases, we'll be using the Commands or Procedures categories in the Help file.

Working with Files

Whichever Works tool you're using, you'll use the same commands on the File menu to create, save, open, and close files. Other File menu commands let you temporarily quit Works and run another program; convert files in other formats into Works' format; manage files, disks, and directories; and exit the Works program.

Creating files

If you followed the exercise at the beginning of this chapter, you've already used the Create New File command (Alt-F-N) to make a new word processor file. Every file you create begins with a generic name that indicates the Works tool you used to create it and how many new files you have created with that tool during the current Works session. If the new word processor file was the first file you created with Works this session, Works named it WORD1.WPS. The filename is shown in the title bar at the top of the document window.

Every file named by Works has a three-letter extension that identifies the Works tool that created the file. The extensions are WPS for the word processor, WKS for the spreadsheet, WDB for the database, and WCM for the communications tool.

Newly created files are stored only in your computer's active memory, so if you exit Works or shut off your computer, they can be lost. If you want to keep a file so that you can work with it later, you must save it on disk.

Opening files

When you choose the Open command from the File menu, Works displays a dialog box like this:

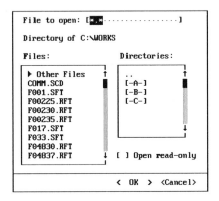

Using this dialog box, you select the name of the file you want to open and then press the Enter key.

The Directory Of line shows the directory from which you loaded Works. Because your data files will probably be stored in a different directory, you must specify the directory in which the file you want is located. To indicate a different directory, you have two options:

- If you want to open a file from a different directory but you don't want to change the current directory, you can type the directory name in front of the filename in the File To Open text box. For example, if the current directory is C:\WORKS and you want to open a file called BUDGET from the directory named BIZ, you would type \biz\budget in the File To Open box. Works would open the file, but the current directory would remain C:\WORKS.

■ If you're opening the first of a series of files that are all located in a different directory, however, you can change the current directory itself. Either type only the directory name in the File To Open box (type *biz* to switch to the \biz directory, for example) or use the Directories box. To change the current directory using the Directories box:

1. Press Alt-I to move the cursor to the Directories box.

2. Press the Down arrow key to move the cursor into the list of available directories.

3. Select the disk or directory you want.

Initially, the list of directories contains only disk drive names. If you want to select a directory that's on the same disk as the current directory:

1. Select the two dots at the top of the list of disks, and press the Enter key. Works displays all the directory names at the same level as the current directory. (Usually, all your directories are on the same level in the main directory of the disk, so selecting the two dots will show you all the directories on your disk.)

2. Select the directory you want, and press the Enter key to change the current directory. The new directory name appears in the Directory Of line.

After you indicate the name of the directory from which you want to open the file, the list of files contained in that directory appears in the Files list box. You can either type the filename you want in the File To Open text box or select the filename from the Files list box.

Works lets you use three different methods to select a file from the list and open it:

■ Double-click on the filename with the mouse. Use the scrollbar to find the file if the list box contains many names.

■ Press the Down arrow key until the filename is selected, and then press the Enter key to open the file.

■ Type the first letter of the filename to select the first filename in the list beginning with that letter, and press the
Down arrow key to select the specific file you want. Then
press the Enter key. Typing the first letter of the filename
is particularly handy when the Files list box contains many
names: The selection jumps right to the group of files beginning with that letter. This way, you don't have to do so
much scrolling to find the file you want.

Saving files

Two commands on the File menu allow you to save files: Save and Save
As. When you choose the Save As command, Works displays a dialog box
similar to the Open dialog box. It lets you enter a different filename or
choose a different disk or directory in which to save the file. It also includes a few other options. When you choose the Save command to save
a file that has been saved on disk before, Works simply saves the file
again at the same location with the same name. When you create a new
file and use the Save command, however, Works presents the Save As
dialog box anyway because you must rename a new file before you save it.
The Save As dialog box looks like this:

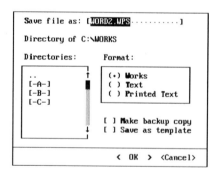

To save a file, type the name of the file in the Save File As box. If
you're saving a new file, the name that Works has given it so far is something like WORD1.WPS. Give it a name that means something to you. If
you're saving an existing file, the current filename will appear here.

The Directory Of line below the filename shows the current disk
directory. As with opening a file, the current directory might not be the
one in which you want to save the file. For example, if you start Works,

create a new file, and then choose the Save As command, the current directory shown will be the one from which you loaded Works. You should not save your data files in that directory because too many files in one directory can be confusing. To save the file in a directory other than the current one, you'll have to select a new directory.

After you type a filename and select a directory, you can save the file and exit the dialog box by pressing the Enter key. You might, however, want to choose one of the other options in this dialog box before leaving it.

The Format options let you save the file in a format that can be used by other programs. The default option here is Works, which means that if you save the file in this format, you can open the file only by using the Works tool that created it. If you choose another option, you'll be able to open the file with another Works tool or with another program entirely. (See Chapter 14 for more information.)

Choosing the Make Backup Copy option tells Works to save your file two times: one time with the usual extension (WKS, WPS, etc.) and one time with a backup extension (BKS, BPS, etc.) so that you can tell the two files apart in a file listing. Making a backup copy is a precautionary measure you can take so that you'll always have an extra copy of a file in the event that the one you normally work with gets damaged or erased. When you choose this option, Works will always save a backup copy each time you save the file.

The Save As Template option is handy when you don't like the standard format settings you get with a new Works document and you want to use different settings. In the Word Processor, for example, new documents have a 1.3-inch left margin and are single-spaced. If you change the format settings of a document to a 1-inch left margin and double-spacing and then save that document as a template, every new word processor document you create from then on will have a 1-inch left margin and will be double-spaced.

You can save only one Template document for each of the Works tools. If you save a new document as a Template when a Template already exists, the new Template settings will replace the old ones. To use this option, first select the Use Templates For option in the Works Settings dialog box. (See "Changing Works' Hardware Settings," later in this chapter.)

For more information about saving files, see the File Save As topic in the Commands category of the Help Index.

Closing files

To close a file, you can either choose the Close command (Alt-F-C) or click the mouse button on the close box in the upper-left corner of the document window. If you try to close a file that has been changed since you opened it, Works displays a dialog box that asks if you want to save the changes to the file and gives you a chance to save them.

Managing files

You might want to perform some DOS-related functions while you run Works, such as formatting a new floppy disk, making a new disk directory, or deleting a file from a disk. The File Management command (Alt-F-F) gives you access to these functions. When you choose the File Management command, Works displays a dialog box listing different file management functions, like this:

After the box is displayed, you can select a function by pressing the Down arrow key to highlight it and then pressing the Enter key, or you can double-click the function name with the mouse. After you select a function, Works displays a dialog box in which you can enter the name of the file to be copied, deleted, or renamed; the name of the directory to be created or removed; the floppy disk to be copied or formatted; or the new date and time you want to set. (Except for the disk formatting and the date and time options, the dialog box for file operations looks much like the Save As dialog box.) After you enter the correct information, press the Enter key to carry out the function. In contrast to most dialog boxes, however, the list of file-management functions doesn't disappear after you carry out an operation. You have to click the Cancel button in the box or press the Escape key to remove the list from your screen and return to the last Works screen. For more information about these functions, choose the File Management topic from the Commands category in the Help Index.

Running other programs

This command lets you exit Works temporarily and run another program. When you quit the other program, return to the DOS prompt and type *Exit*, Works starts up again and the files you had open when you last left Works will be reopened as they were.

When you choose the Run Other Programs command (Alt-F-R), Works displays a dialog box like this:

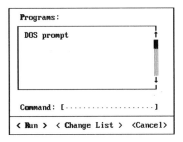

To run another program, press the Down arrow key to select the program name and then press the Enter key. Works displays a message telling you that you're about to exit the program. Press the Enter key again, and the other program runs.

When you first install Works, the DOS prompt is the only "other program" in the list. You can add new programs, however, by choosing the Change List command in this dialog box. For more information about adding or changing programs on the list, see the File Run Other Programs topic in the Commands category of the Help Index.

The Convert command on the File menu lets you convert word processing files from other popular DOS word processing programs into Works' format so that you can edit them with Works. Conversely, you can convert Works Word Processor files into formats for other DOS word processing programs. (See Chapter 14 for more details, or look at the File Convert topic in the Commands category of the Help Index.)

Changing Works' Hardware Settings

When you first select the various hardware options in the Setup program, the Works program is preset to certain default hardware settings. After Works is running, you can use a few specific commands to change some of these hardware settings.

The Works Settings command

The largest group of hardware settings you can control from inside Works is located in a dialog box that appears when you choose the Works Settings command from the Options menu:

1. Hold down the Alt key and press the O key. Works displays the Options menu.

2. Press the W key to choose the Works Settings command. Works displays the Works Settings dialog box, like this:

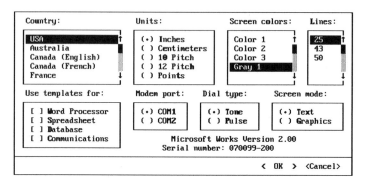

When you make changes to any of these settings, the changes take effect immediately. They apply to any document you open or create from then on, and Works keeps track of them between sessions. How some of the options appear that are displayed under the Country, Units, Screen Colors, and Lines areas in this dialog box depends on which video card you have in your computer, so your Works Settings dialog box might not exactly match the one shown in the above illustration.

Here are the various settings and how they change Works:

- The Country options select a different set of character symbols unique to the country represented. If you choose the dollar symbol ($) with the country set to UK (United Kingdom), for example, Works will produce the symbol for the British pound (£).

- The Units options tell Works which unit of measurement to use when you specify measurements for margin sizes, page sizes, indents, tabs, and other format elements. Normally, Works assumes you mean inches when you specify format measurements. If you change the Units option, however, Works will assume that the numbers you type refer to that unit of measurement.

- The Screen Colors options let you choose different colors or shades of gray to display on the screen. The effect of choosing each of these settings varies, depending on which video card you have installed. Try choosing different options to see which colors or shades are available with your video card.

- The Lines option lets you select a new number of lines to be displayed on the screen. The normal PC-compatible character set will display a total of 25 lines on a Works screen, including the menu names, document name, and other elements of the interface. Depending on your video card, you might be able to display 43, 50, or another number of lines. When you change this setting, Works uses a smaller-sized character to display more lines. It's useful to display more lines when you work with a large document, because you can see more of the document at a time without having to scroll the screen.

- The Use Templates For option activates the opening of a defined template for each Works tool. If you save a document when the Save as template option in the Save As dialog box is checked, the corresponding document type is checked here automatically. To deactivate the open template function, you must uncheck this option for each Works tool. (See "Saving files," earlier in this chapter, for more information.)

- The Modem Port option tells Works which of your serial communication ports to transmit data through when you use the communications tool or the Dial This Number accessory. (See "The Dial This Number accessory," later in this chapter, for more information.)

- The Dial Type option tells Works how to send telephone numbers to your modem when you use the Dial This Number accessory. Most telephone systems use the newer Tone dialing type, and that's the default option here. But, if you have a rotary dial phone, you should select the Pulse option.

■ The Screen Mode option allows Works to display formatting elements on the screen in two different ways, providing your video card can handle them. In Text mode, for example, any italic or underline formatting that you set is indicated by highlighting of the characters on the screen (when you have a monochrome monitor) or by displaying in different colors (when you have a color monitor). In Graphics mode, you would actually be able to see the italic type or underlining on the screen. Although the Graphics mode shows your formatting enhancements more faithfully, it also makes displaying text and scrolling a window a little slower.

The Printer Setup command

The Printer Setup command appears on the Print menu of every Works tool. Use this command to select a different printer brand, model, resolution, and port with which to print your documents. When you choose the Printer Setup command, Works displays a dialog box like this:

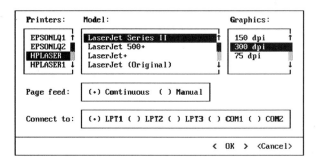

Which printer driver or printer drivers are shown in the Printers list box depends on which printer drivers you installed with the Setup program when you first installed Works. If you didn't install any printer drivers, this list contains the generic printer TTY, which tells Works to send plain, unformatted text out the printer port. (You can always install more printer drivers by running the Setup program again and modifying your installed copy of Works.)

Depending on the printer driver you select, the Model list might contain several different models. And, depending on the printer model you select, the Graphics resolution options will vary. If you plan to print or display spreadsheet charts, you'll have to be sure to choose a printer that is capable of printing charts. If you select a daisy-wheel printer, for example, Works might not be able to display or print charts.

The Page Feed option is normally set to Continuous, which means that you use either continuous paper with a dot-matrix printer or that you use a laser printer. With the Continuous option set, Works doesn't stop printing between pages. If you want to be able to insert blank pages one at a time by hand, choose the Manual option so that Works will pause after printing each page.

Finally, the Connect To option lets you choose the printer port to which you've connected your printer. The default setting is LPT1, which is the first parallel printer port in your computer. If you're using a different port, you can specify it here. As you might remember, you set the printer port during the installation process (see Chapter 1).

The Communication and Phone commands

Other hardware settings you can change from inside Works are the serial port and the dial type used by communications documents when sending commands to a modem. These settings are covered in Chapter 13.

Using Accessories

Three accessory programs are built into Works, each of which is available from the Options menu. Let's look at them briefly.

The Calculator

The calculator is an on-screen version of a pocket calculator, complete with buttons and a window to display results. You can use the calculator to do quick calculations at any time while using Works, and you can even copy the calculated results into an open document. When you choose the Calculator command (Alt-O-C), Works displays the calculator on the screen, as shown on the next page.

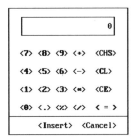

To enter numbers and arithmetic operators, press the number keys or the plus (+), minus (−), multiply (∗), or divide (/) keys on the top row of your keyboard. The result is as if you had pressed the graphic calculator keys shown on the screen. If the Num Lock key is turned on, you can use the numeric keypad keys as well. Finally, if you have a mouse, you can click directly on the calculator's graphic keys. As you type values or operators, the current result appears in the calculator window.

The three other keys on the calculator are CHS, which changes the sign of the number currently displayed in the calculator window; CL, which clears all numbers from the calculator; and CE, which clears the last number you entered.

To copy the displayed number from the calculator to another Works document, press the I key or click on the Insert command on the screen. Works copies the number from the calculator's display and inserts it at the current cursor position in your word processor, spreadsheet, database, or communications document. (Of course, if you have no open documents at the time, this command won't do anything.) For more information about the calculator, see the Options Calculator topic in the Commands category of the Help Index.

The Alarm Clock

The alarm clock lets you instruct Works to remind you of appointments. You can enter short descriptions of the appointments and set alarms to go off on any day or at any time in the future. You can choose to have an alarm go off only one time, or you can set it to go off at the same time every day, weekday, week, month, or year. Here's how to set an alarm:

1. Press Alt-O-A to choose the alarm clock accessory. Works displays the alarm window, as shown on the following page.

```
┌─────────────────────────────────────────────────────────────────┐
│ New alarm:                          Frequency:                    │
│                                    ┌─────────────────────────────┐│
│ Message: [·····················]   │(•) Only once  ( ) Daily     ││
│ Date:    [·····················]   │( ) Weekday    ( ) Weekly    ││
│ Time:    [·····················]   │( ) Monthly    ( ) Yearly    ││
│                                    └─────────────────────────────┘│
│ Current alarms:                         [ ] Suspend alarms        │
│ ┌──────────────────────────────────────────────────────────────┐ │
│ │                                                            ↑   │ │
│ │                                                           ▓   │ │
│ │                                                           ▓   │ │
│ │                                                           ▓   │ │
│ │                                                            ↓   │ │
│ └──────────────────────────────────────────────────────────────┘ │
│ 8/23/89 11:26 AM            < Set >  <Change>  <Delete>  <Done>   │
└─────────────────────────────────────────────────────────────────┘
```

2. The cursor is blinking in the Message text box. Enter a message of up to 60 characters. When you finish, press the Tab key to select the Date box.

3. The lower-left corner of the Alarm Clock dialog box shows the current date and time, as supplied by your computer's internal clock/calendar. (If these times are wrong, reset them with the File Management command. See "Managing files," earlier in this chapter.) Enter the date on which you want the alarm to go off (using the MM/DD/YY format), and press the Tab key to select the Time box.

4. Enter the time at which you want the alarm to go off. When entering the time, be sure to indicate AM or PM and use a colon, like this: *4:00 PM*.

5. Press the Tab key. The cursor moves to the Frequency options box.

6. Press the highlighted letter key for the frequency option you want to choose.

7. Press the Enter key to set the alarm. The Current Alarms box shows the alarm specifications and the message. You can then set another alarm or press Alt-D to exit the dialog box.

When the date and time for the alarm arrive, Works beeps and displays a dialog box containing the alarm message, the date and time, and three options. You can snooze an alarm (Alt-S), which tells Works to sound the alarm again in 10 minutes. You can reset the alarm (Alt-R), which causes Works to display the Alarm Clock dialog box again so that you can enter a new time or date for it. Or you can press the Enter key to choose OK, which shuts off the alarm. When you shut off an alarm that is set to go off only one time, the alarm's setting is deleted from the alarm clock's list.

If the time and date for an alarm pass while you're not running Works or when your computer is turned off, the alarm will sound the next time you start Works. For more information about alarms, see the Options Alarm Clock topic in the Commands category of the Help Index.

The Dial This Number accessory

The Dial This Number accessory lets you use Works to dial telephone numbers for you if your computer is connected to a Hayes-compatible modem. (For information about Hayes-compatible modems and connecting them to your computer, see Chapter 13.)

To prepare Works to use the dialer properly, you must set the appropriate Modem Port and Dial Type options in the Works Settings dialog box. (See "Changing Works' Hardware Settings," earlier in this chapter, for more information.) After you set up Works properly, it's easy to dial a number:

1. Open the Works document that contains the telephone number you want to dial.

2. Select the telephone number in the document.

3. Choose the Dial This Number command from the Options menu (Alt-O-D). Works dials the number and then displays a message asking you to pick up the phone. (If the speaker on your modem is turned up, you'll be able to hear Works dialing.)

If you use Works in an office in which you must dial an initial number to get an outside line, that initial number must be included in the telephone number you select. Works will dial whatever numbers are selected in your word processor, spreadsheet, or database document at the time you choose this command.

Using Macros

Macros provide a powerful way in which to automate repetitive tasks. You can record any series of keystrokes, store the series as a macro under a single keystroke command, and then play the series back later by pressing the macro command. Simple macros play an ordered series of keystrokes when you type the macro command, but you can also create macros that repeat themselves until you tell them to stop or macros that stop at a certain point and wait for you to type before they continue. You can even create macros that execute other macros.

Recording a macro

The Works macro facility is built into the program. To begin recording a macro, press Alt-/. Works displays the Macro options dialog box:

By choosing the appropriate option here, you can record a new macro, play an existing macro, temporarily skip a macro so that the macro's key doesn't activate it, delete a macro definition, change the key used to activate a macro, or turn the macro feature off. After you begin recording a macro, Works remembers every keystroke, so be sure before you begin recording that your document is exactly the way you want it and that the cursor is exactly where you want it. To begin recording a macro:

1. Press Alt-/. The Macro menu appears, and the Record Macro option is selected.

2. Press the Enter key. Works displays a macro definition dialog box, like this:

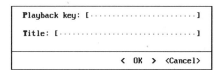

3. Press the key you want to use to activate the macro. Any key you press at this point will be entered in the Playback key text box, so be careful to press only the key you want.

In choosing a playback key for a macro, you can press any single key, or you can press the Ctrl, Shift, or Alt key in combination with another key. It's best to use the Ctrl, Shift, or Alt key in combination with another key to avoid running a macro when you don't mean to. For example, if you define a formatting macro as W, you'll run that macro every time you press the W key. Using the Alt, Ctrl, or Shift keys, though, you can come up with lots of playback key combinations that you'll probably never use in your daily work. Some key combinations, however, can't be used as playback keys. (See Appendix E of the *Microsoft Works Reference* manual for a list of keys you can use.)

4. Type a title for the macro so that you can identify it in the macros list box later.

5. Press the Enter key to begin recording. If you selected a standard letter, symbol, or function key (like W, as described above), Works displays a message asking if it's okay to redefine the key. Press the Enter key to continue.

At this point, Works begins recording the macro. The message RECORD appears at the right side of the message line. Every keystroke you press will be stored in the macro.

When you want to stop recording the macro, do the following:

1. Press Alt-/. Works displays the Macro Options dialog box again, but because you're in the process of recording a macro, its options have changed, and the End Recording option is selected, like this:

2. Press the Enter key to choose the End Recording option.
   The macro is recorded.

Correcting and editing macros

If you press the wrong key while recording a macro, you can cancel recording immediately and re-record the macro from the beginning. Or you can forge ahead, pressing the keys you need to correct the mistake. The second of the alternatives is inefficient because each time the macro runs, it repeats your mistake and the correction. But if you're recording a particularly long macro, it might be easier to make a correction than to start over from scratch.

Another option is to edit the macro. All macros you create are stored in a file called MACROS.INI in the same directory as your Works program files. The MACROS.INI file is stored as a text file, and you can open it as a word processor document. Each keystroke you make is identified inside brackets in the document. In the macro file, for example, *<back>* represents the Backspace key. The versions of every key and keyboard combination that are possible in a macro file are listed in Appendix E of the *Microsoft Works Reference* manual.

If you're adventurous, you can read the macro file, locate the keystrokes you made by mistake, and delete them from the file. In fact, you can write entire macros from scratch by entering them in the MACROS.INI file using the word processor. (For more information about editing macros, see Appendix E in the *Microsoft Works Reference* manual.)

Playing a macro

If you can remember the playback key under which you stored a macro, you can type that key and the macro will execute. As the macro plays, the word PLAYBACK will appear at the right edge of the message line. If you can't remember the playback key, you can select the Play Macro option in the Macro Options dialog box to display a list of the macros you've stored. You can then select the macro you want and press the Enter key to play it.

Other macro options

As you gain experience with macros, you'll want to use some of the other macro options. On the next page, you'll find brief descriptions of them.

- Skip Macro is the macro option you choose when you've defined the playback key for a macro and then want to use that key temporarily for its original purpose. If you define @ (Shift-2) as a macro and find that you need to type the @ sign itself at some point, for example, you can display the Macro options dialog box, choose the Skip Macro command, and then type the @ sign one time without running the macro.

- Turn Macros Off is the option you'll want to use when you have lots of macros defined, you don't want to execute any of those macros, and the work you're currently doing requires you to press a lot of predefined macro playback keys. If you've set up a lot of macros for a specific project, for example, you'll want the macros for that project to be turned on. But when you work on another project, you might want to turn off the macros so that you can use the keyboard normally, without activating any macros by accident.

- You can pause macros for either fixed or variable inputs so that the macro will pause for data entry from the keyboard. For example, you could have a macro that enters the text of a form letter up to the greeting line, pauses while you type the greeting, and then finishes entering the form letter. A fixed-input pause tells the macro to wait for a certain number of keystrokes to be entered before continuing. A variable-input pause tells the macro to wait until the Enter key is pressed before continuing so that you can enter as many characters as you want. When you finish typing, press the Enter key to play the rest of the macro.

- You can create a repeating macro by pressing the macro's own playback key at the end of the macro definition, just before you stop recording.

- You can pause a macro for a specific length of time, which is useful in a repeating macro that will continue until you tell it to stop. By inserting a pause at the end of the macro, you can gain some extra time to stop the macro between repetitions.

■ You can create nested macros, in which the definition for one macro contains the playback key for a second macro. You can either create the second macro beforehand and then press its playback key while you record the first macro or choose Nested Input from the Macro Options screen while you record the first macro. To use Nested Input, you would record the beginning part of the first macro, choose the Nested Input command from the Macro options menu, define and record the nested macro, and then finish recording the first macro.

All these advanced options are explained in detail in Appendix E of the *Microsoft Works Reference* manual.

This completes our overview of the basic Works techniques and procedures. By now, you should know enough to begin exploring the individual Works tools. If you don't feel comfortable yet with the basics of Works, choose the Works Essentials section of the Works Tutorial on the Help menu and work through the lessons.

3

Basic Word Processor Techniques

If you're new to computers, word processing is probably easier to learn than other applications because it's much like using a typewriter. Pressing keys on a typewriter produces characters on a piece of paper; typing with a word processor produces characters on the screen. The biggest advantage of using a word processor is that the text you type can be stored on a disk, recalled later, and easily changed so that you don't have to retype an entire page or an entire document whenever you make a few changes.

The Works Word Processor tool lets you create many kinds of documents, from simple notes to fancy reports. It offers all the editing and formatting features common to most word processing programs, and it includes a built-in spelling checker and thesaurus. In this chapter, you'll run through some simple examples that show how Works handles basic text-editing, formatting, and printing operations.

The Word Processor Screen

To begin, start your Works program if it isn't already running, and choose the commands to create a new word processor file:

1. Press Alt-F to display the File menu.

2. Press the N key to choose the Create New File command. The Word Processor file type is selected in the dialog box that appears. (It's the default selection.)

3. Press the Enter key to choose this file type and to display a new word processor document, as in Figure 3-1.

As with any other Works tool, the screen has a menu bar at the top, a message line at the bottom, and a status line above the message line. You'll also notice a title bar immediately below the menu bar, and scroll bars at the right edge of the screen and at the third line from the bottom of the screen. These features appear on every Works screen (see Chapter 2 for more details).

The ruler, immediately below the title bar, shows you the width of the text in your document. The brackets at the left edge of the ruler and

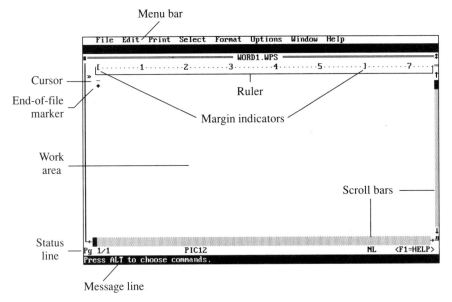

Figure 3-1.
The contents of the word processor screen.

at the 6-inch mark are the margin indicators; they define the default current line length. The area below the ruler and inside the scroll bars is the work area, where the text you type appears.

In a new document, the work area is blank except for the blinking underline character called the cursor and the diamond-shaped marker below it, which is the end-of-file marker. You can never delete the end-of-file marker or move the cursor beyond it. The cursor always indicates where text will appear when you begin typing. As you type, the cursor moves across the screen.

Entering Text

To start a document, you simply begin typing as you would on a typewriter. Type the following sentence:

Sales have been simply stunning during the past quarter at Wonder Widgets, Inc.

Text starts at the left edge of the work area and extends across the screen as you type. When the text reaches the right margin (indicated by the right bracket in the ruler), it automatically wraps down to the next line—you don't have to press the Enter key to move to the next line. This feature is called word wrapping.

Finish this paragraph by adding a few more sentences. The blinking cursor should now be in the space after the period at the end of *Inc.* Press the spacebar one time and then type the following:

Our Ypsilanti factory was flooded with orders for our new Vegi-Saver, and our established lines of kitchen and household hand appliances continued to sell well. Overall, sales were up 15% over the spring quarter of 1989. We added two more Illinois reps to our team of sales go-getters, and we prepared a new advertising campaign that is scheduled to run in the fall. Here are the highlights for the spring, 1990 quarter.

To end this paragraph, press the Enter key. The cursor moves down to the next line. Each time you press the Enter key, you place an invisible paragraph marker in your document. (You can show the invisible paragraph markers, along with space markers and tab stops, by choosing the Show All Characters command from the Options menu.)

Insert two blank lines after this paragraph to separate it from the report's next section by pressing the Enter key two more times. Then type this headline, two blank lines, and the following two paragraphs:

Spring Quarter Sales Update

We had an exceptionally good quarter, better than we would normally have expected after a brisk Christmas season. The Voyager series of self-propelled vacuum cleaners moved well. Our January price increase didn't slow things down at all: HomeCo and Vacuum City both placed large orders.

As for the Leaf Blaster, our improved muffler system has renewed demand for this unit in the Chicago suburbs, so we seem to have turned the tide back in our favor after last fall's passage of noise abatement ordinances in Elmhurst, Park Ridge, and Oak Park.

As you fill the screen with text, the text scrolls up to make room for new text at the bottom of the screen. To return to the beginning of this document, you can use the scroll bar (if you have a mouse) or move the cursor (see Chapter 2 for basic scrolling techniques). The difference is that when you use the scroll bar, you move the text up or down on the screen without changing the cursor position: You can scroll to the top of the document, and the cursor still blinks at the bottom (or wherever you last entered text), which is handy if you want to view another part of a document but continue typing where you left off. If you're typing at the bottom of a document and want to check something at the top, you can scroll up, check the text, and then begin typing again. Works will scroll back to the cursor position as soon as you begin typing.

Moving the cursor

In most cases, you'll want to move the cursor through a document rather than scroll through a document. Works has several cursor-movement keys and shortcuts to handle small and large cursor movements, as shown in the following table:

Key(s)	Moves Cursor
Right arrow	To the right one character
Left arrow	To the left one character
Ctrl-Right arrow	To the right one word
Ctrl-Left arrow	To the left one word

(continued)

Key(s)	Moves Cursor
Up arrow	To the line above
Down arrow	To the line below
Home	To the beginning of the line
End	To the end of the line
Ctrl-Home	To the beginning of the document
Ctrl-End	To the end of the document
Page Down	To the next page
Page Up	To the previous page
Ctrl-Page Up	To the top of the screen
Ctrl-Page Down	To the bottom of the screen

Try some of these commands to move the cursor around in the text you've just entered.

Editing Text

Works' editing features let you erase individual characters or whole blocks of text. You can also move a block of text to a different place in a document and use special keys to delete individual characters. But before you can delete, move, or copy a block of text, you must select it.

To change a few characters or words, it's easiest to use the Backspace or Delete key to remove the incorrect text and then insert new characters to replace it:

- The Backspace key deletes the character to the left of the cursor.

- The Delete key deletes the character at the cursor position.

Delete the word *hand* from the second sentence of your document using the Backspace key:

1. Move the cursor to the space following the word *hand*.

2. Press the Delete key five times.

Now try using the Delete key to change the percent symbol in *15%* to a word:

1. Move the cursor to the percent symbol.

2. Press the Delete key to delete the symbol.

3. Press the spacebar one time, and then type *percent*.

The Delete and Backspace keys are fine for making small changes like these. For larger changes, it's faster to select a block of text and then delete the whole block in one action.

Selecting text

When you want to work on a whole block of text, you must first select it. To select text using a mouse, hold down the mouse button and drag the pointer over the text. To select text using the keyboard, press the Extend key, which is F8, or choose the Text command from the Select menu. For this example, use the keyboard to select the last sentence in the document's first paragraph:

1. Move the cursor to the *H* in *Here*.

2. Press the F8 key. The word EXT appears in the status line, indicating that you have turned on the Extend Selection mode.

3. Use the arrow keys to move the cursor to the end of the sentence. When you move the cursor, the selection highlight extends with it, selecting the text as you go, as shown in Figure 3-2.

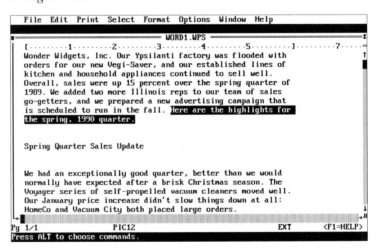

Figure 3-2.
When you select text, the text is highlighted on the screen.

You can select anything from one character to a whole document using the Extend key. In the preceding example, only the arrow keys were used to extend the selection highlight, but you can use any of the cursor-movement keys or commands to extend the selection highlight more quickly. For example, you can use the Ctrl-Right arrow key combination to extend the selection one word at a time or use the Ctrl-Page Down key combination to select everything from the cursor position to the bottom of the screen. Try some of these cursor-movement commands with the EXT mode turned on.

After you finish experimenting with the cursor-movement keys and the selection highlight, cancel the selection:

1. Press the Esc key. The EXT message disappears from the status line, but the sentence remains highlighted.

2. Move the cursor by pressing one of the arrow keys. The highlight disappears. After you cancel a selection, the selection highlight remains until you move the cursor or enter a character using the keyboard. Also, notice that the cursor position moves to the appropriate edge of the highlight, depending on which arrow key you press: If you select a paragraph, for example, pressing the Down arrow key will move the cursor to the end of the paragraph and pressing the Up arrow key will move the cursor to the top of the paragraph.

Works also lets you use the Extend key by itself to select larger blocks of text. If you press the Extend key more than one time, you can highlight a word, a sentence, a paragraph, or the whole document. The following table shows these Extend key shortcuts:

Pressing the Extend Key	Selects
One time	EXT mode
Two times	Current word
Three times	Current sentence
Four times	Current paragraph
Five times	Entire document

Try these shortcuts to get a feel for them.

After you select the text you want to work with, you can delete it, move it, copy it, or format it. Leave the formatting for the upcoming section, "Formatting Text." For now, finish editing this portion of your sample document by deleting and moving some text.

On rereading the example text, the words *simply stunning* don't seem appropriate. Use the F8 key to select the words, and then do the following to replace them with something more businesslike:

1. Move the cursor to the beginning of the word *simply*.

2. Press the F8 key. The EXT mode indicator appears in the status line.

3. Hold down the Ctrl key and press the Right arrow key two times. Work selects the two words and the space after *stunning*.

4. Press the Delete key to delete these words.

5. Type the word *excellent*, with a space after it, to replace the selection.

Along with the Delete key, the word processor's Edit menu also includes a Delete command. Depending on your keyboard skills, it might be faster to press Alt-E-D to choose the Delete command from the Edit menu than to find and press the Delete key on your keyboard.

Moving and copying text

Moving and copying text are similar operations. In both cases, you must first select the text you want to work with, choose the Move or the Copy command from the Edit menu, and then indicate where you want the text (or a copy of the text) to be placed. When you move text, you delete it from one place and insert it in another. When you copy text, you insert a copy of the selected text at a second location. Let's move a sentence in your document now:

1. Move the cursor to the beginning of the last sentence in the first paragraph.

2. Press the F8 key three times (one time to turn on the Extend Selection mode and two more times to select the entire sentence).

3. Press Alt-E to display the Edit menu.

4. Press the M key to choose the Move command. The word MOVE appears in the status line, and the message line prompts you to position the cursor where you want to place the moved text.

5. Move the cursor to the beginning of the second paragraph (so that it's under the *W* in *We*).

6. Press the Enter key. The selection moves to its new location.

If you had chosen the Copy command instead of the Move command, the sentence would have remained in its original place, and a copy of it would have appeared in the new location.

In addition to using the Edit menu to access the Move and Copy commands, you can use the F3 function key to select either command:

■ F3 chooses the Move command.

■ Shift-F3 chooses the Copy command.

When you choose a new location for moved or copied text and then press the Enter key, you insert the text. You can insert other types of data in addition to copied or moved text:

■ You can copy paragraph formats and character formats from one section of text to another.

■ You can insert special characters that tell Works to insert the current date, time, or filename in a file when that file is printed.

These special ways of copying and inserting are handled with the Insert Special command on the Edit menu. You'll see this command in action in Chapter 5. (For more information now, choose the Edit Insert Special command from the Help Index on the Help menu.)

To clear the screen and get ready for the next exercise, select the entire document and delete it. You can quickly select an entire document by choosing All from the Select menu (Alt-S-A) or by pressing the Extend key five times. For this example, use the menu keys.

1. Press Alt-S-A to choose the Select All command.

2. Press the Delete key. The screen is now clear, as it was when you started.

Formatting Text

You'll find three levels of formatting in the Works Word Processor: by character, by paragraph, and by page. Different groups of commands apply to each formatting level. The commands that affect character and paragraph formatting are on the Format menu. The commands that affect the entire page are on the Print menu.

Character and paragraph formats are so named because these commands can affect as little as one character or one paragraph. As a result, you must select the characters or paragraphs you want to format before you choose a character or paragraph formatting command. (Actually, you can "select" a single paragraph for formatting by simply moving the cursor to any place in that paragraph. You need to select paragraphs by highlighting them only when you want to format more than one.) Page formats affect whole pages, so you don't have to select anything before changing these settings.

Character formatting

When you first begin typing in a new word processor document, the text appears in Plain Text style, which is much like the text you see in any DOS program. But in Works, you can apply different styles to your text (such as boldface, italic, underlined, and superscript), and you can print text using different fonts and font sizes.

On the screen, Works highlights text that has been given different character formats so that you'll know it will appear different from other text when printed:

- Boldface characters always appear highlighted on your screen, no matter what type of display setup you're using.

- Italic and underlined characters will appear highlighted, with different intensities from each other and from boldface characters. If your computer has a color or graphics display card and you have selected the Graphics display mode with the Works Settings command, you'll be able to see actual italic and underlined type on your screen.

You can always tell which character style you have applied to text by moving the cursor to the text in question and glancing at the status line: It will show to the left of the font and size indicator a letter that corresponds to the style you've chosen, as shown in the following table:

Style	*Indicator*
Plain text	No indicator
Bold	B
Italic	I
Underline	U
Superscript	+
Subscript	=

All of the character format commands are available from the Format menu. You can also use keyboard shortcuts to apply styles. Instead of choosing the Bold command from the Format menu (Alt-T-B), for example, you can press Ctrl-B to apply that style to selected characters. For a complete list of all the keyboard shortcuts that are available for character formatting commands, choose the WP Keys topic in the Keyboard category of the Help Index on the Help Menu.

Works supplies two procedures for applying character formats. You can apply styles one at a time by choosing individual commands, or you can apply several styles or font changes at one time using the Font & Style dialog box. To examine each option, type the following three sentences:

This is **bold** text.
This is *italic* text.
This is underlined and subscript text.

Now apply the appropriate style to the first sentence:

1. Move the cursor to the first sentence.

2. Press the F8 key three times to select the sentence.

3. Press Alt-T-B to choose the Bold command. The sentence now appears in boldface on the screen, and the status line shows the B indicator, as shown on the following page.

4. Press the Esc key to cancel the Extend Selection mode.

For the second sentence, use a keyboard shortcut to apply the character style:

1. Move the cursor to the second sentence.

2. Press the F8 key three times to select the sentence.

3. Press Ctrl-I. The sentence now appears in either high-lighted type or in italics, depending on your display card and Works' display settings. The I indicator appears in the status line.

4. Press the Esc key to cancel the Extend Selection mode.

To the third sentence, apply the underlining and subscript styles to the words *underlined and subscript* at the same time. You use the Font & Style command from the Format menu:

1. Move the cursor to the *u* in *underlined* in the third sentence.

2. Press the F8 key to turn on the Extend Selection mode.

3. Hold down the Ctrl key and press the Right arrow key three times to select the words *underlined and subscript*.

4. Press Alt-T-F to choose the Font & Style command. The Font & Style dialog box appears, like this:

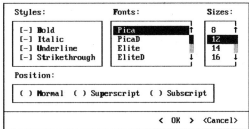

5. Press the U key to select Underline style.

6. Press the C key to select Subscript style.

7. Press the Enter key to confirm these settings. The three words in this sentence change to a different color or intensity (on nongraphics screens) or appear underlined and subscripted (on graphics screens). Both style indicators appear in the status line.

In the Font & Style dialog box, you'll also notice a list of available fonts and font sizes. Depending on which printer you have selected and on which fonts are available for that printer, you can select different fonts and sizes (as well as the other styles) for your text.

Before moving on to the next exercise, clear your screen by selecting the three sentences and deleting them.

Paragraph formatting

Paragraph formatting refers to the way text is placed on a page in terms of tabs, indents, line spacing, and alignment or justification. All these options affect the entire paragraph in which the cursor is located (or the paragraphs that are currently selected) at the time you choose a formatting option. Each paragraph can have its own format settings, but Works assumes you want to continue with the current paragraph format settings when you begin a new paragraph. To see how this formatting works, set a paragraph format or two on some sample text. Type the following sentence:

The Leaf Blaster is a portable, gas-powered blower that quickly removes unsightly leaves from your lawn, driveway, or gutter.

The text begins at the left edge of the screen and continues to the 6-inch mark, which is the default right margin. Now change the left and right indents to make this paragraph narrower:

1. The cursor should be at the end of the sentence, immediately after the period. If it isn't, position it there now.

2. Press Alt-T-A to choose the Indents & Spacing command. The Indents & Spacing dialog box appears, like this:

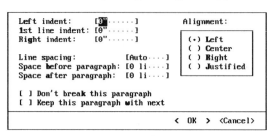

3. The cursor will be blinking in the Left Indent box. Type .5 to indicate a 0.5-inch indent.

4. Press the Tab key two times to move the cursor to the Right Indent box.

5. Type .5 to indicate a 0.5-inch indent.

6. Press the Enter key to accept these new settings. The sentence is now indented 0.5 inch from the right and left margins, like this:

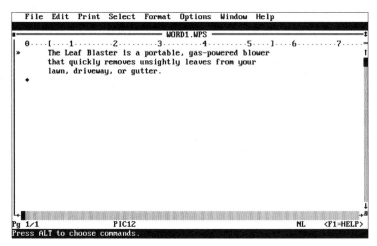

As you can see, the two brackets indicating the left indent and right indent in the ruler have moved: The left indent is now at 0.5 inch, and the right indent is now at 5.5 inches.

When you use the Left Indent setting, you specify an indent for the entire paragraph. If you want to indent only the first line of a paragraph, use the 1st Line Indent setting in the Indents & Spacing dialog box. You can also use the 1st Line Indent setting to create a hanging indent, in which the first line begins farther to the left than the rest of the paragraph. See "Indenting A Paragraph" in the *Microsoft Works Reference* manual for more information.

Now use the Indents & Spacing dialog box again. First you'll set the indents on this sentence back to normal and change the line spacing and justification:

1. Be sure the cursor is still at the end of the sentence.

2. Press Alt-T-A to choose the Indents & Spacing command. The Indents & Spacing dialog box appears.

3. Type *0* in the Left Indent box.

4. Press the Tab key two times to move to the Right Indent box, and type *0*.

5. Press the Tab key again to select the Line Spacing box, and type *2* to indicate double spacing.

6. Press Alt-R to select Right in the Alignment options box.

7. Press the Enter key to accept these settings. The sentence now appears as double spaced and right aligned.

To see how the paragraph formats are carried over from one paragraph to the next, make a new paragraph after the current one:

1. Be sure the cursor is still at the end of the sentence.

2. Press the Enter key two times to end the paragraph and to insert a blank line before the new paragraph.

3. Type the following sentence:

The Leaf Blaster weighs only 12 pounds, and its backpack harness ensures hours of effortless blowing.

As you can see, this sentence also appears as double spaced and right aligned because the paragraph formats you applied to the previous paragraph have been carried over to this one. To change the formatting for this paragraph, move the cursor to a position within the paragraph, and then choose the new format settings.

To prepare for the next exercise, first clear the screen:

1. Press the F8 key four times to select the entire paragraph.

2. Press the Delete key to delete the text.

3. Press Alt-T-N to return the paragraph format to normal.

Chapter 5 explores the line spacing, indent, and text alignment commands in more detail. For a list of keyboard shortcuts for these commands, see the WP Keys topic in the Procedures category of the Help Index.

Before you move on to page formatting, take a look at how the tab settings work in the word processor. When you first open a new word processor document, tabs are set at every 0.5-inch mark on the ruler. See for yourself: Press the Tab key three times, and the cursor moves to under the 1.5-inch mark on the ruler.

The default tabs work fine in many situations, but they have two drawbacks. First you have to live with their 0.5-inch–mark settings. Second they make it harder than necessary to move to a tab stop at the right side of the page. If you want to align text under the 5-inch mark on the ruler, for example, and you're using the default tabs, you must press the Tab key 10 times to get there. By setting your own tab stops, you not only place them exactly where you want them, but you remove all the default 0.5-inch tab stops at the same time, so you can tab directly to the position you choose.

Let's look at an example:

1. Type *Chicago* and press the Tab key three times.

2. Type *Jones* and press the Enter key.

3. Type *Detroit* and press the Tab key three times.

4. Type *Smith* and press the Enter key.

5. Type *Dayton* and press the Tab key three times.

6. Type *Brown* and press the Enter key.

You now have two columns of data, with the second column aligned under the default 2-inch tab stop. Next reset the tab stops so that the right-hand column is aligned under the 3.3-inch tab stop. Remember, because you pressed the Enter key at the end of every line, each of these lines is a separate paragraph, so you'll have to select all three lines to reset their tab stops.

1. Move the cursor to the beginning of *Chicago.*

2. Press the F8 key to turn on the Extend Selection mode.

3. Press the Down arrow key three times to select all three lines.

4. Press Alt-T-T to choose the Tabs command. The Tabs dialog box appears, like this:

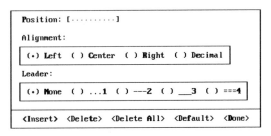

5. Type *3.3.*

6. Press Alt-I to insert the tab stop at the 3.3-inch position. An *L* appears at the 3.3-inch mark on the ruler to indicate that you've set a left-aligned tab stop there.

7. Press Alt-D to return to the document screen.

The right-hand column now appears to be left aligned at the 4-inch mark on the ruler, which might seem confusing because you just set the new tab stop at the 3.3-inch mark. Remember that when you typed the sample text, you separated the second column from the first column with three tab stops. Formatting a new tab stop for this paragraph created the effect of setting the first tab stop at the 3.3-inch mark and leaving all subsequent tab stops at the default 0.5-inch marks. As a result, what appears on the screen is the first tab stop at the 3.3-inch mark, the second at the default 3.5-inch mark, and the third at the default 4-inch mark. It is better to establish where you want to align a column prior to entering text so that you only have to press one tab stop between columns. To fix the text you typed earlier, delete the two extra tabs in each line to make the second column line up at the 3.3-inch mark.

1. Press the Esc key, and then move the cursor to the *J* in *Jones.*

2. Press the F8 key to turn on the Extend Selection mode.

3. Press the Ctrl-Left arrow key two times to select the two tab stops.

4. Press the Delete key to delete the tab stops from the text.

5. Repeat these steps for the *S* in *Smith* and the *B* in *Brown.*

Now the right column is left aligned under the 3.3-inch mark. For more information about the different types of tabs, choose the Help Index command from the Help menu, choose COMMANDS from the Help categories, and select the Format Tabs command topic. Or see the "Tabs and Tables" section in the *Microsoft Works Reference* manual. Prepare for the next exercise by selecting the three sentences and deleting them.

Page formatting

The last means of formatting in Works is at the page level, in which you choose options that determine how your text will appear on the printed page. These options include margins, page breaks, headers and footers, and page size. Because all these options have to do with how your text will look when printed, their commands are located on the Print menu. You'll learn more about what these options are on the following pages.

One of the big differences between typing at a typewriter and writing using a word processor is that with a word processor you aren't typing directly on the paper. You see text on the screen as it will print on the paper, but you can't tell where that text will appear in relation to the edges of the paper. Using the margin commands lets you tell Works where to print text in relation to the edges of the paper.

Works needs to know how large your top, bottom, left, and right page margins are to be and how large the paper is to determine where to print your lines of text on paper. The margin and paper size commands are grouped together in the Page Setup & Margins dialog box.

To see how these formatting options work, start by typing a couple of sentences on the screen:

The Leaf Blaster's whisper-quiet exhaust system conforms to all known noise abatement ordinances nationwide. You'll be the envy of every blowhard on your block with your new Leaf Blaster.

The word processor window on your screen should be set to the default margin settings, so this text appears on 6-inch lines, like this:

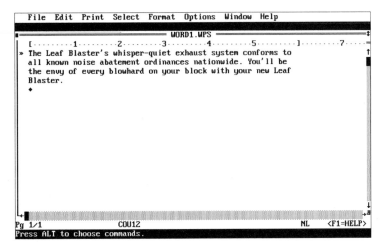

The right-margin marker in the ruler is at the 6-inch mark and the left-margin marker is at the 0-inch mark. (If your ruler doesn't have these settings, close your current word processor file without saving the changes, and open a new word processor file using the steps explained at the beginning of this chapter. Then type the sample paragraph.)

With these margin markers, you know that your lines of text will be 6 inches long and will print as you see them on the screen. But you can't tell by looking at the screen how large your left and right margins will be. To display the margin settings on the screen:

■ Press Alt-P-M to choose the Page Setup & Margins command from the Print menu. A dialog box appears:

```
Top margin:     [1"   ···]  Page length:  [11"  ···]
Bottom margin: [1"   ···]  Page width:   [8.5" ···]
Left margin:   [1.3" ···]
Right margin:  [1.2" ···]  1st page number: [1 ···]
Header margin: [0.5" ···]
Footer margin: [0.5" ···]

                        <  OK  >  <Cancel>
```

Using this box, you can enter settings for the top, bottom, left, and right margins. You can also use it to determine the header and footer margins (the distance that headers and footers will print from the top and bottom of a page), the page size, and the starting page number.

The default page size is 8.5 inches wide by 11 inches long, which is the standard size of U.S. letter paper, so you can leave that setting as it is. Also leave the 1st page number setting as it is. But go ahead and change the left-margin and right-margin settings:

1. Be sure the Page Setup & Margins dialog box is displayed. (Press Alt-P-M if it isn't.) The cursor should be blinking in the Top Margin position box.

2. Press the Tab key two times to move the cursor to the Left Margin position box. (You can also press Alt-E to move the cursor there.)

3. Type *1* to set the left margin to 1 inch.

4. Press the Tab key one time to move to the Right Margin position box.

5. Type *1* to set the right margin to 1 inch.

6. Press the Enter key to accept these settings and to return to the document screen.

Now the left and right margins are 0.5 inch narrower than before, so the right-margin marker in the ruler now appears at the 6.5-inch mark, like this:

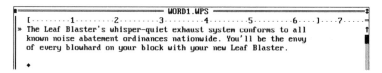

Because the right-margin marker has moved, your text lines are 0.5 inch longer and the text has been reformatted. This change occurs because the length of text lines on the screen is calculated by Works as the width of the paper (8.5) minus the total of the left and right margins (2). With the default left and right margins totaling 2.5 inches, the line length is 6 inches (8.5 − 2.5 = 6). But when you change the left and right margins so that they total 2 inches, an extra 0.5 inch of space is created on the line for text, so the line length increases to 6.5 inches.

The other two page-formatting options in Works are for headers and footers and for page breaks. Headers and footers are lines of text that appear in the same position on every page of a document. They usually contain identifying information such as the document title, section title, page number, date, author's name, and revision number. Headers and footers don't appear when you edit a document, but they do show up when you preview or print a file.

The Works Word Processor lets you create two different kinds of headers: standard headers and footers, which are limited to one line each, and header and footer paragraphs, which can contain as many lines as you like up to the length of the page. Headers appear at the top of the page above the text margin, and footers appear at the bottom of the page below the text margin, as in Figure 3-3.

```
                         Spring Sales Update - Page 1


    Sales have been simply stunning during the past quarter at
    Wonder Widgets, Inc. Our Ypsilanti factory was flooded with
    orders for our new Vegi-Saver, and our established lines of
    kitchen and household hand appliances continued to sell
    well. Overall, sales were up 15% over the spring quarter of
    1988. We added two more Illinois reps to our team of sales
    go-getters, and we prepared a new advertising campaign that
    is scheduled to run in the fall.

    Spring Quarter Sales Update
```
```
    capable of freeze-drying an entire mea-          arter.
    in less than two hours. Our team in research ha..
    slightest idea how GG has accomplished this feat, and our
    reps, particularly in the farm belt, have been experiencing
    buyer resistance from stores and chains that anticipate
    April or May shipments of the Vegi-Blaster.

    Our best bet at this point is to delay the release of the
    Vegi-Blaster by filing a trademark infringement lawsuit on
    the basis of the use of the word "Blaster" at the end of the
    name. The folks in Legal tell me that our chances of
    prosecuting such a suit successfully are slim, but the
    publicity surrounding such an action will raise the spectre
    of doubt among our potential Vegi-Saver customers, and
    hopefully bring them once again back into our camp.



    Wonder Widgets, Inc. -      Page - 1
    Spring Quarter Sales Update - COMPANY CONFIDENTIAL
```

Figure 3-3.
A standard header (top) and a footer paragraph (bottom).

Standard headers can only be one line high, and they require that you use special formatting commands to align your text at the left or right margin or to insert the page number, filename, time, or date. Create a standard header to see how this works. Suppose you want your header to contain the following text, aligned at the left margin:

This is a header - Page <the current page number>

Here's what to do to create this header:

1. Open a new word processor document, or use the one you now have on your screen.

2. Press Alt-P-H to choose the Headers & Footers command from the Print menu. A dialog box appears, like this:

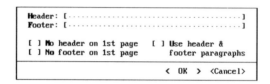

3. Type: *&LThis is a header - Page &P*

4. Press the Enter key to store the header.

Because you used the format command, &L, at the beginning of your text, the text that follows it will be left aligned. And because you used the command to insert page numbers, &P, after the word "Page," the page number will be printed on every page. For more information about standard header formatting commands and about header and footer paragraphs, see the Print Headers & Footers command in the Help Index on the Help menu.

Printing

When you're ready to print a file from the word processor, you can print it three different places: to the screen, to a file on disk, or to a printer. All these options are available from the Print menu.

To do this last exercise, use the document you have on your screen. If no text is showing, type some so that you'll have something to print.

1. Press Alt-P-V to choose the Preview command. The Preview dialog box appears.

2. Press the Enter key to preview the file on the screen. The page appears on the screen in a reduced size, with the exact headers, footers, character styles, margins, and paragraph formats that it will have when printed on paper.

The Preview dialog box contains exactly the same options as does the Print dialog box in Works. These options are available here because you can print directly from the Preview screen that displays your document. See the Print Preview command in the Help Index on the Help menu for more information.

By now you should have a good idea of how to use the Works Word Processor. You haven't yet covered many of the extra features, including searching for and replacing text, correcting text using the spelling program, and using the Thesaurus. Remember, you can get specific information about any command by choosing its name from the Help Index on the Help menu. You'll see most of the word processor's commands at work in the projects covered in Chapter 5.

CHAPTER 4

Word Processor Tips

The Works Word Processor gives you a lot of flexibility in preparing documents, but some word processing approaches are faster or more efficient than others. In this chapter, you'll look at several strategies for making the most of the Works Word Processor. After considering a few general tips, you'll look at some of the word processor's limitations and how, if possible, to work around them.

Making the Most of the Word Processor

Every user has his or her own way of getting along with a computer program, but if you're new to computing or new to Works, reading the tips in this section can help you develop some habits that will make you more productive. The tips are divided into functional groups that are based on the various aspects of word processing, such as entering and editing text or formatting.

Entering and Editing Text

Because most word processing involves entering and editing text, it's not surprising that most of the methods you can use to improve your word processing productivity fall into this category. Here are some techniques to consider as you work with your documents.

Keyboard or mouse?

One choice you'll often make as you use the word processor is whether to use the keyboard commands or the mouse to control the program. (If you don't have a mouse you can skip this section.)

Because word processing mainly involves typing text from the keyboard, using keyboard commands might seem to be the best way to control the program in every situation. But typing text (or, at least, touch-typing) requires you to keep your fingers centered around the "home row" keys in the middle of the keyboard. Unless you have very large hands, you'll have to move your fingers away from the home row to use any of the arrow or function keys. And because you'll be moving your hands off the home row anyway, you might as well use the mouse, which is a faster tool than the keyboard in many situations. Here are some general guidelines:

- Using the mouse is generally a faster, more accurate way to select text. For example, it's much faster to select a word by pointing to it and clicking the right mouse button than it is to select a word by positioning the cursor using the arrow keys and then pressing the F8 key. Using the mouse, you can easily select irregular blocks of text, and it's faster to drag the mouse across even a few characters than it is to select them by using the keyboard.

You'll find only two situations in which it makes sense to select text using the keyboard:

- When you want to select an entire document (Alt-S-A is the quick keyboard command here.)

- When the cursor is already at the beginning of a selection and you want to select a specific block of text by repeatedly pressing the F8 key (See "Selecting text" in Chapter 3 to see how to select blocks of text by using the F8 key.)

Finally, don't ignore the right mouse button. Both the left and right mouse buttons can select blocks of text quickly, depending on where you point when you click each button. Here are the text-selection shortcuts that you can use with the mouse buttons:

When You Click	On	You Select
The left button	A word	A character
The left button	The left margin	A line
The right button	A word	A word
The right button	The left margin	A paragraph

- The mouse is faster than the keyboard at window management. The Works windowing system was designed with the mouse in mind, so it's not surprising that moving and re-sizing windows or scrolling through a document generally goes more quickly when you use the mouse. If you're moving only a screen or two up or down, the Page Up and Page Down keys work fine, but for larger jumps or for moving or resizing windows, the mouse is much faster.

Likewise, the arrow keys are a good choice when you're moving only a few characters in any direction, but the mouse is faster when you're moving farther than that. (Works' Go To command is the fastest, most precise method of all, but you have to remember to use it. See the upcoming section, "Use the Select menu.")

- Choosing menu commands goes more quickly when you use the keyboard. The Alt key is part of the main keyboard area that includes the letter keys, so you don't even have to move your hands away from the home row to use Alt. At first, you'll have to hunt through the menus to remember the right letter keys to use for each command, but soon the commands you use frequently will be etched in your mind and using them will become second nature.

- Commands that require dialog box selections are a toss-up. Depending on the complexity of the dialog box and the number of selections you want to make, the keyboard is sometimes faster and the mouse is sometimes faster. If you want to accept the defaults in almost any dialog box, for example, the keyboard is the quicker route because you normally have to press only the Enter key to accept the defaults and issue the command. But if you want to choose a lot of different options—particularly those that require selecting from a list, as in the Font & Style dialog box—it's faster to click your way through using the mouse.

Save a step with the Typing Replaces Selection command

Normally, you must select text and delete it before you can replace it with something else. Using the Typing Replaces Selection command on the Options menu (Alt-O-Y), however, can save you a step. With the Typing Replaces Selection command turned on, you can simply replace selected text with new text you type without having to first delete the original text. If you want to change *bank* to *gorilla*, for example, you can simply select *bank* and then type *gorilla*.

Use the keyboard shortcuts

Throughout this book and the Works manuals, you'll find many suggestions for keyboard shortcuts. If you find yourself repeatedly choosing the same menu command, learn its keyboard alternative and use that instead. If you normally make items boldface by choosing the Bold command from the Format menu, for example, learn to use Ctrl-B instead. Works has keyboard shortcuts for inserting special characters and for most of the character and paragraph formatting commands. See the Keyboard category in the Help Index for lists of these shortcuts.

Use the Select menu

The Select menu offers a powerful set of commands that you can use for several types of editing tasks. The Search and Go To commands let you move quickly to a certain place in a document. By using descriptive bookmark names and the Go To command, you can make notes to yourself and then display a list of reminders about a document. The Replace command lets you quickly make a series of changes to a document.

First of all, using the Search command is faster than scrolling back and forth and manually scanning the document to find the spot for which you're looking. It's often easier to remember a subheading, proper name, or topic name in the area of the document to which you want to move. When you enter a string of text to search for, try to be as specific as possible, and use the Match Whole Word and Match Upper/Lower Case options to avoid finding unwanted occurrences of a text string. If you search for the word *Ban*, for example, and you don't use the Match Whole Word or Match Upper/Lower Case options, Works finds every occurrence of that text string, including *bank*, *abandon*, and *Banducci*.

Along with text, you can type special characters in the Search For text box to search for tabs, spaces, or other special characters in a document. For a list of the special characters for which you can search, see the section "Searching and Replacing" in the *Microsoft Works Reference* manual.

Also remember that it isn't necessary to choose the Search command to find each successive occurrence of the same string. You can press the F7 key to continue a search.

Using the Go To command, you can jump directly to a certain page by entering its number, or you can select a named bookmark and jump to that. Works' Bookmark Name command in the Edit menu lets you insert invisible, named bookmarks in a document and then almost instantly return to them. When used with the Go To command, a bookmark is a good way to make a note to yourself about a section of text. If you have a question about some text you wrote, for example, leave a bookmark there and give the bookmark a descriptive name. You'll see a list of the bookmarks you've created when you choose the Go To command (the shortcut key is F5). By selecting the proper bookmark name from the list in the Go To dialog box, you'll be able to jump quickly to that place in the document. Remember that when you create bookmark names, they can be only 15 characters long. Works lets you enter more characters than that, but only the first 15 characters appear in the Go To dialog box.

Finally, using the Replace command is a good way to make global changes to your document. If you've left two spaces after the period at the end of each sentence and you decide you want only one, for example, you can use special characters to search for all periods followed by double spaces in a document and replace each of them with a period and a single space.

Recycle information

One of the best features of computers is their ability to store your work and let you recall, change, and reuse it later. Writing projects are hard enough to complete without having to force yourself to redo them unnecessarily. You'll find a lot of ways to reuse your work in the word processor. If you regularly produce similar documents such as weekly reports or standard letters, save them using the Save As command from the File menu each time you change them, and give them different names. That way, the original version of the file will remain intact for you to use later. It's much faster to open an existing file of a memo or report and make changes to it than it is to re-create the file from scratch.

Save files to speed things up

Works uses your computer's memory to store information about the various parts of your file and where those parts are located on the disk. As your file grows and you edit it in more and more places, Works must store more and more information about where you are working in the document at any given time. When you are working with several documents and you're close to the limit of your system's memory, Works slows down as it tries to keep track of all your changes or additions. To free some memory, save the document, close it, and then open it again. If you're working with several documents, try saving, closing, and then reopening each document. You'll find that you have more memory to work with afterward and Works will operate faster.

Use macros to speed text entry

Works' macro feature can automate complex tasks that you perform repeatedly. Here are some examples:

- If you always begin your day with a look at certain files, such as a calendar or a "to-do" list, you can store a macro that automatically opens those files for you.

- If you always enter your name and address at the top of a letter, you can store that information as a macro and have Works type it for you.

- In fact, you can use macros to automatically type long or complex strings of text that you use frequently, allowing you to use macros to give Works a glossary feature.

Formatting

The first tip in this section is a general one that applies to nearly any computer application. The others are more specific to the Works Word Processor.

Edit first, format later

One time-honored rule in computing is to get the information into the computer first and then worry about how it looks. In word processing, it's important to enter your text as you think about it. Pausing to make a sentence or a paragraph look nice will only interrupt your train of thought and make writing harder.

Because some formatting can make the screen easier to read (and thus make it easier for you to write), you can set up most overall formatting in advance. If your eyes are more comfortable with double-spaced text or spacing between paragraphs, for example, you can specify these options before you ever start writing. After your train of thought is in high gear, however, don't complicate matters by playing with the character or paragraph formatting options.

Use page breaks to separate footnotes

When printing footnotes, Works adds them to the end of your regular document text, beginning on the next available line. Be sure that you insert a manual page break (Ctrl-Enter) or a few blank lines to separate the notes from the end of your text. You can also use the Borders command on the Format menu to insert a horizontal line that separates the notes from the text.

Allow enough room for paragraph headers and footers

You can use Works' paragraph headers or footers to create multiple-line headers or footers in your documents. When you choose the option in the Headers & Footers dialog box to use header and footer paragraphs, Works inserts header and footer paragraphs at the top of your document. Each paragraph contains one line, but you can add lines to either paragraph by pressing Shift-Enter. (Pressing the Enter key alone won't add a line to a header or footer paragraph.)

When you create multiple-line headers and footers, though, be sure that you have allowed enough room for them in your top or bottom page margins, or else they won't print completely. You must set the header or footer margin in the Page Setup & Margins dialog box to allow enough room. The default header and footer margins are set for 0.5 inch, and the top and bottom page margins are set for 1 inch, so one-half inch of space separates a one-line header (or footer) and the top (or bottom) of your text. One-half inch of space leaves about enough room for three lines of header or footer text. If your header or footer paragraph is more than three lines high with these margin settings, Works warns you that the header or footer is too tall. If you continue without changing the appropriate margin, any additional lines will not print (because they would obscure text on the page if they did).

To accommodate larger headers or footers, you need to increase the header or footer margin and reduce the top and bottom page margins accordingly. If you're working with a 1-inch header margin, for example, you should set a page margin of at least 1.25 or 1.5 inches so that some space separates the header text and the text at the top of the page. Header and footer margins can't overlap text margins. As a result, the header or footer margin can never be larger than the top or bottom text margin. To see if multiple lines of header or footer text are properly positioned on the page, use the Preview command on the Print menu to view the document on the screen.

Use macros to simplify formatting

If you like to use certain complex character or paragraph formats, you can record them as a macro when you select them the first time. Then you can apply them after that by using only one keystroke.

Use a Template to store a default format

Works' Save As Template feature lets you store a document's custom format settings and then apply those settings to each new word processor document you open. If you don't like the default font, style, spacing, margin, tabs, indent, or other format settings in new word processor documents, you can set them the way you want and then save the document as a formatting template. To use the Save As Template feature, follow these steps:

1. Open a new word processor document.

2. Choose the format settings you want.

3. Press Alt-F-A to display the Save As dialog box.

4. Press Alt-A to choose the Save As Template option.

5. Press the Enter key to save the file. (You don't need to enter a filename because the file is a template that is opened for you whenever you choose the Create New File command.)

Now, whenever you open a new word processor document, it has the format settings you saved as a template. Works can store only one template per tool in a given disk directory, so when you save a new document as a template, it replaces the existing one.

Printing

The following printing tips show you what happens when you print with Works. Knowing this printing information in advance can help you anticipate potential printing problems.

Actual vs. virtual page numbers

Works has two different ways of tracking page numbers. The status line shows the total number of actual pages in the document and which actual page you are on at any time. But when you include page numbers in a header or footer or when you specify certain pages to be printed in the Print dialog box, Works uses the page numbering scheme that you set by using the 1st Page Number text box in the Page Setup & Margins dialog box.

Normally, Works starts numbering pages in a document with the number 1, so the default setting for the 1st page number in the Page Setup & Margins text box is *1*. But if you change a document's first page number, you must allow for that change when you specify which pages you want printed. For example, suppose you change the first page number in your document to *3* and you want to print the first and second pages of that document. To do so, specify in the Print dialog box's Print Specific Pages option that pages *3* and *4* are the pages to be printed.

Specify character fonts, sizes, and styles with Works, not with your printer

Some printers have controls that let you change the font, font size, or font style being printed. Works ignores these settings, however, and uses whatever settings you have chosen in the Font & Style dialog box in the Format menu to determine how it will print a document. If you use the Font & Style command to choose the Courier font for a document, for example, and your printer is set to print with the Prestige font, Works cancels the Prestige setting and prints the document in Courier.

When you choose a font in the Font & Style dialog box, Works shows only the fonts and font sizes your currently selected printer is capable of printing. You can use the Printer Setup command to choose a different printer. When you use the Printer Setup command, Works displays every printer for which you have installed a printer driver. (For more information about installing printers in Works, see Chapter 1.)

What You Can't Do and What to Do About It

Although it's a capable tool, the Works Word Processor lacks some of the features you'd find in stand-alone word processing programs. This part of the chapter looks at these limitations in groups that are organized according to specific functions: editing, formatting, and printing. As we consider each limitation, we'll look at the possible ways to get around it.

Editing Limitations

You can enter and move text in Works as easily as you can using any other word processor, but Works doesn't include some extra editing features. The Works Word Processor doesn't

- Count the number of words, lines, or characters in a document
- Have an outlining function
- Automatically generate a table of contents
- Automatically generate an index
- Include a glossary feature

Counting

Counting the number of words, lines, or characters in a document is important when you're trying to create a document of a precise length. Works' status line shows you the total number of pages a document will have when printed using the current Page Setup settings, and it shows you which page is currently displayed, but it doesn't keep track of other document statistics. You can, however, get statistics manually.

The average word length is about six letters, so dividing a file's total size in characters by six will give you an approximate word count for many documents. To estimate the number of words in a document, you'll need to first determine the file size of your document and then divide that number by six. (This approach is effective because Works stores approximately one character per byte.) Here's how to count words using Works' Run Other Programs command along with its calculator accessory:

1. Press Alt-F-S to save the document on disk.

2. Press Alt-F-R to choose the Run Other Programs command. You'll see a dialog box that lists the other programs stored on your hard disk.

3. Press the Down arrow key to move to the list of programs, and select DOS.

4. Press the Enter key to run DOS. Works shows a dialog box that asks you to confirm your selection. Press the Enter key again, and DOS loads. The current directory is the one in which you just saved your document. (If you're running Works from floppy disks and you don't have a DOS disk in a disk drive, Works asks you to insert it.)

5. Type *dir* and press the Enter key. DOS displays a list of the files on the disk or in the directory. Directly to the right of each filename, you'll see a series of numbers that indicate the file size, like this:

```
C:\REPORTS>dir

 Volume in drive C has no label
 Directory of  C:\REPORTS

 .              <DIR>      6-21-90    3:43p
 . .            <DIR>      6-21-90    3:43p
QTRRPT    WPS     29716    6-21-90    3:43p
MORPT     WPS     27796    6-21-90    3:44p
XPNSE     WPS     22036    6-21-90    3:44p
        5 File(s)   35633152 bytes free

C:\REPORTS>
```

6. Write down the file size for the document whose words you want to count.

7. Type *exit* and press the Enter key. Works loads again, and the document you were working on is opened to the exact place at which you left it.

8. Press Alt-O-C to display the Works Calculator.

9. Type the file size you noted from the DOS directory. The numbers appear in the calculator window.

10. After you type the number, type / to indicate division.

11. Type 6 to divide the file size number by 6, and then press the Enter key to display the result. This number is the approximate number of words in your file.

Remember that this method gives you only an approximate word count, and not an exact one. Other formatting elements such as tabs, spaces, special characters, and markers for inserted charts or fields also count as characters in the file size. If your document has a large number of these characters, the word count you get from dividing the file size by 6 will be a little higher than the actual number of words in the document.

Outlining

An outlining function lets you build the structure of a document as an outline and then convert it to text. Microsoft Word, for example, lets you build an outline and then display the document in either outline or document mode so that you can quickly jump between a structural (outline) view and the actual text. Works doesn't have an outlining function. If your heart is set on using an outliner, you can buy a separate program such as *Grand View, Think Tank,* or *Ready.* The *Ready* program is an accessory that you can use without quitting Works. The others are programs that you can access by using the Run Other Programs command on Works' File menu.

Table of contents

Table-of-contents generators use the headings in a program's built-in outliner as chapter and section names to create a table of contents. Because Works doesn't have an outliner, it won't create a table of contents.

Index

Automatic indexing is a feature that lets you insert special, invisible characters in a document to mark words that you want included in an index. The indexer can then gather all the words so marked into one file. Works doesn't have such a feature.

Glossary

A glossary feature is handy for storing complex names or other strings of text that you use repeatedly. If you're writing a report about the Athabasca Glacier, for example, you could easily get tired of typing that name over and over. Instead, you could store the name in a glossary and insert it when needed. Works doesn't have a glossary feature, but you can use its built-in macro capability to record any string of text as you type it and then reproduce that text string by pressing a key or two.

Formatting Limitations

The Works Word Processor won't

- Number the lines in a document
- Display text in separate columns
- Display different type fonts on the screen
- Let you create style sheets that store specific paragraph or character formats

Line numbering

Line numbers, which are printed in the margin next to each line, are used mostly in legal paperwork. This function is so specialized that most people don't miss it in Works. It can be useful, however, to know how many lines your document contains, especially when you're trying to create a specific number of lines to fill space in a flier or a newsletter. You can manually count lines on a page. To do so, use Works' Preview command to display a page of your document, count the lines on one page, and then multiply that number by the number of pages in the document. You'll have to count any partially full pages by hand.

Columns

To display text in separate columns, set tab stops to create the columns and then press the Tab key to fill in each column, one line at a time. Works offers no way to display and edit separate, newspaper-style columns. It is possible in Works, however, to print text in multiple, side-by-side columns if you're prepared to do a little juggling. Here's how you'd print two 3-inch newspaper-style columns side by side:

1. Enter all the text for the page.

2. Set the left and right margins at 1 inch.

3. Set a right indent of 3.5 inches. Because of the large right indent, the text will be formatted in one 3-inch column on the left side of the page.

4. Display the text on the screen by using the Preview command.

5. Make a note of the contents of the last line on the page.

6. Return to the editing screen, and move the cursor to the beginning of the line that's after the last line on the first page.

7. Press the Enter key to move this line and all the lines below it into a new paragraph.

8. Set the right indent back to 0, and set the left indent at 3.5 inches. Because of the large left indent, this move will produce a column of text 3 inches wide on the right side of the page.

9. Using the Print command, print only the first page of the document. Works prints the left-hand column of text.

10. Put the printed page back into the printer, and print only the second page of the document. Works prints the right-hand column of text on the same page so that both columns are now printed. Because of the left and right indents, each column will be 3 inches wide, with a half-inch of gutter space between them.

This method is a little tedious and requires some trial and error if you're using a printer in which paper is fed with a platen or tractor mechanism. For high-volume production, this technique will not work well, but it's handy if you need to prepare multiple-column documents only occasionally.

Fonts

Displaying different type fonts on the screen is a feature that's beyond the practical capabilities of standard DOS-based systems. Graphic screen environments such as Microsoft Windows are required to support this feature, and Works was designed to operate on any DOS-based computer. Works doesn't show different fonts on the screen, but then neither does any other program that runs in a non-graphic environment.

Style sheets

Style sheets provide a means to name and store complex paragraph or character formats so that they can be applied with ease elsewhere. If you create a paragraph of text to which you apply 10-point Elite boldface type and a half-inch first-line indent, for example, you might give this group of formatting settings a name such as "Indent style." Then you could apply all these settings at one time by specifying Indent style. Works doesn't support style sheets, but you can copy character and paragraph formats from one part of a document to another by using the Copy Special command. Also, you can store a series of style selections as a macro and then apply that collection of styles by running the macro.

Printing Limitations

The following limits concern operations that take place when a document is printed. The Works Word Processor doesn't support

- "Facing pages" printing of headers and footers or left and right margins

- Changing header or footer text in different parts of a document

- File-chaining during printing

Facing pages

Facing pages printing options let you alternate the positions of headers or footers or of left and right margins so that they are laid out attractively when pages are printed on both sides and bound like a book. A single-sided document that was bound with a staple might have a right-aligned header and a wider left margin, for example. But if you printed that document on both sides of the paper and bound it like a book, the right-aligned header wouldn't look good on the left-hand pages. Also, the wider margin in a book should always be the one that's toward the spine of the book, so it would alternate between the left and right sides of the pages. Works doesn't offer the option to alternate headers or margins for facing pages.

Changing header or footer text

Changing header or footer text in a document can be helpful when a document contains several sections or chapters. With each new section or chapter, the header or footer can show the name of that specific part of the document. If you have several pages of front matter (such as a table of contents, a copyright page, and a dedication), for example, you might want those pages to be printed without a header at all, and then have a header containing page numbers in the main text. All headers and footers in Works remain the same for the entire document (except for the page numbers, which change with each page).

To use different headers, you have to divide the document itself into separate Works files and then use a different header in each one. In a document that has front matter, for example, you would copy the front matter into a separate document and then delete it from the document that contains the main text. You could then print the front matter document without a header. If you simply want to suppress the printing of a header or footer on the first page of the document, use the No Header On 1st Page option in the Headers & Footers dialog box.

File chaining

File-chaining features let you print several documents in succession as if they were one. You could print several chapters of a book one after the other, for example, and have the page numbers continue in succession from one chapter to the next. Works doesn't have a file-chaining feature, but it's possible to approximate file-chaining by noting the ending page number of each document and then setting the first page number of the following document so that it is consecutive. Here's the procedure:

1. Create a header or footer for the first document in the group, and include a command to include page numbers in the document.

2. In Preview mode, scroll to the end of the first document and note the ending page number. (Be sure you note the *printed* page number if it will be different from the actual page number because you have changed the 1st page number option.)

3. Create a header for the second document in the group, and include a page numbering command.

4. Change the second document's first page number in the Page Setup & Margins dialog box to be the number that comes after the first document's ending page number. (If the first document ends at page 15, for example, the second document will begin at page 16.)

5. Repeat the preceding two steps for the other documents in the group.

After you set up the page numbering so that it will be consecutive, you can print all the files separately. The separate files can be assembled into one consecutively numbered document when you finish.

These tips will help you work more productively with the Works Word Processor. As you gain experience with Works, you will undoubtedly come up with more shortcuts and strategies of your own. If you're ready to try some typical business projects with the word processor, continue to Chapter 5.

CHAPTER 5

Word Processing Projects

In this chapter, we'll look at the Works Word Processor in action. We'll use it to create a letterhead template, a form letter, a mailing list and labels, a flier, and a monthly report template. By completing these projects, you'll learn how to use most of the word processor's features.

A Letterhead

In this exercise, we'll use Works' font selection and formatting commands to create a personalized letterhead and then save it. With the file on disk, you can open the letterhead file each time you write a letter and then save the document with a different name, thus preserving the letterhead in its original state on the disk.

Entering and formatting the text

To begin, we'll open a new word processor file and enter the name and address that will make up the letterhead:

1. Press Alt-F-N to open the File menu and choose the Create New File command.

2. Press the Enter key to create a new word processor document.

3. Press Alt-W-X to open the Window menu and choose the Maximize command.

A new document appears on the screen. Type the following:

Acme Toys
123 Walden Place
Centerville, CA 12345
(404) 555-1111

When you finish typing, press the Enter key one time. Now we'll change the alignment and apply other formatting commands to make this text appear more like a letterhead. First we'll center the text:

1. Move the cursor to the *A* in *Acme*.

2. Press the F8 key.

3. Press the Down arrow key four times, and then press the Left arrow key one time to select all four lines in the address.

4. Press Ctrl-C to center the text on the page.

Next we'll make all the letterhead text boldface:

☐ Press Ctrl-B to set the Bold style. (The Bold style indicator, B, appears in the status line.)

Finally, we'll place a border beneath the bottom line of the address to separate the letterhead from the rest of the letter:

1. Move the cursor to the line that contains the telephone number.

2. Press the F8 key three times to select the entire line.

3. Press Alt-T-O to choose the Borders command from the Format menu.

4. Press the M key to choose a Bottom border.

5. Press the B key to choose the Bold style for the border.

6. Press the Enter key to confirm these settings and return to the document.

7. Press the Down arrow key to move the cursor below the border line.

Now the letterhead looks like this:

```
  File  Edit  Print  Select  Format  Options  Window  Help
═══════════════════════════ WORD1.WPS ═══════════════════════════
  [ · · · · · · · · 1 · · · · · · · 2 · · · · · · · · 3 · · · · · · · 4 · · · · · · · · 5 · · · · · · · · ] · · · · · · · 7 · · · · ·
»                           Acme Toys
                         123 Walden Place
                        Centerville, CA 12345
                          (404) 555-1111
                  ─────────────────────────────────

  •
```

The letterhead text and the border are both displayed in highlighted characters, indicating that they will print in boldface type.

You could stop here with this letterhead project, but depending on the printer you're using, you might want to choose a different font or type size. For example, using an 18-point type size for the store name would make it stand out a little more from the address below it.

Changing the font

If you haven't selected a printer by using the Printer Setup command, your document is set to print on a generic printer called TTY with the Pica 12 font. If you choose the Font & Style command from the Format menu with this printer selected, your only font and font size choice is Pica 12. When you select a different printer with the Printer Setup command, however, the Font & Style dialog box displays all the fonts and font sizes that the selected printer is capable of printing.

To set a different font or font size for selected text, simply select the text you want to change, press Alt-T-F to choose the Font & Style command from the Format menu, choose the font and font size (and style, if you like) that you want to apply to the selected text, and then press the Enter key to confirm the new choices. The Works screen won't show the text in the font and font size you have selected. You can see an approximation of the font and font size when you preview the document using the Preview command on the Print menu, but you really need to print the document on paper to see exactly how it will look.

The selection of printers available in the Printer Setup dialog box depends on which printer driver files you have installed with Works. (See Chapter 2 for more details about printer installation.)

Saving the file

Save this letterhead so that you can use it each time you write a letter. To save this letterhead:

1. Press Alt-F-S to save the file. The Save As dialog box appears.

2. Type *LETTER* as the filename. LETTER replaces the default filename in the Save File As text box.

3. Press the Enter key to save the file.

Now the letterhead file is on your disk. Each time you want to write a letter, you can open the LETTER file, write a letter, and then save the file with a different name. The original letterhead template will remain unchanged on your disk.

A Form Letter

Form letters are useful when you need to send the same basic information to several different individuals. You might want to notify selected customers of a special sale, tell your friends about a new address, remind people of appointments they have made, or even issue invitations.

You can use Works' mail-merge features to combine data from a database file with a form letter you've created in the word processor. To complete this exercise, you'll need to use the ADDRESS.WDB database file as a data source. Chapter 12 shows you how to create this file from scratch, or you can use the file with the same name on your program disk or in the Works program directory on your hard disk. Note that the ADDRESS.WDB file included with the Works program uses slightly different field names. You can choose the field names that best fit the purposes of this exercise. Before starting the letter, open the ADDRESS.WDB file.

Opening the letterhead file

Begin by opening the letterhead file (if it is not already open) so that we can use it for this form letter.

1. Press Alt-F-O to display the Open Existing File dialog box.

2. If the file is in a different directory or on a different disk include the appropriate drive and pathname in the File To Open box, and then press the Enter key to change the disk, the directory, or both.

3. Press the Down arrow key to move the cursor into the Files list, and then select the LETTER.WPS file from the list.

4. Press the Enter key to open the file.

5. Press the Enter key three times to leave three blank lines between the border and the first line of letter text.

Inserting the address fields

At the top of the letter, enter the current date, and then press the Enter key three times to skip two lines. Next, we'll insert field markers to merge the database data into the address block. The fields from the ADDRESS.WDB database file will be merged into the address block, like this:

FirstName LastName
Company
Street
City, ST, Zip

These are the actual field names used in the ADDRESS.WDB file from Chapter 12, so you can refer to this example as you insert the field markers. Now insert the first field marker:

1. Press Alt-E-F to choose the Insert Field command from the Edit menu. The Insert Field dialog box appears, like this:

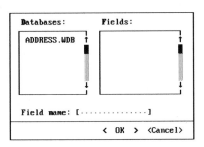

2. Press the Down arrow key to select the ADDRESS.WDB database.

3. Press the Right arrow key to move the cursor to the Fields list.

4. Press the Down arrow key to select the FirstName field.

5. Press the Enter key to insert this field in the letter. Works places a field marker in the document, like this:

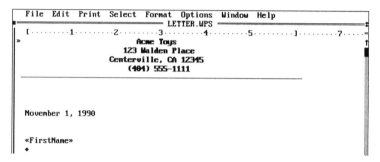

It helps to think of field markers as actual text when you place them in documents. If you merged the wrong field by mistake, simply delete the marker. You can also copy or move field markers, as we'll see below.

Because we've just placed the first name from an address, your next step will be to insert a space after it and then insert the last name from the address:

1. Press the spacebar one time.

2. Press Alt-E-F to display the Insert Field dialog box again. The ADDRESS.WDB database name should still be selected, so you don't have to press the Down arrow key to select it.

3. Press the Right and Down arrow keys to select the LastName field, and then press the Enter key to insert the field marker.

To merge the rest of the address block, press the Enter key to move down to each successive line, and then merge the field or fields on that line. Here's the general procedure if your cursor is now at the end of the LastName field:

1. Press the Enter key to begin a new line.

2. Insert the Company field marker.

3. Press the Enter key.

4. Insert the Street field marker.

5. Press the Enter key.

6. Insert the City field marker.

7. Type a comma at the end of the City field marker, and then press the spacebar to leave a space.

8. Insert the ST field marker (the state code).

9. Press the spacebar to leave a space between the state and zip code.

10. Insert the Zip field marker.

After you insert all the field markers for the entire address block, the letter will look like this:

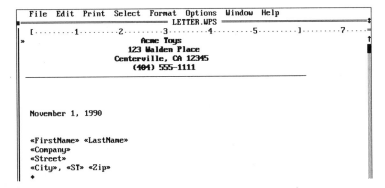

The next step is to leave a couple of blank lines and then type the greeting. Because it's a form letter, you can use a merged field to create a personal greeting. The cursor should now be at the end of the Zip field in the address block. If it isn't, move it there, and then follow the steps on the next page.

1. Press the Enter key three times to leave two blank lines below the address.

2. Type *Dear* and press the spacebar one time.

3. Insert the FirstName field marker from the ADDRESS.WDB database.

4. Type a colon (:) after the field marker to complete the greeting line.

Now press the Enter key two times to leave a blank line between the greeting line and the letter text, which you'll enter next.

Entering the letter text

Type the following text exactly as you see it here. Be sure to include the four blank lines between the words *Sincerely* and *Frank Acme* at the end of the letter. (Some mistakes are deliberately included in this text so that we can use Works' spelling commands to correct them later.) Here's the letter text:

It's only November, but it's not too early to plan your holiday shopping. As an Acme Toys Prefferred Customer, I'd like to give you an advance preview of some great new toys we'll be offering this season.

From 6:00 to 10:00 PM on Monday, November 6, our store will be closed to the public for a special invitation-only, adults-only preview. Because you're a valued customer, you'll be able to visit us during the preview and examine our new lineup of toys. We'll have our full sales staff on hand to demonstrate toys and answer your questions. You'll be able to place layaway orders, and we'll even arrange to store your cash or credit purchases until Christmas.

Some of the featured items at the special preview will include:

*Thunder Ducks, the new line of action figures from Bonzono. The Thunder Ducks cartoons have delighted children this season, and now your children can stage realistic action sequences of their own with Thunder Ducks action figures. The line includes Quacko, Biller, Pinfeather, and Fantail, along with the Duck Blind action vehicle. Prices start at only $9.99.

*Little Miss Workout, the fit, fun, and fashionable doll from Frabbage International. The fitness craze has taken America by storm, and now

Little Miss Workout brings it to children's playtime. Each Little Miss Workout comes with a headband, jump rope, and exercise booklet. Accessory sets include the Race Walking action course and the Aerobic Dancing audio cassette and leotard. Prices start at $7.99.

*Gonzo Gamesman, the latest video game system from Akido. Gonzo Gamesman comes with high-resolution graphics and stereo sound for realistic play action. Games like Demon Dentist, Martian Landing, and Dribble-Man will delight kids for hours. Recommended for ages 3 and up, the Gamesman video system sells for $99.99; games are $35.99 to $54.99.

These are just a few of the hot holiday toys we'll be previewing on November 6. These toys will not be offered for sale to the public until November 7, so take advantage of our Prefferred Customer preview night to beat the rush. I hope to see you there.

Sincerely,

Frank Acme
President, Acme Toys

After you enter the text, it's time to check the spelling.

Checking the spelling

Works has a built-in spell-checking program that scans your document for spelling errors, matching each word against a dictionary that comes with the program. To check the document's spelling:

1. Press Ctrl-Home to move the cursor to the beginning of the document. (Works checks a document's spelling from the cursor position forward. If the cursor is in the middle of a document when you start a spelling check, Works pauses at the end of the document and asks if you want to continue checking from the beginning of the document. You can avoid this pause by moving the cursor to the top of the document before choosing the Spelling command.)

2. Press Alt-O-S to choose the Spelling command from the Options menu. Works begins checking the document's spelling. In a few seconds, the Spelling dialog box appears, like this:

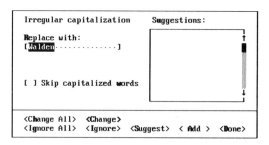

```
Irregular capitalization    Suggestions:

Replace with:
[Walden.............]


[ ] Skip capitalized words



<Change All>  <Change>
<Ignore All>  <Ignore>  <Suggest>  < Add >  <Done>
```

The Replace With text box displays a suspect word (*Walden*) that was not found in the Works spelling dictionary. In this case, the word is a proper name that is part of the store's address. We could simply tell Works to ignore this word, but we might as well add the word to the spelling program's dictionary so that Works will consider it correct in the future:

☐ Press Alt-A to add the word to the Works dictionary. Works continues checking the document.

The next suspect word displayed in the dialog box is *Centerville*, another proper name. Add it to the dictionary by pressing Alt-A again. The next word displayed is *FirstName*, the field marker in the address line. This isn't a correct word, and it isn't a proper name, so tell Works to ignore this word and—because the field marker appears again in the greeting line—all future occurrences of the word:

☐ Press Alt-G to choose the Ignore All option. Works continues checking the document.

Works next finds *LastName* as a suspect word. We also want the program to ignore all occurrences of this word, so:

☐ Press Alt-G to choose the Ignore All option again. Works continues checking the document.

The next suspect word displayed is *Prefferred*, which is misspelled. But suppose we're not sure if the word is misspelled or we don't know the correct spelling. In this case, we can ask Works to suggest the correct spelling.

□ Press Alt-S to choose the Suggest option. Works displays
two words in the Suggestions list box, like this:

```
┌─────────────────────────────────────────────────────┐
│ Misspelled Word          Suggestions:                │
│                         ┌──────────────────┐         │
│ Replace with:           │ Preferred        ↑│        │
│ [Preferred··········]   │ Preferrer        ▓│        │
│                         │                  ░│        │
│                         │                  ░│        │
│ [ ] Skip capitalized words                ░│        │
│                         │                  ░│        │
│                         │                  ↓│        │
│                         └──────────────────┘         │
├─────────────────────────────────────────────────────┤
│ <Change All>  <Change>                               │
│ <Ignore All>  <Ignore>  <Suggest>  < Add >  <Done>   │
└─────────────────────────────────────────────────────┘
```

The first word in the list is selected, and it is the correct spelling. Because
we know that the word is spelled incorrectly, we can choose to replace it
with the correct spelling wherever the incorrect spelling occurs in the
document. To replace all occurrences of the misspelled word with the
correct version suggested by Works:

□ Press Alt-H to choose the Change All command. Works
replaces *Prefferred* with *Preferred* throughout the document
and continues the spelling check.

The next four suspect words are the proper names *Bonzono, Quacko,
Biller,* and *Frabbage.* Press Alt-G each time one of the words is displayed as
suspect to tell Works to ignore these spellings. After these words, Works
presents *children's* as a misspelled word in the Replace With box. The
Works spelling dictionary does not contain every word available. As a
result, the spelling operation will not recognize some acceptable spelling structures. In this case, the possessive use of an apostrophe disguises
the word "children" and is flagged so that you can accept or change the
spelling. Because this word isn't misspelled, press Alt-G to tell Works to
ignore it. The last three unrecognized words found in the document are
the proper names *Gonzo, Gamesman,* and *Akido,* so press Alt-G to tell
Works to ignore them.

At the end of the spelling check, Works displays a dialog box that
announces the completion of the spelling check. Press the Enter key to
return to the document. If you did not start the spelling check at the beginning of the document, Works asks if you want to continue checking
the spelling from the beginning of the document. Press the Enter key to
continue the spelling operation, or press the Esc key to cancel it.

Our text is now letter-perfect, so we can move on to formatting.

Paragraph formatting

Now we'll use Works' formatting commands to make the text look exactly right in a printed letter. First, we'll align the paragraphs differently. Use a first-line indent on all the paragraphs of text, except for the three descriptions of specific toys:

1. Move the cursor to the beginning of the letter text.

2. Press the F8 key.

3. Press the Page Down key to select the first three paragraphs of text. (If the selection highlight on your screen doesn't end exactly at the end of the third paragraph, move it there by pressing the arrow keys.)

4. Press Alt-T-A to choose the Indents & Spacing command. The Indents & Spacing dialog box is displayed.

5. Press the Down arrow key to move the cursor to the 1st Line Indent box.

6. Type .5.

7. Press the Enter key to confirm the setting. The first lines of the three paragraphs of the letter are now indented by 0.5 inch.

We'll use a different indent with the three paragraphs that describe specific toys, but we want to apply the same first-line indent to the final paragraph of the letter. We could select that paragraph and then specify the same setting using the Indents & Spacing command, but Works makes it easier. Because we've already set this format on the first three paragraphs, we can copy the format from one of those paragraphs to the last paragraph in the letter:

1. Move the cursor into any of the first three paragraphs.

2. Press Alt-E-S to choose the Copy Special command.

3. Move the cursor into the last paragraph in the letter, and then press the Enter key. Works displays a dialog box in which you can choose to copy the character or the paragraph format. The Paragraph format option is selected.

4. Press the Enter key to copy the format. The last paragraph in the letter will have a 0.5 inch first-line indent, exactly like the first three paragraphs.

The next formatting task will be to indent the three paragraphs that describe toys so that they'll stand out from the rest of the letter text. Because you want each of the three paragraphs to begin with an asterisk for emphasis, it would be nice if the asterisk that begins each margin could extend a little to the left of the rest of the left paragraph margin. To accomplish this formatting, we'll have to indent the whole paragraph and then specify a first-line indent that is slightly less than the indent for the rest of the paragraph. This type of format is called a hanging indent. Here's how to indent the three paragraphs:

1. Move the cursor to the beginning of the Thunder Ducks paragraph, and press the F8 key.

2. Press the Page Down key to extend the highlight down one screen.

3. Press the Down arrow key four times to extend the selection over the last three lines in the Gonzo Gamesman paragraph.

4. Press Alt-T-A to display the Indents & Spacing dialog box.

5. Type .5 in the Left Indent box, and then press the Tab key to move the cursor to the 1st Line Indent box.

6. Type −.2 in the 1st Line Indent box, and then press the Enter key to confirm the selections.

7. Press the Down arrow key to remove the selection highlight. The three paragraphs now have hanging indents:

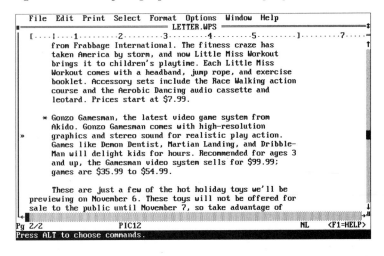

We created the hanging indent by specifying a first-line indent that was 0.2 inch less than the left indent for the rest of the paragraph, which is why the value entered in the 1st Line Indent box was a negative number.

These paragraphs now look good, but we can set them off a little more by making the toy names and asterisks stand out in boldface type:

1. Move the cursor to the asterisk (*) that begins the Thunder Ducks paragraph.

2. Press the F8 key.

3. Hold down the Ctrl key and press the Right arrow key three times to highlight *Thunder Ducks.*

4. Press Ctrl-B to make this text boldface.

5. Repeat this process with the asterisks and toy names at the beginning of the Little Miss Workout and Gonzo Games-man paragraphs.

Now the paragraphs about the toys will really stand out from the rest of the document.

Page formatting

We're almost finished, and it's time to think about how the letter will look when it's printed:

1. Press Ctrl-Home to move the cursor to the beginning of the document.

2. Press Alt-P-V and then press the Enter key to preview the document on the screen. Works displays the first page of the letter in a reduced size.

3. Press the Page Down key to view the second page of the letter.

4. Press the Esc key to return to the document.

We know that this letter is two pages long, so it would be nice to include a header that contains the page number on the second page. Add a simple, one-line header:

1. Press Alt-P-H to choose the Headers & Footers command from the Print menu. The Headers & Footers dialog box appears, and the cursor is in the Header box.

2. Type *&C-&P-*. The *&C* is a formatting command that tells Works to center the text that follows. The *&P* is a formatting command that tells Works to print the current page number. So this entry tells Works to center the header - *pagenumber* -. (For more information about header formatting commands, see the Print Headers & Footers command in the Commands category of the Help Index on the Help menu.)

3. Press Alt-N to choose the No Header On 1st Page option, which tells Works not to print the page number on the first page of the letter.

4. Press the Enter key to enter the header. The header won't appear on the screen, but you can see it if you use the Preview command to display the second page of the letter.

You might have noticed when previewing the document that the third toy paragraph is split between page 1 and page 2. It would be better if this entire paragraph were moved to the second page. To move the paragraph, you can insert a page break:

1. Move the cursor to the blank space between the Little Miss Workout paragraph and the Gonzo Gamesman paragraph.

2. Press Alt-P-I to choose the Insert Page Break command from the Print menu. Works inserts a page break between these two paragraphs so that the second page will begin with the first line of the Gonzo Gamesman paragraph. A manual page break, as you can see, appears as a dotted line across the screen. The page breaks that Works inserts automatically are indicated by a double arrow (>>) symbol at the left edge of the window. To remove a manual page break, simply backspace over it.

This letter is now ready to print. When printing the letter, remember that we want to merge data from a database file into the places indicated by the field markers. To merge the data, we must choose a special printing command from the Print menu and indicate the database file from which the word processor will pull data as it prints.

1. Press Alt-P-F to choose the Print Form Letters command from the Print menu. Works displays a dialog box that lists all the database files that are currently open.

2. If the ADDRESS.WDB file is the only file open, it will be selected in the list. If more than one database file is open, use the Down arrow key to select the ADDRESS.WDB database.

3. Press the Enter key to confirm the selection.

4. Works displays the Print dialog box. Press the Enter key, and Works prints the form letters, making one letter for each record currently displayed in the database file. (For a tip on printing only one form letter or a small group of form letters from a database file, see Chapter 11.)

Before leaving this project, save the form letter file as FORMLTR. We'll use part of it in the project that follows this one. To save the file:

1. Press Alt-F-A to save the file. The Save As dialog box appears.

2. Type *FORMLTR* as the filename. FORMLTR replaces the default filename in the Save File As box.

3. Press the Enter key to save the file.

You can try different formats for the letters you write by experimenting with the Indents & Spacing command and the other commands on the Format menu. Works lets you merge other database information into your form letters by inserting fields that contain other data such as amounts owed or prices or names of products. We'll see more examples of data-merging later in this chapter and in Chapter 14.

Mailing Labels and a Directory

In this project, we'll create some mailing labels and a directory that can serve as a desk reference. You'll need a database file that contains names and addresses such as the ADDRESS.WDB file used in the Form Letter project to complete this project. If you installed Works with Setup, you can open the ADDRESS.WDB file in the Works program directory. Otherwise, follow the instructions in Chapter 12 for creating the ADDRESS.WDB file. In any case, the ADDRESS.WDB file must be open before you continue with this project.

Creating a mailing label document

The word processor document we'll create to make mailing labels contains only field markers. The first step in creating this document is to tell Works which data fields you want to merge into a word processor file. For our labels, we'll use the same merged fields in the same layout that we used in the Form Letter project. Instead of using the Insert Field command to place the fields in our new document one at a time, we'll copy the whole address block (which contains all the field markers we want to use) from the form letter document we completed in the preceding project. (If you haven't yet done the form letter project, follow the instructions in the earlier section, "Inserting the address fields.") Here are the steps if FORMLTR is not already open:

1. Press Alt-F-O and select the FORMLTR file from the list of files.

2. Press the Enter key to open this file.

If FORMLTR is open but is not the active window, then:

3. Select FORMLTR from the Window menu.

Now that FORMLTR is the active window, continue:

4. Press Alt-F-N to make a new file.

5. Press the Enter key to select a new word processor file in the dialog box that appears. A new word processor document opens on the screen.

6. Select the FORMLTR document from the Window menu. The FORMLTR document appears on the screen.

7. Move the cursor to the beginning of the FirstName field marker.

8. Press the F8 key and then press the Down arrow key four times to select all four lines of field markers in the address block.

9. Press Shift-F3 to copy the selected data.

10. Select the new word processor document from the Window menu. The document appears, with the cursor at the top.

11. Press the Enter key to complete the copy. All the field markers from the address block of the FORMLTR file are now copied to the new document.

This new document will be our basic label document, so let's save it as LABEL:

1. Press Alt-F-A to save the file. The Save As dialog box appears.

2. Type *Label* for the filename. LABEL replaces the default filename in the Save File As box.

3. Press the Enter key to save the file.

To print the labels properly, we must tell Works how large the labels are. For this exercise, assume that we are printing labels one across, and that the labels are 1 inch high and 3 inches wide. We'll have to set the label spacing so that Works knows how much space to leave between each address it prints:

☐ Press Alt-P-L to display the Print Labels dialog box. The ADDRESS.WDB database file should be open at this point and its name showing in the Databases list box, like this:

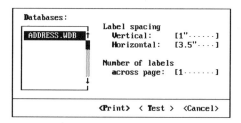

As you can see, the default height for labels is 1 inch. All you need to change is the value in the Horizontal box:

1. Press the Tab key two times to select the Horizontal box.

2. Type *3"*.

3. Insert one-across label stock in your printer.

4. Press Alt-T to test-print one label.

5. Works displays the Page Setup & Margins dialog box. Type the correct margins and page measurements for your one-across label stock, and then press the Enter key.

6. Works displays the Print dialog box. Press the Enter key again.

7. After Works prints the test label, you can adjust the alignment of the label stock in the printer if necessary and press Alt-T to choose Test again.

8. When you are satisfied with the alignment of the label stock in the printer, press Alt-P to print a label for each database record in the ADDRESS.WDB file.

Printing a label directory

You can also use the mailing labels feature to print an address directory. Because you can print more than one label across for two-across or three-across label stock, you can use this feature to print a directory of addresses in two, three, or more columns across a page. We'll use the same LABEL document to create an address directory that has two columns of addresses. The only change is in the Print Labels dialog box:

1. Press Alt-P-L to display the Print Labels dialog box. The ADDRESS.WDB database filename is displayed and selected in the Databases list box.

2. Press Alt-A to select the Number Of Labels Across Page box.

3. Type 2 to set Works for printing two labels across.

4. Press the Enter key to select the Print option.

5. Adjust any margins in the Page Setup & Margins dialog box, and then press the Enter key.

6. To print the labels, press the Enter key when the Print dialog box is displayed.

You can print several columns of labels across a page by selecting the field markers and changing the font to a smaller size. Simply select the whole block of field markers, and use the Font & Style command to select a smaller font. Be sure to adjust the label width in the Print Labels dialog box.

You can use this basic LABEL document to create labels from any database file as long as the database file you select contains fields that have the same FirstName, LastName, Street, City, ST, and Zip field names as does ADDRESS.WDB.

A Promotional Flier

Works doesn't have multi-column formatting or built-in drawing tools, but you can use its Borders and Tabs commands along with its font and font size choices to produce fliers for business, school, or home uses. In this exercise, we'll create a flier that advertises a sale at Acme Toys. The finished flier looks like the one in Figure 5-1.

Entering the text

To begin, open a new word processor document and type the title and the first paragraph of the text shown in Figure 5-1. Don't worry about font sizes, borders, or character styles for now. When you reach the end of the paragraph, press the Enter key two times to move the cursor down two lines.

Next, set some tab stops for the columns that show the before-and-after prices. We want to set two center-aligned tabs for the *Was* and *Now* column headings:

1. Press Alt-T-T to display the Tabs dialog box.

2. Type *4.3* to specify a tab stop at 4.3 inches on the ruler.

3. Press Alt-C to indicate Center alignment for the tab stop.

4. Press Alt-1 to indicate a dotted-line tab leader.

5. Press the Enter key to insert the tab stop. A *C* appears at the 4.3-inch mark on the ruler at the top of the window.

6. Type *5.3* to specify a tab stop at 5.3 inches on the ruler. Because the last tab stop we set was centered, Works assumes that we want to center this tab also, so it isn't necessary to specify Center alignment again.

7. Press Alt-N to indicate no tab leader: We don't want dotted lines between the *Was* and *Now* column labels.

8. Press the Enter key to insert this tab stop. A *C* appears at the 5.3-inch mark on the ruler.

9. Press Alt-D to return to the document editing screen.

```
        ACME TOY COMPANY'S PRE-HOLIDAY BLOWOUT SALE!!!

To clear our shelves for the truckloads of new holiday toys
that will soon be arriving at our store, we're SLASHING
PRICES on our remaining stock. Here are just a few examples:

Item ................................... Was        Now

Alice Action figures ................... 11.99       6.99
Alice Action Chase Plane ............... 29.99      13.99
Bouncing Boris dolls ................... 18.99      11.99
Bouncing Boris Doll Accessory Kits ....... 9.99      4.99
Cribbage Porch Kids dolls .............. 34.99      19.99
Deputy Duck Rocking Horses ............. 79.99      45.99
Elegance Tea Party Set ................. 9.99        4.49
Floating Freddie Water Pistols .......... 2.39        .89
Gloria Trent Mystery Game .............. 15.99      10.99
Homemaker Gerome Cooking Sets .......... 23.99      11.99
Legal Beagles Game ..................... 19.99      12.99
Mr. Mondo Water Wrestling Kit .......... 44.99      36.99
Nemco Girls' Bikes ..................... 99.99      79.99
AXYS R/C Stunt Car ..................... 99.99      79.99
Samurai Snail figures .................. 13.99       7.99
Samurai Snail Shell Fortress ........... 54.99      39.99
Squish Boys' Stunt Bikes .............. 129.99      89.99
Rad-Cal Skateboards .................... 99.99      64.99
Triple Trax Raceway ................... 124.99      79.99
Videoid Game Systems ................... 99.99      69.99
Whammer Volleyball Sets ................ 33.99      14.99

These and many other toys MUST BE SOLD to make room for our
new holiday inventory, so COME ON DOWN!!! Along with the
city's lowest prices, you'll get:

                * Free Parking
                * Free Balloons (kids under 5)
                * Daily Door Prizes
                * Friendly Service

      HOLIDAY BLOWOUT HOURS (Nov. 1 through Nov. 16 only):

            Monday - Thursday:     10 AM - 6 PM
            Friday:                10 AM - 9 PM
            Saturday:              10 AM - 5 PM
            Sunday:                Noon  - 5 PM

************************************************************
            A c m e   T o y   C o m p a n y
    123 Walden Court * Centerville, CA 12345 * (404) 555-1111
```

Figure 5-1.
You can use Works' formatting options to create fliers like this one.

Now we can enter the text for these column labels:

1. Type *Item* and press the Tab key. The cursor moves to the 4.3-inch tab stop, and dotted lines fill up the space left by the tab.

2. Type *Was* and press the Tab key. The cursor moves to the 5.3-inch tab stop.

3. Type *Now* and press the Enter key two times to move the cursor down two lines. The flier now looks like this:

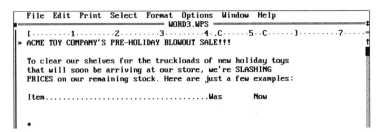

Works always continues the current paragraph format in any new paragraphs that you create when you press the Enter key, so the line at which the cursor is now located will contain the same tab stops as the line above it. For the lines that will contain the actual sale items and prices, however, we want the tab stops for the prices to be decimal tabs so that all the price numbers will align properly. We'll have to reset these tab stops to make the change:

1. Press Alt-T-T to display the Tabs dialog box again.

2. Type *4.3* to set the tab at the 4.3-inch mark on the ruler.

3. Press Alt-E to change the alignment from Center to Decimal.

4. Press Alt-1 to indicate a dotted-line tab leader.

5. Press the Enter key to insert the changed tab stop.

6. Type *5.3* to set the tab at the 5.3-inch mark on the ruler.

7. Press Alt-N to indicate no tab leader.

8. Press the Enter key to insert this change.

9. Press Alt-D to return to the document editing screen.

With these tabs reset, you can now enter all the text for the sale items and prices. This is the procedure:

1. Type the item name, and press the Tab key. The cursor moves to the 4.3-inch tab stop, and the space between the item text and the tab stop fills with dot characters.

2. Type the *Was* price, and press the Tab key to move the cursor to the 5.3-inch tab stop.

3. Type the *Now* price, and press the Enter key to move down to the next line.

Complete these steps for all the sale items listed on the flier. When you finish the last line of sale items, press the Enter key to move to the next line. Now we want to clear the custom tab stops that we set so that they won't affect the paragraphs of text below:

1. Press Alt-T-T to choose the Tabs command.

2. Press Alt-A to delete all the custom tab stops.

3. Press Alt-D to return to the document.

When you choose the Delete All command in the Tabs dialog box, Works deletes only the custom tab stops. The default tab stops, which occur every 0.5 inch, are still there.

Now press the Enter key one more time, and then enter all the text down through the line that begins with *HOLIDAY BLOWOUT HOURS* and ends with a colon. To enter the store hours, we'll use Works' default tab stops:

1. Type *Monday - Thursday:* and then press the Tab key two times.

2. Type *10 AM - 6 PM* and then press the Enter key.

3. Type *Friday:* and then press the Tab key four times.

4. Type *10 AM - 9 PM* and then press the Enter key.

5. Enter the Saturday and Sunday hours in the same way. After you enter the Sunday hours, press the Enter key two times to move the cursor down two lines. The flier window now looks like the example on the next page.

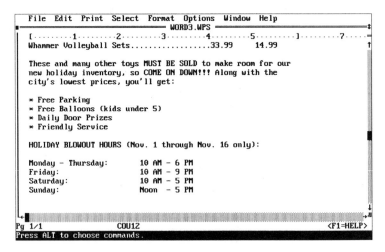

To enter the line that separates the sale items from the store name and address, type asterisk characters (Shift-8) across the screen until the cursor reaches the end of the line and moves down to the next line. Then delete enough asterisks so that the asterisks appear on only one line, stretching all the way to the right margin. (The cursor should be blinking at the end of the line of asterisks.)

After you enter the line of asterisks, press the Enter key and then type the store name and address. Notice the extra spaces between the letters in the Acme Toy Company name.

Formatting the flier text

Now we'll use Works' formatting tools to dress up the text on this page. First, make the first line centered and boldface:

1. Move the cursor to the beginning of the first line of text.

2. Press Ctrl-C to center this line.

3. Press the F8 key three times to select the entire line.

4. Press Ctrl-B to make the line boldface.

We also want to boldface the words *SLASHING PRICES* in the first paragraph, along with the column titles in the table of sale items:

1. Move the cursor to the beginning of *SLASHING*.

2. Press Shift-Ctrl-Right arrow key two times to select *SLASH-ING PRICES*.

3. Press Ctrl-B to make these two words boldface.

4. Move the cursor to the beginning of the word *Item* in the line of column labels.

5. Press the F8 key three times to select the entire line.

6. Press Ctrl-B to make this line boldface.

Apply the boldface style to the following text in the flier. Select the phrases *MUST BE SOLD, COME ON DOWN!!!*, *city's lowest prices, HOLIDAY BLOWOUT HOURS*, and *Acme Toy Company*, and make them boldface.

The four lines that detail extra attractions are currently aligned with the left margin, but they would look better if they were positioned more toward the center of the flier. We could use the Center alignment command, but then each line would be centered, and the beginnings of the lines wouldn't line up. Instead, use the default tab stops:

1. Move the cursor to the asterisk that begins the Free Parking line.

2. Press the Tab key four times. The line moves to the center of the page.

3. Repeat steps 1 and 2 for the other three lines in this section.

While you're at it, you can use the same technique to indent the four lines of store hours. Move the cursor to the beginning of each store hours line, and press the Tab key three times to move each line to the center of the page.

The last alignment adjustment we'll make is to center the HOLIDAY BLOWOUT HOURS line, the line of asterisks, and the store name and address:

1. Move the cursor to the beginning of the HOLIDAY BLOWOUT HOURS line.

2. Press Ctrl-C to center the line.

3. Move the cursor to the first asterisk in the line of asterisks.

4. Press Shift-Ctrl-End.

5. Press Ctrl-C to center these lines.

Now that the text is arranged the way we want, we'll put a border around the whole page:

1. Press the F8 key four times to select the entire document.

2. Press Alt-T-O to choose the Borders command. The Borders dialog box appears, like this:

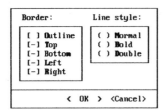

3. Press *O* to select an Outline border, which will surround the whole document.

4. Press *N* to select a normal border.

5. Press the Enter key to confirm these settings. A single-line border appears around the document on the screen.

For our purposes, the flier is finished. The only other changes you might want to make are to select different fonts or font sizes, but your choices will depend on the printer you use. (See Chapter 2 for more information about printers and fonts.)

If you use a printer that offers larger font sizes, you can select the flier's first line and make it larger than the others. Experiment with other font and font size selections that your options permit, but be careful not to mix more than two different fonts on the flier page. Using more than two fonts on this page will only make it less readable. Using the Preview command on the Print menu will show you how different fonts will look, but to really see how font and font size changes will affect this document, you'll have to print it on paper.

Using the flier as a standard format

This flier can be used as a standard format for many other types of documents that have a similar layout. For example, the three-column table is suited for documents such as restaurant menus, parts lists, roll sheets, or inventory listings.

A Monthly Report

In this project, we'll use some of Works' other document formatting commands to create a standard report form. Many people in business create routine reports that are updated each month, or they create reports on different subjects that have essentially the same document structure. With this form, you'll be able to start any report with much of the document organization and formatting work already done.

The purpose of these files is to store standard formatting so that you won't have to enter much text. Because of the way Works prints header and footer information, however, we'll have to break this project up into two documents: one to contain the title page and contents page (the so-called front matter in the report) and the other to contain the text of the report. Let's create the front matter document first. Begin by pressing Alt-F-N and then pressing the Enter key to open a new word processor document and display it on the screen.

Entering the front matter text

Now we're ready to enter the text for this document, which will consist of a title page and a table of contents. The finished title page will look like the example on the following page.

As you can see, the text is generic, so you can fill in the actual text each time you create the report. For now, simply type the report title, byline, and author name without using any formatting. Leave one blank line between each line of the title and byline, and then press the Enter key six times to leave five blank lines between the title and the author information block. Finally, type the text in the author information block.

The cursor should now be blinking at the end of the last line in the author information block. You've reached the end of the title page, so it's time to insert a page break:

1. Press the Enter key to move down one line below the author information block.

2. Press Alt-P-I to insert a page break. A dotted page-break line appears, and the cursor moves to the line below the page break.

```
                    Title of Report

                         by

                     Your Name
```

```
                                Your Name
                                Your Company
                                Your Address
                                Your Phone Number
```

Now we can enter the text for the Table of Contents page. The finished page looks like Figure 5-2:

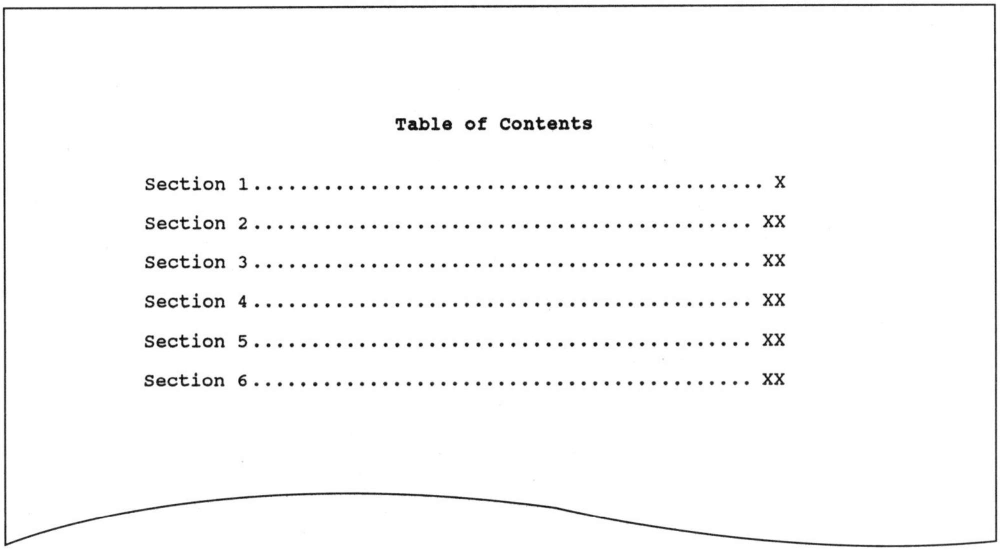

```
                        Table of Contents


    Section 1 ............................................. X

    Section 2 ........................................... XX

    Section 3 ........................................... XX

    Section 4 ........................................... XX

    Section 5 ........................................... XX

    Section 6 ........................................... XX
```

Figure 5-2.
This template contains generic text that will be replaced when each version of the report is written.

We'll need to set a tab stop to separate the page numbers from the section names. As you can see, a tab leader character also fills the empty space between each section name and its page number. Enter the text as explained:

1. Type *Table of Contents*, and press the Enter key three times to leave two blank lines.

2. Press Alt-T-T to display the Tabs dialog box.

3. Type *5.5* to set a tab stop at the 5.5-inch mark on the ruler.

4. Press Alt-R to choose right alignment for this tab stop.

5. Press Alt-1 to choose a dotted-line tab leader.

6. Press the Enter key to insert this tab stop. An *R* appears at the 5.5-inch mark on the ruler.

7. Press Alt-D to return to the document editing screen.

Now you can enter the section names and the page numbers as shown in Figure 5-2:

1. Type *Section 1* and press the Tab key.

2. Type *X* as the page number, and press the Enter key two times.

3. Repeat steps 1 and 2 for the rest of the sections shown in Figure 5-2.

Formatting the front matter text

Returning to the first page of this two-page document, we'll now adjust the alignment of the text on the page. Begin by centering the title and author information and by making the title boldface:

1. Press Ctrl-Home to return to the top of the document.

2. Press the F8 key.

3. Press the Down arrow key five times to select the title and byline information.

4. Press Ctrl-C to center this text on the page.

5. Press the Up arrow key to move the cursor back to the beginning of the title line.

6. Press the F8 key three times to select this line.

7. Press Ctrl-B to make the title boldface.

Next, align the author information block on the right margin:

1. Move the cursor to the beginning of the Your Name line in the author information block.

2. Press the F8 key.

3. Press the Down arrow key four times to select the entire author information block.

4. Press Ctrl-R to right-align this block.

We left some blank spaces between the report title and the author information block, but we want to make sure the text is vertically aligned on the page. To really see this alignment, preview the title page.

1. Be sure the cursor is located somewhere in the text that will be printed on the title page (not in the Table of Contents text).

2. Press Alt-P-V to preview the title page. Works displays the Print dialog box.

3. Press the Enter key to accept the defaults. Works displays the title page on the screen, like this:

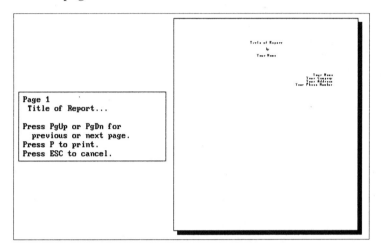

As you can see, the title and author information block are all at the top of the page. To move them down, insert some extra blank lines before the title and between the title and the author information block:

1. First press the Esc key to return to the document.

2. Move the cursor to the beginning of the Report Title line.

3. Press the Enter key 20 times to insert 20 blank lines above the title.

4. Move the cursor to the Your Name line of the author information block.

5. Press the Enter key 15 times to insert 15 more blank lines between the title and the author information block.

Now, if you preview the document again, you'll see that the title is centered on the page and the author information block is located at the bottom of the page.

Finally, center the Table of Contents line on the second page and make this text boldface:

1. Move the cursor to the Table of Contents line.

2. Press the F8 key three times to select this line.

3. Press Ctrl-C to center the text.

4. Press Ctrl-B to make the text boldface.

This document is finished, so we'll save it:

1. Press Alt-F-A to display the Save As dialog box.

2. Type *Front* in the Save file as text box.

3. Press the Enter key to save the file.

Now we can always open the FRONT file when we begin a report. We can change the report title, author, and contents information and then use the Save As command to save the file with a different name. That way, our FRONT file will remain untouched on the disk, ready for the next month's report.

Entering the report text

Like the front matter document, the report document will contain generic text that will serve merely as a placeholder for the real text you'll enter as you create actual reports later. Along with the placeholder text, this report template will use a footer paragraph that also contains text. Begin by opening a new file and creating the footer paragraph:

1. Press Alt-F-N, and then press the Enter key to open a new word processor document and display it on the screen.

2. Press Alt-P-H to display the Headers and Footers dialog box, like this:

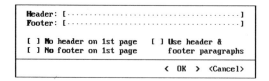

3. Press Alt-U to choose the Use Header & Footer Paragraphs option.

4. Press Alt-N to choose the No Header On 1st Page option.

5. Press the Enter key to return to the document. Works displays header and footer paragraph markers on the screen, like this:

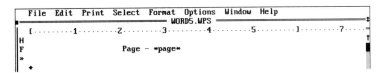

With header and footer paragraphs, Works lets you enter and format the header or footer text right on the screen. Next, create a two-line footer that contains the report name and the page number on the first line and the author's name and the date on the second line. Here's how:

1. Press the Up arrow key to move the cursor into the footer paragraph.

2. Type *Report Title -* followed by a blank space as a placeholder for the actual title of the report.

3. Press the Right arrow key to move the cursor to the *P* in *Page* on the same line.

4. Press the Backspace key to move the *Page - *page** text so that it is one space to the right of the dash after the report title. The line should look like this:

   Report Title - Page - *page*

5. Delete the dash between *Page* and **page**.

6. Move the cursor to the space after **page**.

7. Press Shift-Enter to move the cursor down a line and add a line to the footer paragraph. (Works won't let you press the Enter key alone to add a line to a footer paragraph.)

8. Type *Your Name -* and add a blank space after the dash.

9. Press Alt-E-P to choose the Insert Special command from the Edit menu.

10. Press the D key to choose the Print Date option.

11. Press the Enter key. Works adds the **date** marker to the footer.

Now the footer paragraph looks like this:

```
 File  Edit  Print  Select  Format  Options  Window  Help
                      WORD5.WPS
  [........1.........2.........C.........4.........5.........R.........7.....
H
F Report Title - Page *page*
F Your Name - *date*
»
  ◆
```

It's a two-line, left-aligned footer, and because it contains the *page* and *date* special characters, Works will print the current page number and the date when the document is printed. We haven't entered any text in the header paragraph, so it won't print at all.

Now enter the rest of the text:

1. Press the Down arrow key to move out of the footer para-graph and into the first line of the document.

2. Type *Report Title* and press the Enter key.

3. Type *Section I* and press the Enter key.

5. Type *Section I text goes here.* and press the Enter key.

6. Type *Section II* and press the Enter key.

7. Type *Section II text goes here.* Your document should now look like this:

```
 File  Edit  Print  Select  Format  Options  Window  Help
                      WORD5.WPS
  [........1.........2.........3.........4.........5.........]........7.....
H
F Report Title - Page *page*
F Your Name - *date*
» Report Title
  Section I
  Section I text goes here.
  Section II
  Section II text goes here.
  ◆
```

We'll work only as far as Section II in this project, but obviously, you could add more sections to this document if your report were longer.

Formatting the report

Now set the line spacing and paragraph indents for the paragraphs that will contain text rather than titles:

1. Press the Up arrow key four times, and then press the Home key to move the cursor to the beginning of the Report Title line.

2. Press the F8 key.

3. Press Ctrl-End to select all the text in the document.

4. Press Ctrl-2 to set double spacing for the document.

Now reformat the paragraphs that will contain text so that they will have a first-line indent of 0.5 inch:

1. Move the cursor to the line that contains *Section I text goes here.*

2. Press Alt-T-A to choose the Indents & Spacing command. Works displays a dialog box, and the cursor is in the Left Indent box.

3. Press the Down arrow key one time to select the 1st Line Indent box.

4. Type .5 to specify a 0.5-inch first-line indent.

5. Press the Enter key to confirm this setting.

With the left paragraph indent set on this first paragraph, we can simply copy the format to the text paragraph for Section II:

1. Press Alt-E-S to choose the Copy Special command.

2. Move the cursor to the line that contains *Section II text goes here.*

3. Press the Enter key. Works displays a dialog box that offers a choice of copying either the character or the paragraph format. The paragraph format is selected as the default.

4. Press the Enter key to copy the paragraph format. The text paragraph for Section II is now indented 0.5 inch.

Because the report title falls directly above the Section I title, the document will look better if the report title is centered and underlined:

1. Move the cursor to the Report Title line.

2. Press the F8 key three times to select the whole line.

3. Press Ctrl-C to center the title.

4. Press Ctrl-U to underline the title.

Next we'll set page breaks so that each new section will begin at the top of a new page, and we'll add bookmarks so that it will be easy to jump to the beginning of any new section. The only page break we need to enter right now is the one for Section II:

1. Move the cursor to the beginning of the line that contains the Section II title.

2. Press Alt-P-I to insert a page break above the Section II title. (Note: Because the cursor was at the beginning of the line, Works placed the page break above the current line. Works always places the page break immediately before the cursor position.)

Because we'll fill in this report later, it would be nice to insert some bookmarks so that we can jump quickly to the beginning of any section. Insert a bookmark now so that we can jump to the beginning of Section II:

1. Move the cursor to the line that contains the Section II title.

2. Press Alt-E-N to choose the Bookmark Name command. A dialog box appears.

3. Type *Section II*, and press the Enter key. Works inserts an invisible bookmark in this spot. When you want to jump to the beginning of Section II, you can press Alt-S-G (the Go To command) and select the Section II name from the list that appears. Works will then scroll the document to the beginning of Section II.

The finishing touch for this report will be to right-align the footer paragraph so that the text appears in the lower-right corner of each page:

1. Move the cursor to the beginning of the first line of footer text.

2. Press the F8 key.

3. Press the Down arrow key two times to select both lines of the footer.

4. Press Ctrl-R to indicate right alignment for this text. On screen, the finished template looks like the one on the following page.

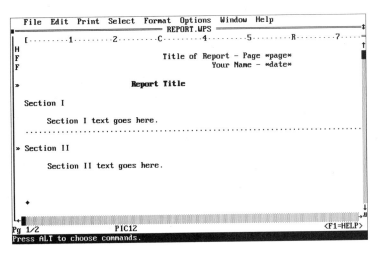

```
  File  Edit  Print  Select  Format  Options  Window  Help
========================== REPORT.WPS ==========================
[..........1.........2.........C.........4.........5.........R.........7....

H
F                              Title of Report - Page *page*
F                                   Your Name - *date*

»                            Report Title

   Section I

         Section I text goes here.
   ...............................................................

» Section II

         Section II text goes here.



   •

Pg 1/2                    PIC12                        <F1=HELP>
Press ALT to choose commands.
```

The report is finished for now, so you can save it with the name REPORT. As before, you can open the REPORT file each month, make changes, and then save the changed file with a different name so that the original version stays unchanged on disk.

Creating monthly reports

To use these files each month, you can open the FRONT or REPORT files and then replace the existing text with the text of your report. If you are doing a monthly report, you might be able to enter some "boilerplate" text that you can reuse every month, and simply change specific facts or sets of data.

When you begin replacing the existing generic text in this template, first choose the Typing Replaces Selection command (Alt-O-Y). Whatever you type will then replace whatever you have selected instead of simply being inserted in front of it, which is Works' normal mode. With Typing Replaces Selection turned on, you can select the text you want to replace, such as the report title, and then simply type the new title in its place. Using this approach lets you avoid having to delete the old text before typing the new text.

As you fill in the text for each section, remember that Works carries the paragraph-format settings from the current paragraph into the next paragraph you create. Unless you deliberately select a paragraph and change its settings, all the text paragraphs will have a 0.5-inch first-line indent, and the whole document will be double-spaced.

If you need to add footnotes to your report, use the Edit Footnote command (Alt-E-T) to insert them. Works places all footnotes at the end of a document, so be sure to separate the notes from the end of your text by inserting a page break or by drawing a horizontal line using the Borders command.

These projects have shown you how to use most of the word processor's commands to work with text in a variety of ways. As you pursue your own projects, you'll develop additional techniques of your own. In Chapter 14, we'll create an expanded report that includes data copied from the Works Spreadsheet and Database.

6

Basic Spreadsheet Techniques

In this chapter, we'll explore the basic features of the Works Spreadsheet. If you're new to spreadsheets, this is a good place to begin learning about how they work and what they can do. By following some simple examples, you'll see how spreadsheets work in general and how the Works Spreadsheet handles fundamental spreadsheet operations.

The Spreadsheet Concept

Computer spreadsheet programs are electronic versions of the paper spreadsheets that have been around for decades. A spreadsheet arranges numbers in a matrix of rows and columns. In a budget, for example, you can use the rows to track figures for income or expenses in several categories, and each column can represent a different period of time. Because numbers are laid out in rows and columns, it's easy to see not only totals but also the individual numbers that make up those totals and the relationships between the two. A common example of a spreadsheet is a budget such as the one shown in Figure 6-1.

The budget shown in Figure 6-1 contains separate rows for rent, utilities, telephone, equipment leases, and salary expenses, and separate columns that show the expenses in these categories for each month. The row at the bottom (the famous "bottom line") shows each month's total expenses. The column at the far right shows the total spent on each category for the entire quarter.

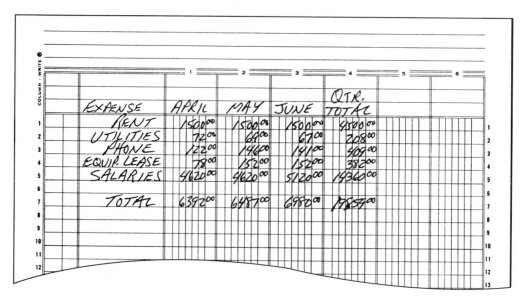

Figure 6-1.
A common type of spreadsheet is a budget.

The totals in this spreadsheet are calculated by adding the numbers, or values, in each row or column. We could produce these same totals using a calculator, but seeing the values that contribute to the totals (as well as the totals themselves) shows us more. Looking only at the monthly totals, for example, we see only that expenses are rising from one month to the next. Because of the spreadsheet format, however, we can see that the salary expenses went up in June and that the equipment lease expenses went up in May. In other words, we know exactly why expenses went up.

Electronic spreadsheets are also composed of rows and columns, so they show the relationships between numbers in the same way. But electronic spreadsheets can also store formulas that calculate numbers automatically. You can change the numbers contributing to a total, for example, and the total itself changes automatically. If we were working on paper and we changed the Rent value for May in Figure 6-1, for example, we'd have to recalculate the Rent total for the quarter and the total expenses for May manually. In an electronic spreadsheet like the one in Works, these recalculations are made automatically.

Along with automatic recalculation, the Works Spreadsheet makes number crunching easier in other ways. You can copy numbers or formulas, for example, so that you don't have to reenter a formula over and over again to use it in other areas in which essentially the same calculation is used. In Figure 6-1, for example, the same basic addition formula is used to sum each month's expenses: In each column, we want to sum the five values above. Formulas that perform calculations can use arithmetic operators (+, −, *, or /), or they can use functions. The Works Spreadsheet tool has dozens of predefined functions that perform various financial and scientific calculations, from summing or averaging a group of numbers to calculating logarithms or cosines.

By using formatting commands, you can set the spreadsheet to display values with dollar signs, commas, percent signs, or decimal points. You can also draw attention to text or numbers by displaying them in boldface. In addition, the Works Spreadsheet can quickly translate numbers into charts that clearly show important relationships.

The features of the Works Spreadsheet can be divided into five groups, according to function: entering and editing data, calculating, formatting, charting, and printing. Let's look at these features one group at a time.

Entering and Editing Data

To start building a spreadsheet, you create a new spreadsheet file:

1. Press Alt-F-N to create a new file. Works displays a dialog box in which you can choose the type of file you want to create.

2. Press the S key to choose a spreadsheet file. Works displays a new spreadsheet document on the screen, as in Figure 6-2.

The spreadsheet itself is divided into a matrix of rows (which are numbered consecutively from 1 through 4096) and columns (which are labeled alphabetically from A through IV). The row and column labels frame the left and top side of the work area. Each intersection of a row and a column is called a cell, and each cell is identified with a column-and-row reference indicating the intersection it represents. The first cell in the upper-left corner of the spreadsheet is cell A1, for example, because it's at the intersection of column A and row 1. The cells make up the work area of the spreadsheet.

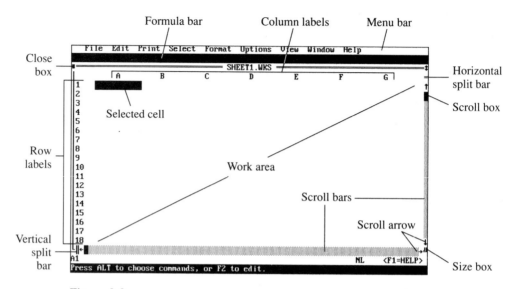

Figure 6-2.
The Works Spreadsheet screen.

Because you often work with groups of cells in the spreadsheet, you can refer to a group of cells as a *range*. A range of cells is a rectangular block of contiguous cells that occupies one or more rows and one or more columns. It is identified in Works by the upper-left and lower-right cells of the block, separated by a colon. If you selected the cells A1, A2, B1, and B2, for example, that range would be designated as A1:B2.

Below the menu bar at the top of the screen, the formula bar displays the contents of any selected cell. As you enter text or numbers in a cell, what you've typed appears in the formula bar. At the right and along the bottom of the work area are scroll bars that you can use (if you have a mouse) to move quickly to other areas of the spreadsheet. In the status line immediately below the bottom scroll bar, Works always shows the cell reference for the currently selected cell or range. At least one cell is always selected in the spreadsheet.

After you open a new spreadsheet file, cell A1 is selected, and when you press an arrow key, the cell selection moves. The table on the following page shows how various keys move the cell selection in the spreadsheet.

Key(s)	Moves Cell Selection
Left arrow	Left one cell
Right arrow	Right one cell
Up arrow	Up one cell
Down arrow	Down one cell
Tab	Right one cell
Shift-Tab	Left one cell
Home	To first filled column in same row
End	To last filled column in same row
Ctrl-Home	To upper-left nonfrozen cell
Ctrl-End	To lower-right filled cell
Page Up	Up one screen
Page Down	Down one screen
Ctrl-Page Up	Left one screen
Ctrl-Page Down	Right one screen
Ctrl-any arrow	In arrow direction to next filled cell

Try these key combinations to move the cell selection around the spreadsheet. The movement keys that move the selection from one block of data or to filled rows or columns won't work unless you've first entered data in the spreadsheet, so you might want to leave those commands for later.

You can use other shortcut keys to select entire rows, columns, or ranges in the spreadsheet. The most important of these is the Extend Selection key, F8, which lets you extend a selection from one cell to adjacent cells by pressing the arrow keys. In the spreadsheet, you can also hold down the Shift key as you press an arrow key to extend a selection. To select cells A1, B1, and C1 in a new spreadsheet, for example, you would select cell A1, either press F8 or hold down the Shift key, and then press the Right arrow key two times. Works lets you use other keyboard shortcuts to select ranges of cells or entire rows or columns. You'll find information about these shortcuts in the *Microsoft Works Quick Reference.*

Let's create a simple budget spreadsheet like the one shown in Figure 6-1 to see how to enter data in the spreadsheet:

1. Select cell A1.

2. Type *Expenses*. Notice that as you type, the letters appear in the formula bar.

3. Press the Enter key to enter this text in cell A1. As you can see, Works places a quotation mark in front of the label name in the formula bar. This mark identifies the data you've entered as a label, or text, rather than as a value or a number.

The Works Spreadsheet considers data as one of three types: labels (text), values (numbers), or formulas. When you begin an entry with a letter, a blank space, or a quotation mark, Works assumes you are entering a label. When you begin an entry with a number, Works assumes you are entering a value. To let Works know you're entering a formula, you must begin the entry with an equal sign (=). After you enter a formula, Works displays the result of the formula's calculation rather than the formula itself. (See "Calculating" later in this chapter.) Works has a default format for each type of data: Labels are left aligned in the cell, and values are right aligned. (See "Formatting" later in this chapter.)

If you make a mistake typing an entry and you haven't yet pressed the Enter key, you can use the Backspace key to back up and correct your mistake. If you discover a mistake later, however, you have to either replace or edit the contents of the cell. To completely replace a cell's contents, simply select the cell, type the new data, and press the Enter key. But if you want to make only a small change to a cell's contents, you can edit the contents without completely replacing them. In cell A1, we entered the label *Expenses*, but we should have entered *Expense* instead. Let's edit this label:

1. Select cell A1, if it isn't already selected. The contents of the cell are displayed in the formula bar.

2. Press the F2 (Edit) key. A blinking cursor appears at the end of the label in the formula bar and the word EDIT appears on the status line.

3. Press the Backspace key one time to delete the *s* at the end of *Expenses*, and then press the Enter key to confirm the change.

Now let's enter the rest of the labels in the top row of this spreadsheet:

1. Press the Right arrow key to select cell B1, and type *April.*

2. Press the Right arrow key again. The entry is confirmed, and the cell selection moves to cell C1.

When you press an arrow key after typing an entry, Works accepts the entry and at the same time moves you in the indicated direction. So, if you're entering a lot of data at one time, you can press an arrow key to confirm an entry and move to the next cell, thus saving the extra step of pressing the Enter key to confirm an entry.

□ Repeat steps 2 and 3 above to enter the labels for *May, June,* and *Qtr. Total,* as in Figure 6-1.

Notice that Works converts the names *April* and *June* to *Apr* and *Jun:* Works interprets month names as dates and treats them accordingly. Because you can perform date and time calculations using the Works Spreadsheet, Works treats dates as values and formats them as such: You'll notice that the month labels are right aligned rather than left aligned as the other labels are.

Now enter the row labels in column A:

1. Use the Left and Down arrow keys to select cell A2.

2. Type *Rent,* and press the Down arrow key to confirm the entry and select cell A3.

3. Enter the labels *Utilities* and *Phone* in cells A3 and A4.

4. Select cell A5, and enter the label *Equip. Lease.*

5. Press the Enter key to confirm the entry. Notice, though, that the label extends beyond the right edge of the cell selection, like this:

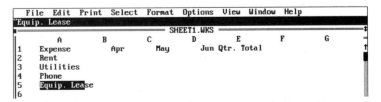

The label contains 12 characters, but the width of column A is the default 10 characters. When you enter more letters than will fit in a spreadsheet column, Works extends the entry into the adjacent cell in the next column, as long as that cell is empty. (If you enter more digits than will fit, Works either displays a series of hatch marks or displays the number in exponential notation.) In this case, the last two letters of this label have been extended into column B. Because we'll want to use column B to store the expense numbers for April, we'll have to widen column A enough to accommodate the entire *Equip. Lease* label:

1. Press Alt-T to display the Format menu.

2. Press the W key to choose the Column Width command. Works displays the Column Width dialog box, like this:

Column A is now 10 characters wide, but we need it to be at least 12 characters wide to contain the label. Let's make it 14 characters wide:

1. Type *14* to change the column width.

2. Press the Enter key to confirm the change. Column A widens, and now the entire label fits inside it.

Now finish entering the labels:

1. Enter the label *Salaries* in cell A6.

2. Enter the label *Total* in cell A8.

Entering numbers is exactly the same as entering labels, except that Works knows they're numbers, so they're right aligned in their cells. To enter numbers, you can use either the number keys in the top row of the keyboard or the number keys in the numeric keypad. If you use the numeric keypad, however, you must be sure that the Num Lock key is turned off; otherwise, the numeric keypad's keys move the cell selection. If the letters NL appear on the right side of the status line next to the Help reminder, Num Lock is on.

Follow the steps on the next page to enter the expense numbers (but not the totals) from the *April* column in Figure 6-1 in the appropriate cells in the sample spreadsheet.

1. Select cell B2.

2. Type *1500*, and press the Down arrow key to enter the number and select cell B3.

3. Type *72*, and press the Down arrow key to enter the number and select cell B4.

4. Type *122*, and press the Down arrow key to enter the number and select cell B5.

5. Type *78*, and press the Down arrow key to enter the number and select cell B6.

6. Type *4620* and press the Enter key.

You can always enter numbers in individual cells as you've just done, but you can also copy cell contents to enter repeated numbers or labels quickly. In Figure 6-1, you'll notice that the Rent expense is the same for all three months. You could enter that number three times, but you can also use Works' Fill Right command to copy it quickly. Let's use Fill Right to enter the May and June Rent expenses:

1. Select cell B2.

2. Press the F8 key to extend the selection.

3. Press the Right arrow key two times to select cells C2 and D2.

4. Press Alt-E-R to choose the Fill Right command from the Edit menu. Works copies the value from cell B2 to cells C2 and D2, like this:

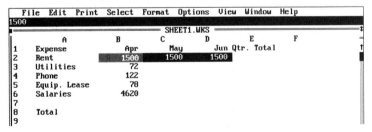

You can use the Fill Right command to copy any cell contents in the spreadsheet, whether they're labels, values, or formulas. The Fill Down command on the Edit menu works in the same way, except that it copies down instead of to the right. The Edit menu also has commands to move data from one cell or group of cells to another and to copy a cell's contents. See the Edit Move and Edit Copy commands in the Commands category of the Help Index on the Help menu.

For now, finish entering all the other values in rows 3, 4, 5, and 6, and in columns C and D. When you finish, we'll enter some formulas to calculate the totals in row 8 and column E.

Calculating

Whenever you want the Works Spreadsheet to perform a calculation, you must enter a formula describing the type of calculation you want performed and pointing out the specific cells or values you want calculated. Every formula starts with the equal sign (=). If a formula simply contains cell references or values, the equal sign must be followed by the cell references, numbers, and arithmetic operators that make up the calculation, like this:

    =B1+A2–3

If you use a function in a formula, the formula must begin with an equal sign, which is followed by a function name and an argument enclosed in parentheses, like this:

    =Function(*Argument1*, *Argument2*, …)

Let's enter a simple formula in cell B8 that calculates the total expenses for April, as follows:

1. Select cell B8.

2. Type an equal sign (=) to tell Works that you're beginning a formula.

3. Type *B2+B3+B4+B5+B6* to indicate which cell contents you want the formula to add.

4. Press the Enter key. The result of this addition formula appears in cell B8.

In this case, we told Works to add the contents of cells B2, B3, B4, B5, and B6, which contain the expense figures for April. We could have just as easily used the actual amounts inside those cells in the formula so that the formula would read *=1500+72+122+78+4620*, but by using the cell references instead we can now change the contents of any of those cells, and the formula will recalculate. Try it.

1. Select cell B3.

2. Type *82*, and press the Enter key.

We have just changed the contents of cell B3 from *72* to *82*, and the total amount shown in cell B8 now reads *6402* instead of *6392*. By using cell references in the formula, we have told Works to add the contents of those cells, so if we change the contents the formula will recalculate the total. If we had used actual numbers in the formula, we would have had to edit the formula itself to produce a different total.

When you're adding lots of values in a formula, it can be tedious to enter each cell reference individually. Fortunately, Works has functions that operate on ranges of cells. Let's use a function and a range argument in a formula to total the May expenses.

1. Select cell C8.

2. Start the formula by typing, *=SUM(*. The SUM function tells the spreadsheet to add all the numbers in the argument, and the open parenthesis begins the argument itself.

3. Type the range *C2:C6*.

4. End the argument with a closing parenthesis, and then press the Enter key to enter the formula. The total for May appears in cell C8.

Another variation on entering formulas is to ''point'' to the cells you want to include in an argument. You can use the arrow keys to select a cell and then use the F8 key to extend the selection to select a whole range and include it in a formula. Let's total the expenses for June using this method:

1. Select cell D8.

2. Start the formula by typing *=SUM(*.

3. Move the cell selection to cell D2 using the Up arrow key. The reference D2 appears in the formula bar, and you'll notice that the word POINT appears in the status line to show that you're pointing to cell references.

4. Press the F8 key to extend the selection. A colon appears after the D2 reference in the formula bar, and the reference D2 appears to the right of it.

5. Press the Down arrow key to extend the selection down to cell D6. After cell D6 is selected, the argument reads *(D2:D6*, which is the range of cells from D2 through D6.

6. Type a closing parenthesis to end the argument, and then press the Enter key to enter the formula. The total amount appears in cell D8.

To finish calculating this sample budget spreadsheet, we'll enter the total formulas for the *Qtr. Total* column, starting with the *Rent* expenses in cell E2:

1. Select cell E2.

2. Start a formula by typing *=SUM(*.

Now select the range of cells for this formula by pointing:

3. Press the Left arrow key three times to select cell B2.

4. Press the F8 key to extend the selection.

5. Press the Right arrow key two times to highlight the range B2:D2. This range now appears in the argument in the formula bar.

6. Type a closing parenthesis to end the formula, and press the Enter key to enter the formula. The total *Rent* expenses now appear in cell E2.

This formula is essentially the same in all six places in which it appears (E2, E3, E4, E5, E6, and E8). The formula tells Works to add the contents of the three cells directly to the left. We'll save time by using Works' Fill Down command to copy the formula from cell E2 to the adjacent cells below it:

1. Select cell E2.

2. Press the F8 key to extend the selection.

3. Press the Down arrow key four times to select the range E2:E6.

4. Press Alt-E-F to choose the Fill Down command from the Edit menu. Works copies the formula from cell E2 to cells E3, E4, E5, and E6.

When this formula was copied into the adjacent cells, it adjusted itself to calculate the cells in the proper row. The range reference that we entered in the original *Qtr. Total* formula (in E2) for the *Rent* row was B2:D2. Try selecting cell E3, E4, E5, or E6, and examine the formula bar for each cell. You'll see that the range reference changes to B3:D3, B4:D4, and so on.

Works adjusted the range references in the original formula when it was copied because the references in the formula were relative references. Spreadsheet formulas can use either absolute or relative references, so it's important to know the difference.

- *Relative references* are the references used when you type a normal column-and-row cell reference in a formula argument or when you enter a reference in an argument by pointing to a cell. Relative references always change to reflect the position of the formula that contains them. In our example above, for instance, the formula in E2 sums the contents of the three cells that are immediately to the left, so it sums cells B2:D2. Because the references are relative, the spreadsheet understands the instructions as "Sum the three cells immediately to the left." When we copy this formula into cells E3, E4, E5, and E6, Works sums the three cells to the left of the formula position and calculates the correct total in each location.

- *Absolute references* are specified by entering a dollar sign ($) in front of the column or row designation in a cell reference. An absolute reference tells the spreadsheet to always use that specific column or row location no matter where the formula that contains it is moved or copied. See for yourself:

1. Select cell E2.

2. Press the F2 key to edit the formula in E2. The cursor is at the end of the formula in the formula bar.

3. Press the Left arrow key until the cursor is under the B in the B2 reference.

4. Enter a dollar sign ($). The dollar sign appears to the left of the B.

5. Enter dollar signs to the left of the other column and row references in the formula. When you finish, the reference should read *$B$2:$D$2*.

6. Press the Enter key to confirm the new formula. The formula argument now contains absolute references, like this:

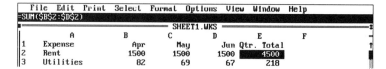

Because these references are absolute—meaning they always refer to the specific range of cells B2:D2—Works always calculates the formula with the contents of those cells no matter where the formula is located. Let's copy the formula to check this out:

1. Select cell E2 if it isn't already selected.

2. Press Alt-E-C to choose the Copy command from the Edit menu.

3. Press the Down arrow key seven times to select cell E9 as the copy destination.

4. Press the Enter key to complete the copy. The sum *4500* now appears in cell E9. As you can see, the formula in cell E9 is identical to the formula in cell E2: The cell references haven't changed to reflect the formula's new position because they are absolute references.

5. Select cell E9 if it isn't already selected, and press Alt-E-E to clear the contents of this cell.

Most of the time you will want to use relative cell references in formulas, but it's important to know how to create an absolute reference when you need one. Note that you can insert a dollar sign in front of only the column or only the row part of a reference so that Works treats only that part of the reference as absolute. We'll see some absolute references in Chapter 9.

The last formula we need to enter is the one in cell E8. We could have copied the formula in E2 here by simply extending the selection down this far when we used the Fill Down command, but doing so would have placed an extra copy of the formula in the empty row at cell E7. Instead, we'll use the standard Copy command to copy the relative formula from cell E6 to cell E8:

1. Select cell E6.

2. Press Alt-E-C to choose the Copy command. Notice the word COPY appears in the status line to show that we're in the middle of a copy operation.

3. Select cell E8.

4. Press the Enter key to complete the copy.

Now we've entered all the labels, numbers, and formulas in this spreadsheet. It should look like the one in Figure 6-3.

The next section looks at some formatting commands that you can use to make this spreadsheet a little easier to read.

```
  File  Edit  Print  Select  Format  Options  View  Window  Help
=SUM(B8:D8)
========================= SHEET1.WKS =========================
         A           B        C        D        E         F
1    Expense        Apr      May      Jun Qtr. Total
2    Rent          1500     1500     1500      4500
3    Utilities       82       69       67       218
4    Phone          122      146      141       409
5    Equip. Lease    78      152      152       382
6    Salaries      4620     4620     5120     14360
7
8    Total         6402     6487     6980     19869
9
10
11
12
13
14
15
16
17
18
E8                                                   <F1=HELP>
Press ALT to choose commands, or F2 to edit.
```

Figure 6-3.
A completed budget spreadsheet containing labels, values, and formulas.

Formatting

The first thing we notice about this spreadsheet is that it's a bit crowded. Works lets us insert or delete rows or columns to add or remove extra space between data in a spreadsheet. Follow the steps on the next page to insert an extra row between the column labels in row 1 and the *Rent* expenses in row 2.

1. Select any cell in row 2.

2. Press Alt-E-I to choose the Insert Row/Column command from the Edit menu. Works displays a dialog box where we can choose whether to insert a row or a column. The default selection is Row, so we don't have to change it.

3. Press the Enter key to accept the default selection and insert a row, as in Figure 6-4.

File	Edit	Print	Select	Format	Options	View	Window	Help	

		SHEET1.WKS				
	A	B	C	D	E	F
1	Expense	Apr	May	Jun	Qtr. Total	
2						
3	Rent	1500	1500	1500	4500	
4	Utilities	82	69	67	218	
5	Phone	122	146	141	409	
6	Equip. Lease	78	152	152	382	

Figure 6-4.
You can insert or delete rows and columns in a spreadsheet to make it easier to read.

When you insert or delete a row or a column in the spreadsheet, Works renames the affected row or column, and any formulas you have entered adjust to their new locations. In our example, the *Rent* expenses row is renumbered to row 3, and the rows below it are renumbered accordingly. If you want to see how the formulas have adjusted, select cell E3 and look at the formula there: The old cell range $B$2:$D$2 is now $B$3:$D$3. (Even if you use absolute references, the row or column references change when you insert or delete a row or a column. The references remain the same only when you move or copy the specific cell containing that formula.)

What you'll notice next about the spreadsheet, as shown in Figure 6-4, is that the *Qtr. Total* label in column E is butted up against the *Jun* month label in column D. The problem is that the *Qtr. Total* label in column E is a label, so it's aligned on the left edge of that column, and the *Jun* label is right aligned against the edge of column D because Works recognizes it as a date.

To fix this problem, we'll change the alignment of the date labels so that they're centered in their columns, opening some space between the *Jun* and *Qtr. Total* labels.

1. Select cell B1.

2. Hold down the Shift key and press the Right arrow key two times to extend the selection across cells C1 and D1.

3. Press Alt-T-S to choose the Style command from the Format menu. Works displays the Style dialog box, like this:

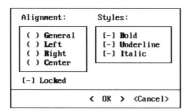

The Style command lets you choose how data in cells is aligned and also whether it is displayed in normal, bold, underlined, or italic type. For the moment, let's change only the alignment of the three selected labels to Center:

4. Press the Alt-C key to choose the Center option.

5. Press the Enter key to confirm the change and return to the spreadsheet.

Now that the month labels are centered, some space is displayed between the *Jun* label and the *Qtr. Total* label. The next formatting change we'll make is to display the values in this spreadsheet as dollars, also giving us the opportunity to select a range of cells:

1. Select cell B3.

2. Hold down the Shift key, or press the F8 key.

3. Press the Right arrow key three times to select the cells across to E3.

4. Press the Down arrow key six times to select all the rows down to cell E9. Now the range of cells B3:E9 is selected.

5. Press Alt-T-U to choose the Currency command from the Format menu. A dialog box appears, allowing us to enter the number of decimal places that we want to appear in the dollar amounts.

6. Type *0* as the number of decimal places.

7. Press the Enter key to confirm the choice and return to the spreadsheet. The numbers are now formatted with dollar signs and commas, like this:

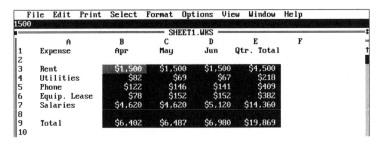

The Format menu offers eight different commands with a variety of options for displaying numbers and text in a spreadsheet. For more information about the different format commands, consult the Help Index on the Help menu.

Finally, we'll set off the column and row labels in this spreadsheet by displaying them in boldface type. Doing so will also give us a chance to select entire rows and columns.

1. Select any cell in column A.

2. Press Shift-F8 to select column A.

3. Press Alt-T-S to choose the Style command from the Format menu.

4. Press B to choose the Bold style option.

5. Press the Enter key to confirm the change and return to the spreadsheet. All the labels in column A are now displayed in boldface, as shown on the next page.

Now we'll make row 1 bold to set off the column labels in the same way.

1. Select any cell in row 1.

2. Press Ctrl-F8 to select the entire row.

3. Press Alt-T-S to choose the Style command from the Format menu.

4. Press B to choose the Bold style from the Style dialog box.

5. Press the Enter key to confirm the change and return to the spreadsheet.

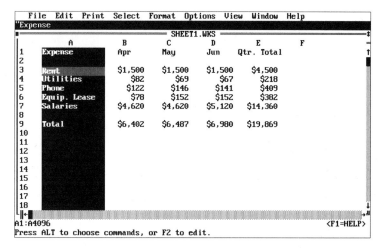

Our spreadsheet is now nicely formatted for presentation, so we'll look at Works' basic charting features next.

Charting

The purpose of using spreadsheet charts is to create a visual display of your data so that you can easily see relationships between different data sets. With the Works Spreadsheet, you can create different types of bar, line, and pie charts. Each chart type displays data in a different way and is suited to showing different relationships between data sets. We'll make a chart here to see how the charting function works.

To create a chart, first select the data you want displayed. If you want to include data legends in the chart, you must also select the row and column labels that identify the data. So, to chart all the monthly expense amounts in our budget with legends, we'll need to select all the row and column labels and the expense amounts for each month:

1. Select cell A1.

2. Extend the selection across to cell D1 by holding down the Shift key and pressing the Right arrow key three times.

3. Extend the selection down to row 7 by pressing the Down arrow key six times.

The next step in charting is to display the chart:

□ Press Alt-V-N to choose the New Chart command from the View menu. Works displays a bar graph on the screen, similar to the one shown in Figure 6-5.

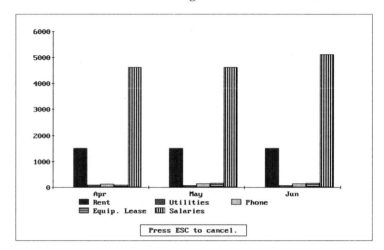

Figure 6-5.
A Works bar graph.

As you can see, this graph presents each month's expenses as a different bar, and it shows the relative increase in expenses from month to month. Because the spreadsheet shows such a large difference between the *Salaries* and *Rent* amounts and the *Utilities*, *Phone*, and *Equip. Lease* amounts, the graph scale in this example must accommodate amounts from $0 to over $5000. Chapter 8 offers some tips for accommodating wide ranges of values in charts.

Bar charts or line charts are best for showing changes in data sets from one period to the next, but what if you want a visual representation of how much each monthly expense category contributes to the total month's expenses? When you want to see how each of the values in one data set contributes to a total, you want to use a pie chart. For more information about creating pie, line, stacked bar, and other chart types, see Chapter 8.

To exit charting mode and return to the normal spreadsheet menus, press the Esc key followed by Alt-V-S to choose the Spreadsheet command from the View menu.

Printing

Now that our spreadsheet is formatted the way we want it, suppose that we want to print it. Using commands on the Print menu, you can print a file on paper, print it into a disk file, or view its printed version on the screen. Let's preview the appearance of our spreadsheet on the screen:

1. Press Alt-P-V to choose the Preview command from the Print menu. The Preview dialog box appears.

2. Press the Enter key to preview the file on the screen. The page appears on the screen in a reduced size, with the exact formats it will have when printed on paper, as in Figure 6-6.

Works displays the page on which the currently selected cell is located. To view preceding or following pages on the screen, use the Page Up key or the Page Down key. If you like what you see, you can print directly from this screen by pressing the P key, or you can return to the spreadsheet itself by pressing the Esc key. For more information about printing specific parts of a spreadsheet and about the options available in the Print and Preview dialog boxes, see the Print Print and Print Preview commands in the Commands category of the Help Index on the Help menu.

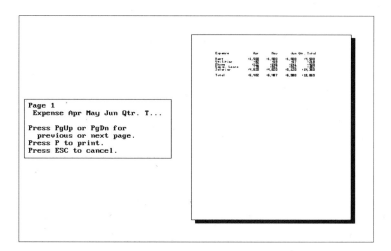

Figure 6-6.
The Print Preview display for a spreadsheet.

By now you should have a good idea about the basics of using the Works Spreadsheet. You already know how to do a lot with numbers using this tool. If you're ready to learn more, turn to the spreadsheet tips in Chapter 7, the charting tips in Chapter 8, or the spreadsheet and charting projects in Chapter 9.

CHAPTER
7

Spreadsheet Tips

The Works Spreadsheet tool does just about everything you would want to do with a spreadsheet program, but some ways of working are faster or more efficient than others. In this chapter, we'll look at some strategies for improving your productivity with the spreadsheet.

Because the spreadsheet's functions fall into several categories, we'll divide the tips the same way—into entering and editing data, calculating, formatting, and printing. (For tips about the charting features, see Chapter 8.)

Entering and Editing Data

Most spreadsheets you create will grow beyond the boundaries of a single screen, and it's easy to get lost. The tips in this section will help you enter data more efficiently, move around in a spreadsheet faster, and bring your data into view more easily.

Plan first, execute later

Before you jump into a new spreadsheet document and start entering labels, values, and formulas, it's a good idea to spend a few minutes thinking about the spreadsheet you want to build and planning how best to do it. If you're new to spreadsheets, you might want to draw a plan on paper, deciding how the rows and columns of data will be laid out. In drawing such a plan, you might often discover that the first layout that occurs to you isn't the best one, and that you can rearrange rows or columns to make the spreadsheet easier to read and use. It's much easier to rearrange a spreadsheet's rows and columns on paper than it is to do so after you begin working in the actual document.

When you make a spreadsheet plan, you should think about the row and column titles you will have, what kinds of formulas the spreadsheet will contain, and how the results will be displayed. In a budget spreadsheet, for example, you should have a good idea of what kinds of expense items you want to list and in what subcategories, if any, you want to place them. You might separate household expenses from installment credit expenses, for example, with a subtotal for each group of expenses.

As you gain experience with spreadsheets, you'll be able to abandon paper and develop plans in your head because you will be able to remember previous spreadsheets that were similar to the new ones that you want to make. But until then, plan ahead.

Keyboard or mouse?

Works was designed to be controlled either by the keyboard or with a mouse, but each of these devices is more efficient at certain operations. Obviously, you must use the keyboard to enter labels and values in a spreadsheet, but when it comes to moving around, selecting cells, choosing spreadsheet commands, or even entering cell references in formulas, you have a choice. Here are some general guidelines for deciding whether to use the mouse or the keyboard in given situations. Of course, if you don't own a mouse, your choice has already been made.

- **Use the keyboard to choose commands.** Even if you begin by choosing commands from menus with the mouse, you'll probably find that it's faster to type commands from the keyboard. Works lets you choose all the menu commands by typing a single letter, and you'll soon come to memorize the Alt-key combinations that open a particular menu and choose the command you want at the same time. To print a file, for example, you type Alt-P-P, and pressing these three keys is faster than using the mouse.

- **Use the mouse for dialog boxes.** Unless you're simply going to press the Enter key to accept the default choices in a dialog box, it's faster to use the mouse to choose dialog box options. It's difficult to remember all the Alt-key combinations for selecting dialog box options, so it will be faster to point to the options you want and click the mouse button. You might come to memorize the single option that you always choose in a familiar dialog box, in which case using the Alt-key combination might be faster, but using the mouse is generally the best way to choose options in dialog boxes.

■ **Use the mouse for selecting cells.** To select cells using the mouse, hold down the left mouse button and drag across the cells you want to select. You can select an entire row or column by clicking on its label. If you use the keyboard, you must hold down the Shift key or press the F8 key and then use the arrow keys to extend the cell selection. The only time it makes sense to use the keyboard for selecting cells is when you're moving the selection from one cell to a cell immediately next to it as you enter data. In that case, it makes more sense to use an arrow key to move the selection than it does to take your hand off the keyboard so that you can use the mouse.

■ **Point to cells as you build formulas.** Whether you use the mouse or the arrow keys on the keyboard, pointing to the cells you want to use in formulas is faster and more accurate than typing the cell references with the keyboard. After you type an equal sign (=) to let Works know you're beginning a formula (and after adding a function name and opening parenthesis to begin an argument, if necessary), you can enter any cell reference in that formula by simply selecting that cell, either by moving the selection to it using the arrow keys or by clicking on it with the mouse. For example, to use the mouse to enter the formula *=Sum(A1:E1)*:

1. Select the cell in which you want to enter the formula.

2. Type *=SUM(* to begin the formula.

3. Click on cell A1 using the left mouse button. The reference *A1* appears inside the formula's argument.

4. Hold down the left mouse button, and drag the mouse to extend the selection to cell E1. Release the mouse button. Works places a colon after the *A1* reference in the formula bar and then inserts the reference *E1* after the colon.

5. Type) to complete the argument for the formula.

6. Press the Enter key to enter the formula.

When you point to cells, you eliminate the possibility of entering an incorrect reference in a formula because of a typing mistake. You can still point to the wrong cell, however, so be sure you point to the cell you really want to include in the formula.

■ **Use the mouse for scrolling and resizing windows.** The window interface in Works was designed to be controlled with a mouse, and it's much easier to use a mouse than it is to use the keyboard for window operations. To move or resize a window using the mouse, for example, point to the window's title bar or its size box, hold down the left mouse button, and drag to the new location or size. Using the keyboard, you must type a Window menu command and then use the arrow keys to move the window around or resize it.

Use navigation shortcuts

It can be time-consuming to move around to various places in a larger spreadsheet. In the *Microsoft Works Quick Reference* you'll find a list of the keyboard shortcuts that you can use to move around a spreadsheet, but you can also use the Go To and Search commands on the Select menu to move quickly in a spreadsheet.

Use the Go To command when you know which cell reference or range name you want to go to. When you can't remember the cell reference or range name, you can use the Search command to find and select a cell based on its contents. You might remember that a cell contains a certain amount—for example, $150.00—but you might not remember the cell's location. In this case, you could use the Search command to have Works search for cells that contain the amount of $150.00.

You can either use the Search command to search the entire spreadsheet or select a specific range of cells and have Works search only the cells in that range. Normally, Works searches by rows, starting at cell A1 and searching across row 1 and then across row 2, and so on. But you can have Works search by columns, starting at cell A1 and searching down column A and then down column B, and so on, by choosing the Columns option in the Search dialog box.

The Works Spreadsheet also lets you use either a question mark (?) or an asterisk (*) as a wildcard character when you can't remember the complete contents of the cell you're looking for. Use the question mark character to replace any single character in a search entry. If you're looking for a value and you can't remember if it's 100, 120, or 150, for example, you could ask Works to search for "1?0". Works would find and select cells that contain those three values in the specified order. In essence, Works searches for any occurrence of a three-character string or value whose first character is a 1 and whose third character is a 0. Works does not distinguish between partial and complete strings. In the above example, therefore, Works would also find "4130 Shoremont Drive."

Use the asterisk to replace any group of characters in a search entry. If you're looking for a formula that contains two occurrences of the SUM function and you don't remember which range of cells it is calculating, you could ask Works to search for "SUM*" to find the appropriate formulas. (The following paragraphs provide more information on searching for formulas.)

Here are some other considerations to keep in mind when using the Search command:

- Works searches only displayed labels and values. If you want to search for a formula, therefore, you must first choose the Show Formulas command from the Options menu to display formulas (rather than the calculated results of those formulas) in the spreadsheet's cells.

- Works will not search cells in hidden columns because the data in those columns is not displayed. (See "Use zero column widths to hide columns" later in this chapter.)

- Works will not search for cell references or range names. You must specify as the search criterion the value, formula, or label that's contained in a single cell. If you know the cell reference or range name, use the Go To command.

Use the copy shortcuts

When you copy the contents of a cell to a series of cells either immediately to the right or immediately below the copied cell, use the Edit menu's Fill Right, Fill Down, and Fill Series commands to copy the whole series of cells in one operation. To copy the same expense amount from the January column through the December column in a budget, for example, it's much faster to select the range of cells from January through December and then press Alt-E-R (the Fill Right command) than it is to copy the contents individually 11 times.

When you copy from a cell to several nonadjacent cells, use the Repeat Copy (Shift-F7) command so that you don't have to select the original cell and copy from it repeatedly. When you use Repeat Copy, Works remembers the data you last copied and puts a copy of it in the selected cell. So you could copy data from cell A1 to A3 using the Copy command and then select cell A5 and press Shift-F7 to place a copy of the same data in A5.

You can also combine the Fill Down or Fill Right command and the Repeat Copy command to speed up copying. Suppose, for example, that you want to copy data from cell A1 to A3 and then copy the same data to each cell in the range A5:A9:

1. Select cell A1 and press Alt-E-C to copy the data.

2. Select cell A3 and press the Enter key to copy the data there.

3. Select cell A5 and press Shift-F7 to repeat the copy.

4. Select cells A5:A9 and press Alt-E-F to choose the Fill Down command.

Finally, using the Fill Series command can make things much easier when you enter a series of numbers or date labels in a range of cells in a row or a column. If you want to enter month labels for January through December in one row, for example, you can simply enter the January label, select the range of cells in which the remaining labels are to go (including the cell that contains the January label), and then use the Fill Series command to insert the series of month labels in the selected cells. This approach is far faster than entering the labels one at a time by hand.

Use viewing options

Because spreadsheets can be so large, and your screen is relatively small, it can be hard to arrange your data so that you can see a large amount of it at all times. Works offers Split and Freeze Titles commands on its Window menu to help you view different areas of your spreadsheet at one time.

You use the split bars at the lower-left and upper-right corners of the spreadsheet window to divide the window in half vertically or horizontally. If you use both split bars at one time, you can divide the window into four separate, independently scrolling panes. If you had a budget spreadsheet that had separate household and installment credit groups of expenses, for example, you could divide the screen in half and scroll each so that you could view both groups of expenses at one time, even if they were located many rows apart on the spreadsheet. If you're using a mouse, you can simply drag the split markers from the corners of the spreadsheet to the locations you want—you don't have to choose the Split command first. (For more information, see the Window Split command in the Commands category of the Help Index on the Help menu.)

The Freeze Titles option lets you lock any number of rows and columns on the screen so that they're always displayed no matter where you scroll in the spreadsheet. One problem with large spreadsheets is that when you scroll to a distant row or column to edit or view data, the row and column labels scroll out of view, making it hard to tell which row or column is which. The Freeze Titles command locks row and column labels on the screen so that you can always see them. (For more information, see the Options Freeze Titles command in the Commands category of the Help Index on the Help menu.)

Use range names to speed formula entry

The Edit menu's Range Name command is a powerful feature that makes referring to groups of cells easy. After you define a group of cells—whether it's a budget total or subtotal or a column that contains income for March—you can define that group as a range by giving it a unique range name. You can then use the range name when you want to calculate the group of cells in a formula or when you simply want to move to and select the group quickly using the Go To command.

If you're new to range names, you might not be sure when it's appropriate to use them. After all, you could name any rectangular group of cells as a range, but ranges are only useful if you'll need to refer to the group of cells as a whole group later. A rule of thumb is that if you find yourself referring to a range of cells more than one time as you create formulas, you should define a range name for those cells. When you've named a range, you'll know that you can accurately refer to a group of cells by specifying the range name, and you'll eliminate the possibility of entering the wrong cell range because of a typing or pointing error.

Range names are also easier to remember than are cell references when you need to use them in formulas.

Turn off automatic recalculation

The Works Spreadsheet is usually set to automatic recalculation, which means that it recalculates formulas whenever you enter or edit the contents of any cell. When you're first building a spreadsheet, however, your main goal is to get a lot of data and labels entered as quickly as possible. As the spreadsheet grows and you add more formulas, it takes longer and longer for Works to recalculate each time you make a change. By choosing the Manual Calculation command on the Options menu, you can stop automatic recalculation while you enter a lot of data and formulas, thereby avoiding having to suspend data entry temporarily while Works recalculates.

Realistically, automatic recalculation doesn't become a problem until your spreadsheet grows to several dozen rows and columns with several dozen formulas. After your spreadsheet does grow, you can eliminate recalculation delays by opting for manual recalculation. The only thing to remember is that after you set Manual Calculation, you must explicitly tell Works to recalculate its formulas. If you forget, your spreadsheet won't show the correct results. A good rule is to set Manual Calculation only when you know you'll be entering a lot of data and, after you've finished, to choose the Manual Calculation command again to turn it off and have Works recalculate after every change.

Use templates

The first tip in this chapter discusses the need for advance planning before you actually begin building a Works spreadsheet document. If you save old spreadsheets as templates, you can speed up the planning process by having some standard spreadsheet layouts on hand. Many budget spreadsheets look much the same, for example, so if you save a budget spreadsheet as a template, you can load that template file the next time you want to create a budget, and change only the values and labels or add some new rows or columns to suit your new budgeting purpose.

When you use templates to construct new spreadsheets, however, be careful to check all the formulas in the spreadsheet to be sure they make the right calculations. The references and formulas you used in the original spreadsheet might not be suitable for your new purpose.

Save files to speed things up

When you are working with one or several documents and you're close to the limit of your system's memory, Works slows down. Works uses memory to store information about the various parts of your file and where they're located on the disk. As your document grows, and you edit it in more and more places, Works must store more information about it. To free some memory, save the file and close it, and then open it again. If you're working with several documents, try the save/close/reopen strategy with each one. You'll find that you have more memory to work with afterward and that Works will operate faster.

Calculating

Calculating shortcuts include not only ways to enter cell references in formulas (see "Keyboard or mouse?" earlier in this chapter) but also ways to build formulas more quickly and efficiently.

Check all formulas and results

Even if you know a formula produced the correct result when you first entered it, you can't be sure that the result will always be accurate. After you enter a formula, you might sort, insert, or delete rows or columns in the ranges included in the formula and thereby change the results of the formula. Before printing a spreadsheet or presenting its calculated values as the truth, be sure you check each formula to verify that it refers to the cells you want to calculate and that the formula itself is making the calculation in the proper way.

Use a reference area

Unless your spreadsheet is for your own personal use, it's a good idea to insert some notes at the top of the spreadsheet so that others can see what it is supposed to accomplish; what assumptions, if any, you're making; and where various parts of the spreadsheet are located. A reference area such as this helps orient other readers to the spreadsheet. Another bonus of a reference area is that it lets you enter amounts one time at the top of the spreadsheet, refer to them in the spreadsheet formulas, and then change the reference area amounts when you want to do "what if" calculations.

Let's say you're making a sales forecast. In the reference area, you might type a line that reads *Assumed annual sales growth, 19%*. If you are careful to enter the 19% value in its own cell to the right of the text, it becomes a value. You can then refer to that cell in calculating the growth rate for the forecast itself. If you want to see how sales will look if the growth rate is 22%, you can simply enter the value 22 in the reference area, and the spreadsheet recalculates.

Reference areas are particularly useful when you have several values that you might want to change or several assumptions that you want to make known. In Chapter 9, we'll build an amortization table that contains a reference area.

Tips on using dates

The Works Spreadsheet treats dates differently from other numbers, and the results can be confusing in cells in which you've entered dates. Here are some ideas to keep in mind about dates in spreadsheets:

- When you enter a date, Works converts it to a value that equals the number of days between the date and January 1, 1900. If you enter 1/1/90, for example, Works stores that date as 32,874. Although Works might not display this sequential number as the contents of the cell, it will present the number when the cell is referred to in a formula. So if you enter the date 1/1/90 in cell A1 and then copy that cell to other cells or use the cell as a reference in a formula, Works copies the number 32,874 to the other cells and uses that as the value of cell A1 in the formula.

- Works won't recognize dates earlier than 1/1/1900 or later than 6/3/2079. If you enter a date outside this range, Works treats it as text.

- As we saw in Chapter 6, Works recognizes the spellings of months as dates and converts them to its longest date format, which writes the month as a three-letter abbreviation. When you enter "January" in a cell, therefore, Works converts it to "Jan". To display the whole name "January" in a cell, begin the entry with a quotation mark (") so that Works knows to treat the entry as text instead of as a date.

- You can use a formula that contains time or date functions to have the spreadsheet calculate the current date at any given time. See Appendix B in the *Microsoft Works Reference* manual for more information.

Use macros to speed repetitive operations

You can use the built-in macro feature in Works to handle operations that you perform repeatedly in the spreadsheet. Works lets you record strings of commands or repetitive data-entry operations. Any time you have to execute a procedure that requires several commands—whether you're copying, reformatting, moving, or inserting data—you can automate the procedure by using a macro. Be on the lookout for repetitive operations, and when you discover one, consider recording a macro to automate it in the future.

Remember, you can name and store separate macro files, so you can use the same macro key sequences over and over. You might store a different macro file for corporate budget macros, for example, and then load that macro file when you begin working on a corporate budget project. For more general information about creating macros, see Chapter 2.

Formatting

Formatting is the last step before printing a spreadsheet. In Chapter 6, we explored some ways to insert rows and columns or to align the contents of cells to make spreadsheets more readable. But Works gives you other ways to arrange spreadsheet data to make it more useful or more easily comprehensible.

Consolidate several spreadsheets

The Works Spreadsheet doesn't allow you to link data between separate spreadsheet files or to automatically consolidate or transfer data from several files to one master file. These features are often used for breaking one large spreadsheet into several smaller ones that are easier to work with. In a corporate budget, for example, you might have one file for the production budget, which you would give to the production manager, and another file for sales, which you would give to the sales manager.

Although Works doesn't support spreadsheet linking and consolidation (allowing values from separate spreadsheets to be copied to a master spreadsheet), you can create separate spreadsheet areas in the same document. Using cell references, range names, and a little layout creativity, you can approximate linking and consolidation functions in Works.

Let's say you're making a corporate expense and income statement, and you want to divide it into separate areas that represent sales, production, administrative expenses, and income. Each area of the budget has several line items and a subtotal. The administrative area might look like this:

| File | Edit | Print | Select | Format | Options | View | Window | Help |

```
============================ ADMINBUD.WKS ============================
              A              B        C        D        E        F
25  Administrative Budget
26                          Jan      Feb      Mar      Apr      May
27  Office Lease            2200     2200     2200     2200     2200
28  Office Utilities        120      121      118      130      132
29  Telephone               342      320      280      299      311
30  Liability Insurance     425      425      425      425      425
31  Workmen's Comp.         200      200      200      200      200
32  Health Insurance        1200     1200     1200     1200     1200
33  Salaries                9200     9200     9200     9200     9200
34  Office Supplies         125      140      132      200      110
35  Equipment Leases        350      350      350      350      350
36
37  Total Admin. Budget     14162    14156    14105    14204    14128
38
```

Along with the three budget areas, however, you want to create an overall budget summary area so that the top brass can see only the total income and total expense figures in each of the three areas.

In the first place, you would lay out each area on a diagonal to the others so that none of the rows and columns in one area would be used in any other area. Taking this approach, you could insert or delete rows or columns in one area as needed without affecting the data in other areas. This diagonal layout might look like the following:

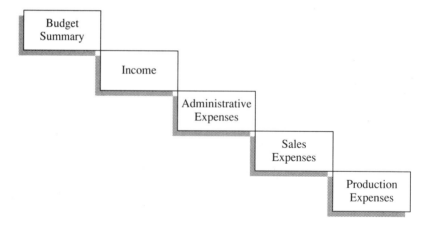

Notice that the budget summary is at the top of the spreadsheet because that's the area that top management would probably want to look at first. Following the budget summary—on the diagonal—are the income area and the three expense areas.

The summary area doesn't contain any values that you would enter manually. Instead, all its cells take their contents from other areas of the spreadsheet through cell references. When you first create the summary area, it might look like this:

```
 File   Edit   Print   Select   Format   Options   View   Window   Help

====================== ADMINBUD.WKS ======================
              A           B       C         D        E        F
 2
 3   Budget Summary:
 4                       Jan     Feb       Mar      Apr      May
 5   Administrative
 6   Sales
 7   Production
 8
 9   Total Expenses
10
11   Total Income
12
13   Profit/Loss
14   Cash Flow
15   »
```

As you create the summary area, you can reference the Total rows in the income and expense areas. If the Income totals for the year are in cells O24:Z24 (on the diagonal starting below the lower-right corner of the summary area), you could enter the appropriate Total Income cell reference for each month in the Income row of the summary area. The January Total Income cell in the summary area (cell B11), for example, would contain the reference =O24. The February Total Income cell in the summary area (cell C11) would contain the reference =P24, and so on. That way, as the income amounts for each category were entered and totaled in the Income area, the total amounts would transfer to the summary area.

The expense areas of the spreadsheet operate on the same principle; the references for the cells in the Total row of each area would be entered as the contents of rows 5 through 7 in the summary area.

To speed navigation from one area to another in this spreadsheet, you can select all the cells in each area and name them as a range. The cells in the income area could be given the range name Income, for example. With these range names, you could use the Go To command, enter the name of the range you want to view, and then have Works scroll the spreadsheet to that area immediately. In fact, if you include a reference area at the top of the spreadsheet (see the preceding section called "Calculating"), you could enter the range names in the same pattern and location that they occupy in the actual spreadsheet. New users will know where each section of the spreadsheet is and what its range name is.

Another benefit of using range names is that you can select each area of the spreadsheet easily. When you use the Go To command, Works not only scrolls the spreadsheet to that area but also selects all the cells in the range. With all the cells selected in this way, it's easy to copy the entire area to a new spreadsheet file and then give that file to the manager responsible for filling in that budget area. After the manager fills in his or her budget area, you can select the manager's spreadsheet, choose the Copy command, and then select the entire budget area in the consolidated spreadsheet and press the Enter key. The filled-in budget you got from the manager replaces the empty budget area in the master spreadsheet.

One final benefit of the diagonal layout of the different areas is that you can insert a page break at the upper-left corner of each area so that each area prints on a separate page.

As you can see, you can use several of the Works Spreadsheet features to create master, consolidated spreadsheets that are easy to use.

Use zero column widths to hide columns

If you want to hide a spreadsheet column from view without deleting it, you can set the column width to zero. The spreadsheet then looks as if it skips the hidden column. If you hide column C, for example, the column labels at the top of the spreadsheet read A, B, D, E, and so on.

If you hide a column, you need only widen it to reveal it again. Of course, after a column is hidden, you can't select any cells in it. And because selecting a column is the first step in specifying a new column width value when you use the Column Width command, you can't select a hidden cell to reveal it again. To reveal a hidden column:

1. Select adjacent cells in the columns on either side of the hidden column. (If column C is hidden, select two adjacent cells in columns B and D, for example.)

2. Press Alt-T-W to choose the Column Width command.

3. Type a positive value for the column width (or simply confirm the current width setting shown).

4. Press the Enter key to change the column width. The hidden column will be displayed again, with the same width as the two columns adjacent to it.

It's useful to hide columns when you want to print the columns on either side of the one you hide.

Watch out when sorting rows or columns

You need to be careful when you sort rows that contain formulas or sort rows whose cells are referred to in formulas: Sorting often changes the results of the formulas or moves the formulas to a different location. Let's look at two examples. Suppose that rows 1 and 2 of a spreadsheet contain values and that row 3 contains a formula that adds the values in rows 1 and 2, like this:

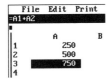

The formula in A3 is $=A1+A2$, and the result it produces is *750*. If you select rows 1 through 3 and sort column A in descending order, however, Works rearranges the rows so that the contents of cell A3 are in cell A1, because 750 is the largest value of the three. When it moves the contents of cell A3, however, Works actually moves the formula $=A1+A2$, and it adjusts the cell references in the formula to reflect the formula's new location.

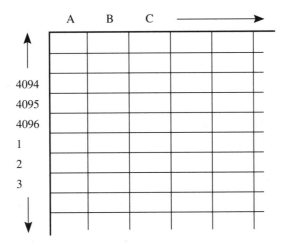

Because a formula in cell A1 can't add the contents of the two cells above it, Works changes the formula to reference the two cells at the bottom of the spreadsheet. In essence, Works spreadsheets aren't linear but are circular, as shown on the preceding page. You can also run into problems when cells referred to in a formula (rather than the formula itself) move following a sort. Suppose you have a SUM formula that adds only the *Phone* and *Utilities* expenses in a budget, like this:

```
  File   Edit   Print   Select   Format   Options   View   Window   Help
=B4+B5
================================= SHEET1.WKS =================================
        A          B          C          D         E         F         G
 1   Expense       Apr        May        Jun  Qtr. Total
 2
 3   Rent         $750       $750       $750    $2,250
 4   Utilities     $60        $69        $67      $196
 5   Phone         $25        $35        $27       $87
 6
 7   Total        $835       $854       $844    $2,533
 8
 9   Util/Phone      $85
10
```

Here the formula adds the contents of cells B4 and B5 to produce a total of $85. But if we sort rows 3, 4, and 5 on the contents of column A in ascending order, the locations of the expense values change, and the formula—which still adds the contents of cells B4 and B5—produces a different result, like this:

```
  File   Edit   Print   Select   Format   Options   View   Window   Help
=B4+B5
================================= SHEET1.WKS =================================
        A          B          C          D         E         F         G
 1   Expense       Apr        May        Jun  Qtr. Total
 2
 3   Phone         $25        $35        $27       $87
 4   Rent         $750       $750       $750    $2,250
 5   Utilities     $60        $69        $67      $196
 6
 7   Total        $835       $854       $844    $2,533
 8
 9   Util/Phone     $810
10
```

As you can see, it's a good idea to avoid sorting rows that contain formulas when those formulas refer to data in other rows. (Sorting a row using a formula that adds across cells in that same row wouldn't affect the formula.) If you sort rows whose cells are referred to in formulas, be sure to check the formulas carefully afterward to verify that Works is still calculating the values you want to calculate.

Format spreadsheet data in the word processor

Works restricts you to one font and one font size for an entire spreadsheet document, but by copying spreadsheet data to a word processor document you can gain the added formatting flexibility the word processor offers. Simply select the spreadsheet data you want to reformat, copy it to a new word processor document, and then select the specific labels or values that you want to reformat, and change them using Format menu commands of the Works Word Processor.

In the word processor, you can select any label or value and change its font or font size, choose other style options such as superscript or subscript, or place borders around groups of numbers. Remember, though, that after you copy spreadsheet data to the word processor, the data can no longer be recalculated because the formulas are not copied. When you copy from the spreadsheet to the word processor, Works copies only the labels and values that are displayed and not the formulas that calculate the values. Chapter 14 contains more information about copying spreadsheet data to the word processor and reformatting it using the word processor's Format options.

Printing

Spreadsheets can be difficult to print properly: Among other challenges, you often have more data than can fit on a single page. Here are some tips that make printing easy and that ensure the legibility of your spreadsheets:

- Use efficient column labels and cell formatting to maximize horizontal space on a page. Typically, you end up with more columns in a spreadsheet than you can print across a page, so the challenge is to squeeze as many columns across the width of a page as possible. You can make the most of a page's width by keeping column labels short and by using efficient cell formats.

- Whenever possible, a column label should be no wider than the numbers in the column itself. If your column contains five-digit numbers, try to use a five-character column label at the top. That way, you can reduce the column width to five or six characters without chopping off part of the column label.

■ Don't format cells for more decimal places than is necessary. If all your figures are in even dollars, for example, don't format the cells for dollars with two decimal places. By eliminating the decimal point and the two zeros from the end of each number, you can save three character spaces in the column width. And, if you use the Fixed cell format instead of the Currency cell format, you'll also save the extra character spaces used for dollar signs and commas in the Currency cell format.

Use page breaks to divide data logically

Before printing a spreadsheet, check the page breaks to be sure that each page contains a logical grouping of data. Spreadsheet page breaks look like vertical and horizontal dashed lines. If one of these breaks falls in the middle of a group of rows or columns, set a manual page break above or to the left of the existing break so that the page doesn't end in the middle of a group. On a budget spreadsheet, for example, you probably won't be able to print all 12 months on one page. Instead, try setting page breaks at each quarter, or after six months, so that the data is more logically grouped on each page.

Choose nonproportional fonts for printing

If possible, choose a nonproportional (monospace) font for spreadsheet printing. The characters in proportional fonts have different widths (an 8 is wider than a 1, for example), and they can cause columns of numbers to be misaligned. When you use a monospace font such as Pica or Courier, every number in every column lines up.

Print extra information to aid other spreadsheet readers

If you're printing a spreadsheet for others, it might be a good idea to use the Print Row and Column Labels option in the Print dialog box. Choosing this option tells Works to include the row and column labels on the printed spreadsheet, which makes it easy to refer to specific cells. If you're in a meeting, for example, it's easier to say "cell B23" than it is to say "the fourth cell below the Income totals, in the second column."

Print only selected parts of a spreadsheet

If you need a printout of some numbers, they'll be easier to read if you don't also print a lot of numbers in which you aren't interested. Works normally prints whole pages from a spreadsheet, but you can use the Set Print Area command on the Print menu to print only a selected part of a spreadsheet. Simply select the group of cells you want to print, and then choose the Set Print Area command (Alt-P-A) and print the page. Works prints only the cells you selected.

These are some of the ideas that you can use to get more out of the Works Spreadsheet. As you gain experience using this tool, you'll discover other shortcuts and techniques that will make Works work a little harder or faster for you.

CHAPTER 8

Charting Tips

A spreadsheet can show you a lot about data relationships, but it's even more useful when you add the visual impact of a chart. The charting example in Chapter 6 explained the basic steps that you follow to create a new chart. In this chapter, we'll look at the types of charts that you can create with Works and how each presents data in its own way. We'll also look at some general charting tips that will help you create better looking charts more efficiently.

The How and Why of Charting

Charts reveal at a glance the approximate relationships among numbers. With a chart, you can choose the important numbers from a spreadsheet and display them visually adjacent to each other. Charts are especially useful for showing how values change over time or how some values compare with other values.

With the Works Spreadsheet, you can create up to eight different charts for every spreadsheet file. To create a chart, you must already have entered some data in the spreadsheet, and must already have selected a range of data cells. Works then charts the data.

After you create a chart, any changes in the spreadsheet data plotted in that chart cause the chart itself to change. As you create new charts, Works names each chart "Chart1," "Chart2," "Chart3," and so on, up to "Chart8," and lists the charts you create on the View menu. Chart definitions don't have to be saved—they're automatically saved with the spreadsheet file when you save it.

The fastest way to create a chart is to select a block of data and labels in the spreadsheet and then choose the New Chart command from the View menu. (See "Charting" in Chapter 6 for a quick example of how this process works.) If you want to chart data that doesn't appear in one contiguous block of the spreadsheet, you can choose menu commands to specify different groups of data as different data sets in Works. (See the Data X- Or Y-Series command in the Commands category of the Help Index on the Help menu for more information.)

Each time you use the New Chart command on the View menu, Works draws a bar chart that shows the contents of the cells that are currently selected in your spreadsheet. After you view the chart, you need to press the Esc key to display the spreadsheet data in Chart mode. Chart mode shows the same spreadsheet cells you normally see in your spreadsheet, but many of the menus and commands at the top of the screen are different. After you're in Chart mode, you can change the chart type by choosing a command from the Format menu. Figure 8-1 shows a budget spreadsheet in Chart mode. You can see that the menus are different from the regular spreadsheet menus.

You can tell by the menu names that you're in Chart mode, and you can also tell because Works displays the word CHART in the status line. You'll notice that the Edit and Select menus are missing in this mode.

```
 File  Print  Data  Format  Options  View  Window  Help

======================= BUDGET.WKS =======================
          A          B        C        D        E        F
1                   Apr      May      Jun    Qtr. Total
2
3    Rent          $750     $750     $800    $2,300
4    Utilities      $42      $39      $37     $118
5    Phone         $122     $146     $110     $378
6    Food          $150     $185     $130     $465
7    Entertainment $100     $160     $200     $460
8
9    Total       $1,164   $1,280   $1,277   $3,721
10
11
12
13
14
15
16
17
18
F1                   CHART                        <F1=HELP>
Press ALT to choose commands, or F2 to edit.
```

Figure 8-1.
In Chart mode, the spreadsheet data is displayed, but the menus at the top of the screen are different.

Although you can edit cell contents, enter values in new cells, and scroll the spreadsheet in Chart mode, you can't copy cells, create range names, or change cell formats in this mode.

After you're in Chart mode, you must choose the Spreadsheet command from the View menu to return to the regular spreadsheet mode and its menus. Any menu commands that you choose when in Chart mode apply to the current chart, which is the chart you displayed on the screen before you pressed Esc to enter Chart mode. The current chart is indicated on the View menu with a bullet next to its name.

The only way to change the options for a chart other than the current chart is by plotting that chart on the screen first (by selecting it from the View menu) and then pressing the Esc key to move back to Chart mode.

Time-Series and Pie Charts

You can plot two types of charts with Works: time-series charts and pie charts. The Works Spreadsheet lets you choose from seven time-series chart types and one pie chart type.

A time-series chart, as shown in Figure 8-2, plots values along horizontal and vertical axes. The vertical axis—a vertical line that is usually

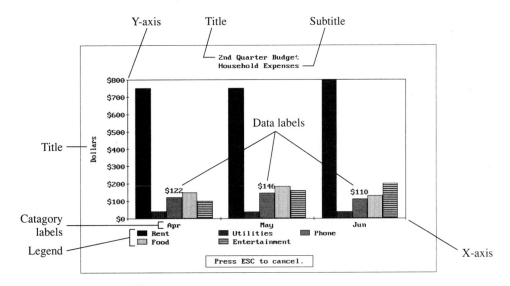

Figure 8-2.
A time-series bar chart.

near the left edge of the screen—contains a scale that typically represents values. The vertical axis is also called the Y-axis. The horizontal axis, called the X-axis, is a horizontal line that Works places at the bottom of the screen. The X-axis contains a scale that typically represents periods of time. (X-Y charts are an exception. See below.)

In a time-series chart, each group of values that you want to plot for one time period is called a Y-series. This group is a range of cells in a row or column of your spreadsheet. Works can plot up to six Y-series of data on a chart. You can also plot one X-series of data in an X-Y chart (see below).

Other features of time-series charts, as shown in Figure 8-2, are titles, legends, and labels:

- A title is identifying text that you can place at the top of a chart or on its axes. Figure 8-2 contains a chart title at the top, a subtitle, and a Y-axis title indicating Dollars.

- A legend describes each Y-series plotted on a time-series chart. Like the legend on a map, a legend is a key that shows which of the bars or lines in a chart refers to which data series. Works differentiates each data series by displaying its bar, line, or points with a different color, pattern, or marker. The legend in Figure 8-2 shows which bar refers to which type of expense. You can use the actual row labels in your spreadsheet as the data legends by selecting them when you select the data to be plotted, or you can enter other legends to identify data by using the Legends command on the Data menu.

- Labels are extra text that you can add to identify categories of plotted data (category labels) or identify the specific amounts each bar or line point represents on a chart (data labels). Category labels might be month names or dates, for example. Data labels can be used at the tops of bars or above points on a plotted line to show the actual value the bar or point represents so that the value stands out from the others. To create category labels, select the spreadsheet cells that contain the labels you want to use (usually the column labels in the spreadsheet).

A pie chart plots values as slices of a pie. It shows just how much of the total amount (the total pie) each value represents. When you plot a pie chart, you must select values in only one time period (one Y-series), which means that you select only one range of cells in a row or column. Pie charts don't contain category labels because category labels are used on the X-axis, and pie charts don't have an X-axis. When you use data labels on a pie chart, they appear next to the pie slices they represent.

Works Chart Types

Although every chart plotted using the New Chart command begins as a bar chart, you can use the commands on the Format menu to change the chart type. Works offers eight different chart types. Let's look at each type of chart and see how it presents data differently:

- A Bar Chart contains an X-axis and one or two Y-axes and plots individual values from a spreadsheet as bars. In each series of data, each value is plotted as a bar of a different color or pattern. If you plot four different expense items for one month, for example, each expense item is plotted as a bar and one set of four bars is included because you selected only one month. If you plot the four expense items for three months, three sets of four bars are included, with each set representing one month's expenses. Figure 8-2 contains a bar chart that shows three months' expenses.

- A Stacked Bar Chart combines all the different values for each series into one bar. Each value in the series represents a part of the bar equal to its proportion of the total amount in the whole series, as shown in the chart at the top of the following page.

  As you can see, the bar's height is determined by the sum of the values it represents, and each value is distinguished by a different color or pattern according to the part of the total it represents. Also, the Y-axis scale changes to accommodate the higher amounts represented by each bar. Because all the values in a series are combined in one bar, one bar per time period is included on the X-axis. Because the plot on the following page shows expenses for three months, three bars are included.

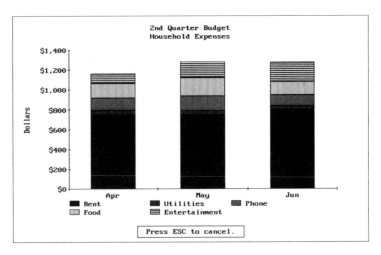

- A 100% Bar Chart is like a stacked bar chart, except that the X-axis scale is in percentages instead of in whole numbers and the bars are always the same height, like this:

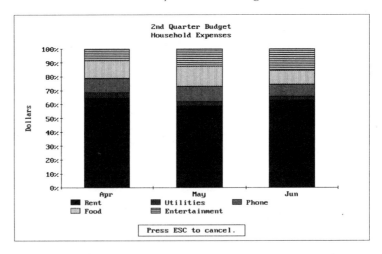

This chart plots the same data as does the preceding stacked bar chart, but you can see here that the bar for each data series is always 100%, and each value in the series is represented by a proportional amount.

- A Line Chart also shows changes in values over time, except that each line on such a chart represents one data series. In a way, a line chart is simply a bar chart in which

Works has drawn lines that connect the tops of similar bars, like this:

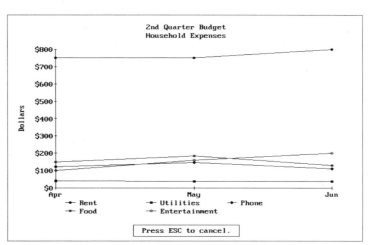

This line chart shows exactly the same expense data as do the earlier bar charts. The advantage of a line chart is that you can easily see when one data series rises above or falls below another because the lines cross.

■ An Area Line Chart also plots changes in data over time, except that all the lines on the chart contribute to a total, so each line shows how the values it represents change in their contribution to the total over time, like this:

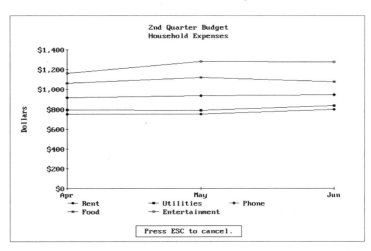

You could think of an area line chart as a stacked bar chart with lines that connect the tops of the bar segments.

■ A High-Lo-Close Chart is also like a stacked bar chart, except that each bar is a vertical line and the bar segments are points plotted on that line, like this:

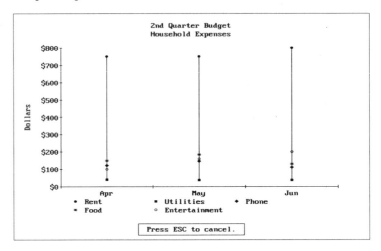

This chart is so named because it is frequently used to show high, low, and closing stock prices during a day.

■ A Pie Chart is a plot of one data series, and each slice of the pie represents one value in that series, like this:

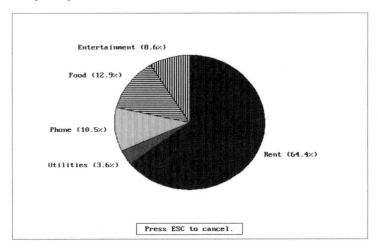

Because they show only one series, pie charts are useful only for showing relationships among values in that series. In a way, a pie chart is like one bar from a 100% bar chart, except that it's round instead of rectangular.

■ An X-Y Chart plots the intersections of X-series and Y-series values. These charts are used to plot the relative positions of different pairs of values so that you can see where each pair of measurement values stacks up against other pairs. When you define an X-Y chart, you first select an X-series of values, which defines the horizontal scale on the chart. Then you select one or more Y-series of values, which defines the range of the vertical scale and plots the sets of points above the X-axis, like this:

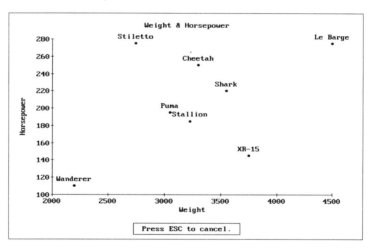

This example shows the horsepower and weight measurements of different cars. To look for the heaviest car with the most horsepower, we would look for the Y-value plot in the upper-right corner of the graph. In the original spreadsheet, the horsepower and weight figures were in two columns: The weight column was selected as the X-axis, and the horsepower column was selected as the first Y-series.

These are the eight types of charts that you can create with the Works Spreadsheet. As you can see, each chart type reveals something a little different about the data being plotted.

Charting Tips

Works gives you a lot of flexibility in creating charts of spreadsheet data. It's easy to make a simple chart, and you can do a lot to dress up your data. On the other hand, the array of options can be a little confusing. The techniques suggested in this section will help you make the most of Works' charting features.

Keep it simple

The whole point of charting data is to use a visual method to show relationships between numbers quickly and dramatically. Works allows you to combine line and bar charts, add right-hand Y-axes, add data labels, and change a chart's colors, patterns, and markers, but be careful that you don't sacrifice clarity to visual complexity. A chart should be no more complex than it needs to be to display the data relationships that you want to show:

- Don't mix line and bar charts unless doing so shows a data relationship that you can't show any other way. If you are plotting one Y-series as a line and three other Y-series as bars, consider whether the line data might be better displayed in a chart by itself.

- Don't use a second Y-axis if you can avoid it. The purpose of a right-hand Y-axis is to present a second scale, which is necessary only when widely diverse ranges of values are being displayed in different Y-series in the same charts.

- Don't use fancy fonts in chart text. A chart is nothing if it isn't easily readable, and it's best to stick with plain fonts that are easy to read such as Pica, Courier, and Helv. Avoid smaller font sizes as well because they're also harder to read.

- Don't explode more than one slice of a pie. Exploding a pie slice away from the rest of the pie is a way to emphasize that particular value in the chart. When you explode more than one pie slice, you emphasize more than one data value equally and therefore do not give special emphasis to any of them.

- Stick with the default colors and patterns. Works does a good job of choosing different colors, patterns, and markers for displaying your data. When you change only one of the default colors, patterns, or markers, the chances are you'll choose a substitute that doesn't fit as well with the others in the chart. When this happens, you'll be tempted to change the color, pattern, or marker settings for other data series, and you'll end up spending a lot of time getting all the combinations right again.

- Minimize titles and data labels. Unless it isn't clear what measure you're using for an X-axis or Y-axis scale or it's critical to show the actual amount represented by a bar, line, point, or pie slice, avoid extra titles and data labels. The more text you put on a chart, the more you divert the reader's attention from the graphic data relationship that the chart was intended to show. When you must use titles, make them as short and clear as possible.

Plot values of the same magnitude

Try to select Y-series whose values are in the same numeric range. If some of the values in a chart are over 10,000 and others are under 100, the scale for that chart must be so broad that it will be difficult to see the difference between bars at either end of the scale. On a chart whose Y-axis scale runs from 0 to 10,000, for example, you won't be able to notice the difference between a bar that shows the value 120 and a bar that shows the value 150. When you must plot two widely separated groups of values, use a chart that has a right-hand Y-axis scale. Then you can show the lower-range values against a lower-range scale in the left-hand Y-axis and the higher-range values against a higher-range scale in the right Y-axis.

Duplicate charts to explore options

If you're going to explore Works' charting options to embellish a chart on which you're working, it's a good idea to make a copy of the chart and modify the copy. That way, if you end up making the chart look ugly and you can't remember how it got that way, you can easily return to the original, simple version. You use the Charts command on the View menu to copy and rename charts.

Make sample printouts

What you see on your screen isn't necessarily what you'll get out of your printer—and this is more often the case with charts than it is with text-only documents. You might start out with a nice pie chart on the screen, only to discover that your printer turns the round pie into an oval when it prints. Or you might find that a pattern that looked good on the screen looks awful on paper. These problems often crop up when you resize charts or change their default colors, patterns, or markers. Always print your charts on paper to make sure that they look the way you want before you consider the job done.

Don't use a chart when data will do

Charts add a lot of visual interest to your reports or presentations, but you can have too much of a good thing. If your data consists of only a few simple numbers, pointing out the numbers might be better than charting them. Using too many charts at one time can make any one chart in the group less effective, so save Works' charting muscle for those situations in which you really want to drive a point home.

Display charts in black and white
to match monochrome printing

If your screen is set to display in color and you've chosen color printing options using the Data Format command in the Format menu, your chart will be displayed in color when you view it on the screen. If your printer prints in black and white, however, it would be better to view the chart in black and white so that you can see how Works will substitute different patterns for colors. To view a chart in black and white, choose the Format For B&W command from the Options menu. (See the Options Format For B&W command in the Commands category of the Help Index on the Help menu for further information.)

Use data labels for added emphasis

The Data Labels command lets you point out specific information in a chart. The data labels in Figure 8-2, for example, call attention to the Phone expenses by showing the exact amount represented by each of the Phone bars on the chart. You apply data labels to a series of data by selecting the series and then choosing the Data Labels command from the Data menu.

For example, cells B5:D5 in Figure 8-1 have been plotted as the Phone expenses for the chart in Figure 8-2, and cells B5:D5 have also been selected as the data labels for this Y-series in the chart. That's why the data labels showing the Phone expense amounts appear above the bars for these expenses in Figure 8-2.

When you apply data labels, Works assumes that you want to select an entire Y-series of data to label in a chart so that each bar has one label. Working from left to right, Works takes the first label you select and places it on the left-most bar, and then takes the second label you select and places it over the second bar from the left, and so on.

This approach works fine as long as you always select the same number of data labels as there are bars in a chart (or if you always want to label the left-most bar in a chart). But what if you want to label only the second or third bar in a group? If you were to select only one cell as the label for a Y-series that contains three bars or points, Works would place the label on the left-most bar or point in the series.

Let's look at Figures 8-1 and 8-2 again to see how this situation would work out. Suppose we wanted to label only the May Phone expense bar in Figure 8-2. To do so, we might select only cell C5 in Figure 8-1, thinking that the label would be applied to the May Phone bar in Figure 8-2. But because Works always applies data labels by position—beginning with the left-most bar or point in a chart—Works would place that label on the left-most bar in the chart, which is the one that represents the April Phone expense.

To label only some of the bars or points in a series when you don't want to label the left-most bar in a series, you must fool Works into placing blank labels over the bars that are to the left of the bars in which you want labels to appear. Let's take the above example again. Suppose you want to label only the May Phone bar (the C5 value) in the chart. To do so, you must create a new range of two cells—one for the April bar label and one for the May bar label—in which the left-hand cell is blank. That way, when Works places the first label in the series (the left-hand cell) over the left-hand bar, it puts a blank label there.

Here's how we might label only the May Phone expense bar in the chart shown in Figure 8-2, using the spreadsheet in Figure 8-1:

1. Be sure that the spreadsheet is in Chart mode.

2. Select cell C11.

3. Type the value =C5 to tell Works to copy the value from cell C5.

4. Select the range of cells B11:C11.

5. Press Alt-D-D to choose the Data Labels command. The Data Labels dialog box is displayed.

6. Press the Down arrow key three times to select the fourth Y-series. (The Phone expenses row is the third row of data in the spreadsheet, but the blank row between the column labels and the data is also a series in the chart, so the Phone expenses row is actually the fourth Y-series.)

7. Press Alt-C to create the data labels for that series.

Now Works will display data labels from the range B11:C11, but because only the right-hand cell in that range actually contains a label, only the second bar for that series (May) will be labeled with its value.

Use grid lines to aid readability

Works' chart options don't include grid lines by default, but you might occasionally want to add them to your charts. To help readers match bar, line, or point positions with the values on the Y-axis, it helps to include a grid that extends from the Y-axis values across the chart. You can add a horizontal grid to the Y-axis by using the Y-Axis command on the Options menu. If you're plotting an X-Y chart, it might also help to add vertical grid lines that extend up from the X-axis. Use the X-Axis command on the Options menu to add an X-axis grid.

These suggestions will help you use charts to add the right visual clarity to your spreadsheet numbers. As you begin building your own charts, you'll discover other techniques that make charting easier and more effective.

Spreadsheet and Charting Projects

In this chapter, we'll see Works' Spreadsheet and Charting features in action as we create a budget and cash flow spreadsheet, an advertising tracking and analysis spreadsheet, and an amortization table. By completing these spreadsheet projects, you'll learn some practical uses for the Spreadsheet's features.

A Budget and Cash Flow Spreadsheet

A budget is probably the classic spreadsheet because the column-and-row structure of a spreadsheet is ideally suited for tracking various expenses or income sources over a designated period. Also, nearly everyone can benefit from a budget and cash flow spreadsheet because such a tool shows us exactly what our cash position is each month and because it can help us predict our financial needs in the future. We built a simple budget spreadsheet in Chapter 5, but now we'll create a more sophisticated model. The finished budget and cash flow spreadsheet is shown in Figure 9-1.

To complete this spreadsheet, we'll fill in sample expense and income categories and sample dollar amounts. We'll save the spreadsheet as a template so that you can open it later as a new document and then fill in your actual expense and income categories and amounts. The spreadsheet's structure suits it for both business and personal use.

Budget - 6/15/90 - Page 1

	A	B	C	D	E	F	G
1		Jan	Feb	Mar	Apr	May	Jun
2	Home Expenses						
3							
4	Food	300	300	300	300	300	300
5	Garbage	12	12	12	12	12	12
6	Health Ins.	150	150	150	150	150	150
7	Home Ins.	50	50	50	50	50	50
8	Life Ins.	35	35	35	35	35	35
9	Maintenance	15	15	15	15	15	15
10	Medical	25	25	25	25	25	25
11	Phone	45	45	45	45	45	45
12	Rent	750	750	750	750	750	750
13	Utilities	75	74	70	68	65	60
14	Water	7	7	7	7	7	7
15							
16	Subtotal Home	1464	1463	1459	1457	1454	1449
17							
18	Auto Expenses						
19							
20	Auto Exp.	50	50	50	50	50	50
21	Auto Ins.	65	65	65	65	65	65
22	Auto Loan	145	145	145	145	145	145
23							
24	Subtotal Auto	260	260	260	260	260	260
25							
26	Credit Expenses						
27							
28	Amer. Express	25	25	25	25	25	25
29	Dept. Store	15	15	15	15	15	15
30	Mastercard	25	25	25	25	25	25
31	Visa	25	25	25	25	25	25
32							
33	Subtotal Credit	90	90	90	90	90	90
34							
35	Savings/Cash						
36							
37	Cash	200	200	200	200	200	200
38	Savings	200	200	200	200	200	200
39							
40	Subtotal Sav/C	400	400	400	400	400	400
41							
42	Total Expenses	2214	2213	2209	2207	2204	2199
43							
44	Income						
45							
46	Dividends	25	0	0	25	0	0
47	Interest	5	5	5	5	5	5
48	Other	0	0	0	0	250	0
49	Wages	2300	2300	2300	2300	2300	2300
50							
51	Total Income	2330	2305	2305	2330	2555	2305
52	Total Expenses	2214	2213	2209	2207	2204	2199
53	Cash Flow	116	208	304	427	778	884

Figure 9-1. *(continued)*
This spreadsheet can help track expenses and income so that you can project future financial needs.

Budget - 6/15/90 - Page 2

	H	I	J	K	L	M	N	O
	Jul	Aug	Sep	Oct	Nov	Dec	Total	Avg
1								
2								
3								
4	300	300	300	300	300	300	3600	300.0
5	12	12	12	12	12	12	144	12.0
6	150	150	150	150	150	150	1800	150.0
7	50	50	50	50	50	50	600	50.0
8	35	35	35	35	35	35	420	35.0
9	15	15	15	15	15	15	180	15.0
10	25	25	25	25	25	25	300	25.0
11	45	45	45	45	45	45	540	45.0
12	750	750	750	750	750	750	9000	750.0
13	50	40	50	60	65	75	752	62.7
14	7	7	7	7	7	7	84	7.0
15								
16	1439	1429	1439	1449	1454	1464	17420	1451.7
17								
18								
19								
20	50	50	50	50	50	50	600	50.0
21	65	65	65	65	65	65	780	65.0
22	145	145	145	145	145	145	1740	145.0
23								
24	260	260	260	260	260	260	3120	260.0
25								
26								
27								
28	25	25	25	25	25	25	300	25.0
29	15	15	15	15	15	15	180	15.0
30	25	25	25	25	25	25	300	25.0
31	25	25	25	25	25	25	300	25.0
32								
33	90	90	90	90	90	90	1080	90.0
34								
35								
36								
37	200	200	200	200	200	200	2400	200.0
38	200	200	200	200	200	200	2400	200.0
39								
40	400	400	400	400	400	400	4800	400.0
41								
42	2189	2179	2189	2199	2204	2214	26420	2201.7
43								
44								
45								
46	25	0	0	25	0	0	100	8.3
47	5	5	5	5	5	5	60	5.0
48	0	0	0	0	0	0	250	20.8
49	2300	2300	2300	2300	2300	2300	27600	2300.0
50								
51	2330	2305	2305	2330	2305	2305	28010	2334.2
52	2189	2179	2189	2199	2204	2214	26420	2201.7
53	1025	1151	1267	1398	1499	1590	10647	887.3

Entering the spreadsheet labels

To begin this project, we'll open a new spreadsheet file and enter all the row and column labels.

1. Press Alt-F-N to choose the Create New File command from the File menu. Works displays a dialog box that gives us a choice of creating a new word processor, spreadsheet, database, or communications document.

2. Press the S key to choose a new spreadsheet. Works opens a new spreadsheet file.

Most of the column labels are months of the year, and we can use Works' Fill Series command to enter them quickly.

1. Press the Right arrow key to select cell B1.

2. Type *Jan*, and press the Enter key to enter the label for this column.

3. Press the F8 key to extend the selection.

4. Press the Right arrow key 11 times to select the 11 cells to the right of B1.

5. Press Alt-E-L to choose the Fill Series command from the Edit menu. Works displays the Fill Series dialog box, like this:

As you can see, Works' Fill Series command lets you specify a series of labels or values to be entered in a selected range of cells:

1. Press the M key to select Month units. The Step By value is set at the default of 1, which tells Works to enter a series of month labels, moving from one month to the next. We want column labels for every month, so this setting is correct.

2. Press the Enter key to confirm the selection. Works fills the selected cells with month labels from Feb through Dec in cells C1 through M1.

The final two column labels will show total and average amounts in each expense and income category, respectively:

1. Press the Right arrow key 12 times to select cell N1.

2. Type *Total*, and press the Right arrow key to enter this label and select cell O1.

3. Type *Avg*, and press the Enter key.

Now we'll enter the expense and income category labels in column A. Before we do, however, we'll widen column A so that it will have enough room for the labels we're about to enter:

1. Press the Home key to select cell A1.

2. Press Alt-T-W to choose the Column Width command from the Format menu. Works displays a dialog box in which we can enter the number of characters that we want to set for the column width.

3. Type *15*, and press the Enter key. Works widens column A.

When you create a new spreadsheet, you usually don't enter labels in exactly the order in which you want them. For this exercise, we'll deliberately enter the labels out of order so that we can use Works' sorting and editing features to fix them.

1. Press the Down arrow key to select cell A2.

2. Type *Expenses*, and press the Down arrow key two times. Works enters the label in cell A2, skips a row, and selects cell A4.

3. Type *Rent*, and press the Down arrow key.

4. Repeat Step 3, entering the rest of the expense and income labels shown in Figure 9-2 on the following page.

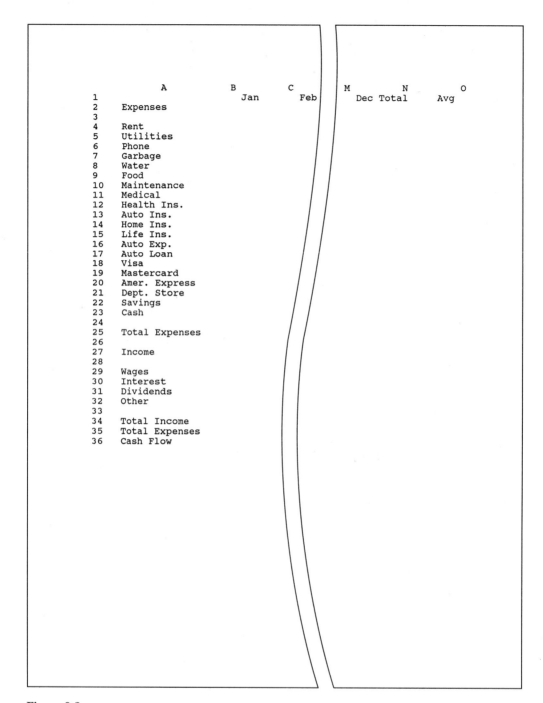

```
                    A            B        C       M       N         O
 1                           Jan      Feb       Dec Total     Avg
 2        Expenses
 3
 4        Rent
 5        Utilities
 6        Phone
 7        Garbage
 8        Water
 9        Food
10        Maintenance
11        Medical
12        Health Ins.
13        Auto Ins.
14        Home Ins.
15        Life Ins.
16        Auto Exp.
17        Auto Loan
18        Visa
19        Mastercard
20        Amer. Express
21        Dept. Store
22        Savings
23        Cash
24
25        Total Expenses
26
27        Income
28
29        Wages
30        Interest
31        Dividends
32        Other
33
34        Total Income
35        Total Expenses
36        Cash Flow
```

Figure 9-2.
Spreadsheet labels don't usually start out in the order in which you want them. These must be sorted before they'll look like the labels in Figure 9-1.

After all the labels are entered, it appears that the expenses would be easier to comprehend if we could divide them up into Household, Auto, and Credit groups and if they were alphabetically sorted in each of those groups. Let's add some subcategory labels and move the expense labels around to make this change:

1. Select cell A17 and press Alt-E-I to choose the Insert Row/Column command from the Edit menu. Works displays the Insert dialog box, in which the option to insert a row is already selected.

2. Press the Enter key to confirm the selection and to insert a blank row. The *Auto Loan* label and the labels below it all move down, and a blank row appears.

3. Repeat steps 1 and 2 four times so that five blank rows separate the *Auto Exp.* and *Auto Loan* labels.

4. Press the Down arrow key to select cell A18.

5. Type *Subtotal Home*, and press the Enter key to enter this label.

6. Press the Down arrow key two times to select cell A20.

7. Type *Auto Expenses*, and press the Enter key.

8. Select cell A23 (the *Visa* label), and repeat steps 1, 2, and 3 to insert five rows between the *Visa* and *Auto Loan* labels.

9. Select cell A24, type *Subtotal Auto*, and then press the Down arrow key two times to select cell A26.

10. Type *Credit Expenses*, and press the Enter key to enter this label.

11. Select the *Savings* label in cell A32.

12. Repeat steps 1, 2, and 3 to insert five rows between the *Dept. Store* and *Savings* labels.

13. Insert the *Subtotal Credit* and *Savings/Cash* labels as shown in Figure 9-1.

14. Select the *Total Expenses* label in cell A40.

15. Repeat steps 1, 2, and 3 to insert two rows only between the blank cell A39 and the *Total Expenses* label.

16. Type *Subtotal Sav/C* as a label in cell A40, and press the Enter key.

17. Select cell A2 (where the *Expenses* label is now located), and type *Home Expenses*. Then press the Enter key to enter the changed label.

With all the rows and labels now correct, we need to be sure that expenses are located in the appropriate categories, and we also need to sort each group of expense labels. First, because the *Auto Ins.* label in cell A13 really belongs in the *Auto Expenses* category, we'll move it:

1. Select cell A13, which contains the *Auto Ins.* label.

2. Press Ctrl-F8 to select all of row 13.

3. Press the F3 key to choose the Move command.

4. Select cell A23, and press the Enter key. Works moves row 13 to row 23, the *Auto Ins.* label moves with it, and the rows between row 13 and row 23 move up one row to fill the remaining space.

5. Select cell A15, which contains the *Auto Exp.* label.

6. Press Ctrl-F8 to select all of row 15.

7. Press the F3 key to choose the Move command.

8. Select cell A21, and press the Enter key. Works moves row 15 to row 21. The *Auto Exp.* label moves with row 15, and the rows between row 15 and row 21 move up one row to fill the remaining space.

Now let's sort the labels in each expense category. We can't simply select all the labels in column A because Works would sort the category titles and subtotal rows into the wrong order. Instead, we have to select the labels within each category:

1. Select cell A4.

2. Press the F8 key to extend the selection.

3. Press the Down arrow key 10 times to select all the labels through cell A14.

4. Press Alt-S-O to choose the Sort Rows command from the Select menu. Works displays a dialog box like that shown on the following page.

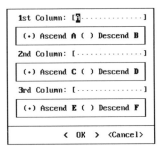

Works lets you sort on up to three columns at one time, but in this case we want to sort only on the labels in column A. We want them to be in ascending alphabetic order. These options are already selected as the defaults, so:

1. Press the Enter key to confirm the default sort settings. Works arranges rows 4 through 14 so that the labels are in ascending alphabetic order.

2. Sort the *Auto Expenses*, *Credit Expenses*, *Savings/Cash*, and *Income* category labels in the same way.

Now our labels are arranged in the way that we want them. We could apply some formatting enhancements to improve the labels' readability, but we'll save these finishing touches for the end of the project.

Entering the spreadsheet values

Now we'll enter the initial spreadsheet values. In a real budget spreadsheet, we would first enter our best estimates of our expenses and income and then adjust those values to actual values as each month passes. Here we'll enter some projected amounts, using Works' Fill Right command to help.

1. Select cell B4.

2. Type *300*, and press the Enter key.

3. Press the F8 key.

4. Press the Right arrow key 11 times to select the range B4:M4.

5. Press Alt-E-R to choose the Fill Right command from the Edit menu. Works fills the *Rent* expense cells for every month with the value, *300*.

As you can see in Figure 9-1, many of the expense and income category amounts in this spreadsheet are the same for every month or at least for several months at a time. You can use the Fill Right command to enter like amounts more quickly. In fact, where several adjacent rows have like amounts—as in rows 5 through 12 here—you can select all the rows at the same time and use the Fill Right command to fill them. Here's how:

1. Type all the values in cells B5:B12 as shown in Figure 9-1.

2. Select cell B5.

3. Press the F8 key.

4. Press the Down arrow key seven times to select cells B5:B12.

5. Press the Right arrow key 11 times to select cells in the range B5:M12.

6. Press Alt-E-R to choose the Fill Right command. All the rows will be filled, each with the value it contained in column B.

Practice using the Fill Right command to insert the values from Figure 9-1 in the other rows where you can, and enter the values individually where necessary. When you finish, the values should match those in Figure 9-1. Don't enter values in the Total, Subtotal, or Avg cells—we'll fill these cells by entering formulas in them.

Entering the spreadsheet formulas

Now we'll enter the formulas that will calculate the subtotals, totals, and averages in this spreadsheet. First we'll do the monthly subtotals for each expense and income category:

1. Select cell B16, which is the Home Expenses subtotal for January. We want to total all the home expenses in cells B4 through B14, so we'll use Works' SUM function to add this range of cells.

2. Type *=SUM(* to begin a formula.

3. Press the Up arrow key 12 times to select cell B4.

4. Press the F8 key to extend the selection.

5. Press the Down arrow key 10 times to extend the selection down to cell B14. As you select the range, Works enters it in the formula's argument.

6. Type) to end the formula, and then press the Enter key to enter it. Works calculates the formula, and the total of the home expenses for January appears in cell B16.

Because this formula is the same for every month-total cell in row 16, we can copy it to the right using the Fill Right command, exactly as we copied the values earlier:

1. Select cell B16.

2. Press the F8 key.

3. Press the Right arrow key 11 times to select the range B16:M16.

4. Press Alt-E-R to choose the Fill Right command. Works fills all the subtotal cells in row 16 with copies of the formula in cell B16 and calculates the totals. Because we used relative cell references in the formula, each copy of the formula Works made with the Fill Right command contains the correct cell references. (See Chapter 6 for more information about relative cell references.)

You can fill in the Subtotal Auto (row 24), Subtotal Credit (row 33), Subtotal Sav/C (row 40), and Total Income (row 51) rows the same way. Here's the general procedure:

1. Select the cell in column B that will contain the January subtotal for that group of expenses.

2. Type =SUM(to begin a formula.

3. Select the range of cells that represents the individual expense categories for January in that group by pointing to the first cell in the range (in column B) and extending the selection down to the last cell in the range. As you select the range, Works enters it in the formula's argument.

4. Type) to end the formula, and press the Enter key to enter it.

5. Select the formula and the 11 cells to the right of it in the same row using the F8 key.

6. Press Alt-E-R to fill the cells to the right with copies of the formula.

Next, we'll enter the formulas to calculate each month's total expenses in row 42:

1. Select cell B42, and type = to begin a formula. For this formula, we will add together individual cells that aren't located in a contiguous range, so we won't use the SUM function.

2. Press the Up arrow key to select cell B16, which is the cell that contains the Subtotal Home expenses for January. Works adds this cell reference to the formula.

3. Type +. Works adds the + sign to the formula after the B16 cell reference and returns the cell selection to cell B42.

4. Press the Up arrow key to select cell B24. Works adds it to the formula.

5. Type +. Works adds the + sign to the formula and returns the cell selection to cell B42.

6. Using the same method, add cells B33 and B40 to the formula, being sure to include a + sign between their references.

7. Press the Enter key to end the formula entry. Works calculates the sum of cells B16, B24, B33, and B40 and displays the total in cell B42.

This formula also uses relative cell references, so use the Fill Right command to copy it into the Total Expenses cells for Feb through Dec in the range C42:M42.

The summary area at the bottom of the spreadsheet compares total expenses with total income and shows the monthly cash flow. The total expenses in row 52 are the same as the values in row 42, so we can tell Works to copy them:

1. Select cell B52.

2. Type = to start a formula.

3. Press the Up arrow key to select cell B42. This cell reference appears in the formula bar.

4. Press the Enter key to enter this formula.

The formula in cell B52 now reads *=B42*, which tells Works to copy the value from cell B42. Because this is a relative reference, we can now use the Fill Right command to copy the formula in cell B52 to the range C52:M52.

To calculate the cash flow in column B, we subtract the total expenses in cell B52 from the total income in cell B51:

1. Select cell B53, and type = to start a formula.

2. Press the Up arrow key two times to select cell B51. This reference is added to the formula.

3. Type − to indicate subtraction. The operator appears after B51 in the formula, and the cell selection moves back to cell B53.

4. Press the Up arrow key one time to select cell B52. The reference is added to the formula.

5. Press the Enter key to enter the formula. Works subtracts the amount in cell B52 from the amount in cell B51 and displays the result in cell B53.

In a real budget, a cash flow will probably carry over from the previous month (December). To figure January's cash flow accurately, the carryover amount would have to be added to the Total Income figure represented by cell B51, and then the Total Expenses figure in cell B52 would be subtracted from the total. In this case, the formula in cell B53 would look like this:

```
=(carryover amount+B51)–B52
```

Because we're calculating cash flow in row 53, we'll want the February cash flow to show any remaining cash in January, plus February's income minus February's expenses. To enter this formula:

1. Select cell C53, and type =(to begin the formula.

2. Press the Left arrow key to select cell B53 (January's cash flow), and then type +.

3. Select cell C51 (February's Total Income), and then type).

4. Type −, and then select cell C52 (February's Total Expenses). The formula now reads:

=(B53+C51)−C52

5. Press the Enter key. Works calculates the formula and displays the result in cell C53.

Now you can copy this formula in cell C53 into the Cash Flow cells for March through December (D53:M53) using the Fill Right command. All the vertical formulas are complete for this spreadsheet, and we can enter the horizontal totals in columns N and O. Exactly as we used the Fill Right command to speed up formula entry before, we will now use the Fill Down command to speed it up here:

1. Select cell N4, and type =SUM(to begin a formula.

2. Select cell B4, and press the F8 key to extend the selection.

3. Press the Right arrow key 11 times to select the range B4:M4.

4. Type) to complete the formula.

5. Press the Enter key to enter the formula. Works calculates the total Food expenses and displays the result in cell N4.

Now we'll enter the formula to calculate the average monthly expense for Food in cell O4:

1. Select cell O4.

2. Type =AVG(to begin the formula. AVG is a function name that tells works to average the amounts in the range of cells contained in the formula's argument.

3. Select the range of cells B4:M4, as with the SUM formula above.

4. Type) to complete the formula, and press the Enter key to enter it. The average amount, which is *300*, appears in cell O4.

Again, these formulas use relative cell references, so we can copy them using Works' Fill Down command. And, as we have seen, we can select the two columns at one time and use Fill Down on both of them simultaneously.

1. Select cell N4, and press the F8 key.

2. Press the Right arrow key one time to extend the selection to cell O4.

3. Press the Down arrow key to extend the selection down to row 53.

4. Press Alt-E-F to choose the Fill Down command. Works copies the formulas in cells N4 and O4 down the spreadsheet into every row through row 53.

The spreadsheet now displays totals and averages for every row from row 4 through row 53. The problem is that some of those rows are supposed to be blank in order to provide spacing between groups of expense or income categories. Because these rows have no value, the AVG formula displays an error message. (The SUM formula treats the empty cells as zero values, so it results in a value of zero.) Also, the total in row 53 (Cash Flow) is meaningless because this is a measure of month-to-month cash available. We can eliminate the extra formulas by selecting the cells that contain them and using the Clear command. Our first extra formulas are in cells N15 and O15. To clear them:

1. Select cell N15, and press the F8 key.

2. Press the Right arrow key one time to extend the selection to cell O15.

3. Press Alt-E-E to choose the Clear command. Works clears these cells.

When more than two cells are together in a contiguous group—as in the range N17:O19—you can select the entire block and use the Clear command one time to clear them all. Finish clearing all the extra cells in the spreadsheet now.

Formatting the spreadsheet

Now let's make the spreadsheet a little more readable, both on the screen and on paper. First, we'll make all the column labels boldface:

1. Select any cell in row 1.

2. Press Ctrl-F8 to select the entire row.

3. Press Alt-T-S to display the Style dialog box.

4. Press the R key to specify right alignment for these labels.

5. Press the B key to specify boldface style for these labels.

6. Press the Enter key to confirm these settings and to return to the spreadsheet. The labels in row 1 now appear right aligned in their cells and in highlighted characters to indicate the boldface style.

Now add some other boldface style enhancements on your own. Select the Home Expenses, Subtotal Home, Auto Expenses, Subtotal Auto, Credit Expenses, Subtotal Credit, Savings/Cash, Subtotal Sav/C, Total Expenses (both of them), Income, Total Income, and Cash Flow labels, and make them boldface. Because most of these labels aren't adjacent to each other, you'll have to select them and make them boldface individually. In rows 51–53, however, you can select three labels as a group and make them all boldface at the same time.

Next, let's change the numeric formatting for the average amounts in column O. Right now, Works' General format shows the average amounts calculated to several decimal places of accuracy. We probably don't need to see such detail, and all those decimal points make the column harder to read. We'll change the formatting to show only one decimal place:

1. Select any cell in column O.

2. Press Shift-F8 to select the entire column.

3. Press Alt-T-X to choose the Fixed command from the Format menu. Works displays a dialog box in which we can enter the number of decimal places.

4. Type *1*, and press the Enter key to confirm this setting. The numbers in column O are rounded off to one decimal place.

The next formatting chore concerns getting the spreadsheet ready to print. As it is, this spreadsheet will require three sheets of paper to print. Each page will contain all the rows, but more columns are included than will fit across one page. So, using the current layout, the first page will print through the April expenses, the second page will print from May through October expenses, and the third page will print the remaining months and the Total and Average columns.

We aren't able to squeeze all these columns across only one sheet of paper, but we can make the columns narrower so that a little space remains between each column and yet the whole spreadsheet fits across two pages. We can't make column A narrower because some of the labels fill all of the column's 15 characters, but we can make all the number columns narrower because not one of them holds more than five digits:

1. Select any cell in column B.

2. Press the F8 key to extend the selection.

3. Press the Right arrow key until columns B through O are selected.

4. Press Alt-T-W to display the Column Width dialog box.

5. Type 7 and press the Enter key. Works narrows all the number columns to seven characters, and the spreadsheet now fits across two pages. To see this change for yourself, press Alt-P-V to preview the spreadsheet on the screen.

Finally, because this is a two-page spreadsheet, we'll add a header that contains the spreadsheet name and the page number:

1. Press Alt-P-H to choose the Headers & Footers command. The Headers & Footers dialog box is displayed, and the cursor blinks in the Header text box. (Notice that in the spreadsheet, the Use Header & Footer Paragraphs option is unavailable. You can have only one-line headers and footers in the spreadsheet.)

2. Type &RBudget - &D - Page &P, and press the Enter key. When you print this file, Works prints a right-aligned header like this:

Budget – current date – Page X

In the above example, the current date will be the date shown by your computer's system clock when you print the file. The X will be the current page number. The &R, &D, and &P are special header formatting codes that tell Works to right-align the header (&R), insert the current date (&D), and insert the current page number (&P). For more information about header formatting commands, choose the Print Headers & Footers command from the Commands category in the Help Index on the Help menu.

Saving and using the template

To reuse this budget spreadsheet for your own finances, you can save it and then use it later as a template:

1. Press Alt-F-A to choose the Save As command. Works displays the Save As dialog box.

2. Type the filename BUDGTEMP.

3. Press the Enter key to save the file.

Now you can open this file when you want it, make the changes you need, and then save the changed file with a different name. The template will remain unchanged on the disk.

For your own purposes, you'll probably want to make some modifications to this spreadsheet such as adding or changing expense or income categories. Here are some tips for doing so:

■ Edit the existing category names to change them to the names you want, rather than delete rows.

■ If you must insert additional rows, insert them in alphabetic order to maintain the alphabetic sort of the expense and income categories. Do not sort this spreadsheet again because it could make the formulas that refer to the sorted rows inaccurate.

■ Check all formulas when you're finished to be sure that they still refer to the cells you want to calculate.

Now let's move on to a different analytical task that puts Works' charting features to use.

An Advertising Analysis

In this project, we'll see how Works' charting features can reveal different bits of information about our data. In this spreadsheet, a mail-order business is tracking the responses it has gotten from various advertisements. The ads are running in the September, October, November, and December issues of four different monthly magazines, and the spreadsheet shows the number of responses for each month. By plotting those response results in different ways, we can reveal different trends.

Creating the tracking spreadsheet

To begin this project, we'll need to create a spreadsheet from which to chart the data. The spreadsheet we'll use is shown in Figure 9-3.

```
 File  Edit  Print  Select  Format  Options  View  Window  Help

                              ADVANAL.WKS
          A            B          C         D        E        F
  1   Magazine        Sep        Oct       Nov      Dec    Totals
  2
  3   Young Modeler    11          8         9       24       52
  4   Kit Craft        17         14        14       18       63
  5   Model Maven      13         28        19       18       78
  6   Car Modeling     25         35        45       40      145
  7
  8   Totals           66         85        87      100      338
  9
 10   ████████████████
 11
 12
 13
 14
 15
 16
 17
 18
A10                                                        <F1=HELP>
Press ALT to choose commands, or F2 to edit.
```

Figure 9-3.
This spreadsheet tracks responses to advertisements in various magazines.

After we enter the first label in cell A1, we'll use the Fill Series command to enter each of the month labels for the tracking period:

1. Open a new Works spreadsheet. Cell A1 is selected.

2. Type *Magazine*, and press the Right arrow key to select cell B1.

3. Type *September*, and press the Enter key. Works recognizes September as a month name and converts it to *Sep*, changing the cell to date formatting.

4. Press the F8 key.

5. Press the Right arrow key three times to select cells B1:E1.

6. Press Alt-E-L to choose the Fill Series command. Works displays the Fill Series dialog box. The Day interval is selected, but we want each successive cell in the series to contain the next month name.

7. Press the M key to select the Month interval. The Step By value is already set to 1, which is what we want because we want the month labels to be increased one month at a time from cell to cell in the range.

8. Press the Enter key to confirm these settings. Works fills cells C1, D1, and E1 with Oct, Nov, and Dec labels and converts those cells to date format.

Next, widen column A to accommodate the labels we'll enter:

1. Select any cell in column A.

2. Press Alt-T-W to display the Column Width dialog box.

3. Type *15*, and press the Enter key to change column A's width to 15 characters.

Now enter the other labels and values as shown in Figure 9-3, except for the total amounts. Notice that the Totals label in cell F1 is right aligned; you can align the label this way by selecting cell F1, choosing the Style command from the Format menu (Alt-T-S), and choosing the Right option under Alignment in the Style dialog box.

The totals in column F and row 8 are all produced by SUM formulas. We can enter one formula in cell B8 and copy it to the right, and we can enter one formula in cell F3 and copy it down:

1. Select cell B8, and type *=SUM(B3:B6)*.

2. Press the Enter key.

3. Press the F8 key.

4. Press the Right arrow key four times to select the range B8:F8.

5. Press Alt-E-R to choose the Fill Right command. Works copies the formula to the other four cells in row 8.

6. Select cell F3, and type *=SUM(B3:E3)*.

7. Press the Enter key.

8. Press the F8 key.

9. Press the Down arrow key three times to select the total cells for the other magazines (F3:F6).

10. Press Alt-E-F to choose the Fill Down command. The total formula is copied into the other rows, and Works displays the total amounts.

Now let's save this spreadsheet.

1. Press Alt-F-A. Works displays the Save As dialog box.

2. Type *ADVANAL*, and press the Enter key to save the file.

With the spreadsheet safely on disk, we're ready to begin charting our data.

Creating charts

The spreadsheet shows monthly response figures for each of four magazines, but displaying this data in charts will help us spot some key relationships and facts. Let's suppose we want to plot a chart that shows which magazines did the best each month. To begin charting, we must choose the New Chart command from the View menu. First, however, we need to select the data we want to chart. Because we want to compare the monthly response figures for each magazine each month, we'll select all four months' data from all four magazines:

1. Press Ctrl-Home to select cell A1.

2. Press the F8 key, and then press the Right arrow key four times to select cells A1:E1.

3. Press the Down arrow key five times to select rows 1 through 6. The entire block of response figures, magazine labels, and month labels is selected. We've selected the month labels in row 1 and the magazine names in column A so that Works will use them in the chart as the X-axis labels and the data legends, respectively.

4. Press Alt-V-N to view the chart. Works displays a Bar Chart on the screen, as shown at the top of the next page.

This chart makes it clear that *Car Modeling* magazine is the response leader every month. And, if we could afford to advertise in only two magazines each month, this chart plainly shows us the two best magazines each month.

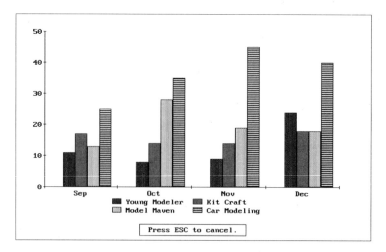

Let's change the chart format to a Stacked Bar chart so that we can get a better idea of exactly how much of the total response volume each magazine represents every month:

1. Press the Esc key to display the Chart mode screen.

2. Press Alt-T-S to choose a Stacked Bar chart format.

3. Press Alt-V-1 to display Chart1 again. (The only chart we've viewed from this spreadsheet is the bar chart that we just saw, so Works names it Chart1.) In Stacked Bar format, the response data looks like this:

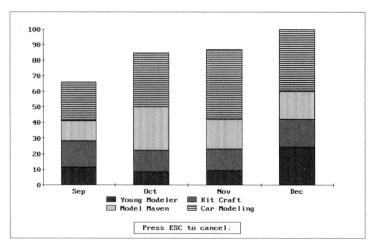

Now we can easily see that *Car Modeling* magazine represents from one third to one half of the total response volume every month—it's obviously a good advertising vehicle for us. The chart also shows that although *Kit Craft* was fairly consistent from month to month, *Model Maven* had its biggest month in October, and *Young Modeler* had a strong finish in December. Finally, we can easily see that the largest number of responses came in during November and December, so if we could afford advertisements during only two months, November and December would be the best choices.

Now let's suppose that we want to see how each magazine contributed to the total number of responses for the entire period so that we can determine whether the most expensive magazine is delivering the most orders. To see how each magazine contributes to total response volume for the four-month period, we'll make a Pie Chart:

1. Press the Esc key, and then select cell F3.

2. Press the F8 key, and press the Down arrow key three times to select the totals in the range F3:F6.

3. Press Alt-V-N to display a new chart based on this data selection. Works displays a rather boring bar chart that has four bars. Works names this chart Chart2 because it's the second chart we've viewed from this spreadsheet.

4. Press the Esc key to display the Chart mode screen.

5. Press Alt-T-P to select the Pie format, and press Alt-V-2 to display Chart2. It is now a pie chart:

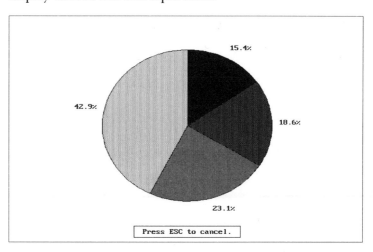

This chart clearly shows that *Car Modeling* magazine's share of the total responses is 42.9%, but it would be nice if the name of each magazine were listed next to each pie slice. To do so, we must add category labels to the chart.

Unlike the chart title, X-axis or Y-axis Titles, or subtitles—all of which can be created from scratch—category labels must be the contents of cells that you select in the spreadsheet. We want to use the magazine names in column A as the labels for our pie slices, so:

1. Press the Esc key to return to the Chart mode screen.

2. Select the magazine labels in the range of cells A3:A6.

3. Press Alt-D-X to choose the X-series command from the Data menu. Doing so tells Works to use that range of cells (the magazine names) as the labels for the X-series data. In a pie chart, each slice is one value in the X-series—pie charts have no Y-series—so the labels will be applied to the chart slices.

4. Press Alt-V-2 to view the chart again. It now has labels on the pie slices, like this:

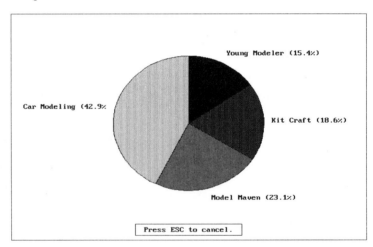

To finish this chart, let's add a title and subtitle:

1. Press the Esc key to return to the Chart mode screen.

2. Press Alt-D-T to choose the Titles command. Works displays the Titles dialog box, like this:

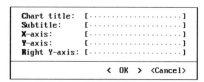

```
Chart title:  [......................]
Subtitle:     [......................]
X-axis:       [......................]
Y-axis:       [......................]
Right Y-axis: [......................]

              <  OK  >  <Cancel>
```

3. The cursor is already blinking in the Chart title text box, so type *4th Quarter Ad Campaign.*

4. Press the Down arrow key to select the Subtitle box.

5. Type *Share of Total Responses*, and press the Enter key to confirm these titles.

6. Press Alt-V-2 to display the pie chart again. Now it contains the title and subtitle.

These few examples have shown how different kinds of charts can reveal different facts about collections of data. For more information about charting, see the Charting Reference in the *Microsoft Works Reference* manual.

An Amortization Table

In this project, we'll build an amortization table that you can use to determine the payment, principal, and interest amounts for loans. To make it easy to change the amount, interest rate, and term of the loan, we'll use a reference area at the top of this spreadsheet in which these amounts will be entered and then refer to that area when making the calculations elsewhere in the spreadsheet. This way, you will be able to change the amount, rate, and term values in the reference area, and Works will recalculate the new loan payment immediately.

Creating the Loan Summary area

The Loan Summary area is at the top of the spreadsheet, so we'll create it first. Before we enter any new data in our spreadsheet, we'll adjust the column widths so that we can display the spreadsheet's formulas as well as its values. Two views of the finished amortization spreadsheet are shown in Figure 9-4.

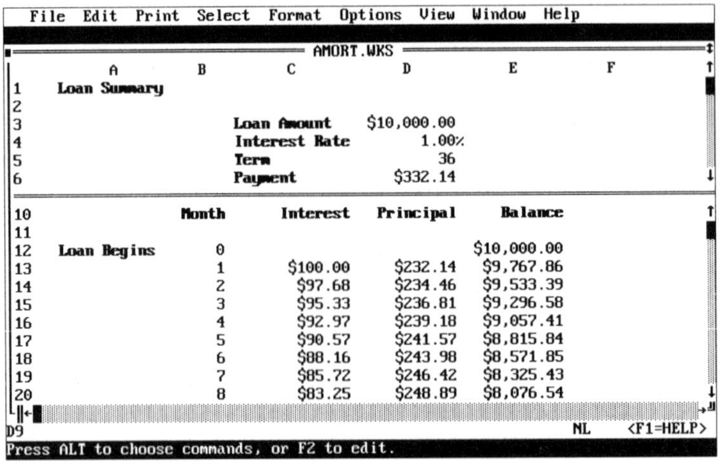

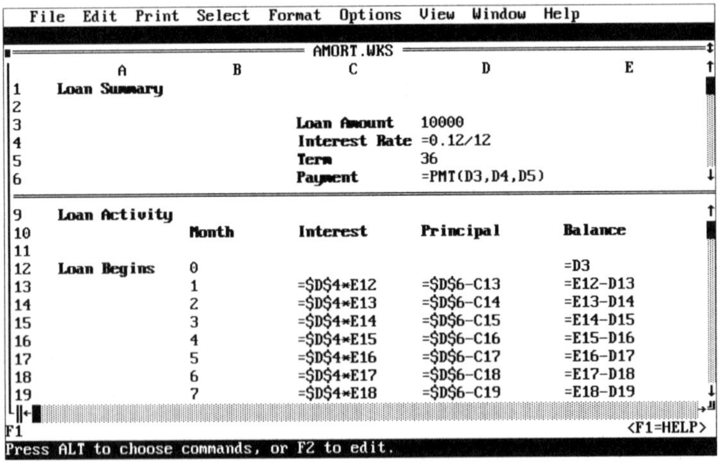

Figure 9-4.
Two views of the amortization spreadsheet: values (top) and formulas (bottom).

1. Open a new spreadsheet file. Cell A1 should be selected. If it is not, select it.

2. Press Alt-T-W to choose the Column Width command. The Column Width dialog box appears.

3. Type *14* as the new column width, and press the Enter key.

4. Select a cell in column B, and make this column six characters wide, using the Column Width command as above.

5. Select a cell in column C, and make this column 14 characters wide.

6. Select cells in both columns D and E, and make these columns 12 characters wide.

Now we'll enter labels and formulas to complete the Loan Summary area:

1. Select cell A1 and type *Loan Summary.*

2. Select cell C3 and type *Loan Amount.*

3. Select cell C4 and type *Interest Rate.*

4. Select cell C5 and type *Term.*

5. Select cell C6 and type *Payment.*

To give us something to work with, let's determine the payment for a loan of $10,000 at the rate of 12 percent for three years:

☐ Select cell D3 and type *10000.*

Because we want to know the monthly payment on this loan, the interest rate must be specified as a monthly rate. And because we know that the yearly rate is 12 percent, we'll divide that rate by 12 to determine the monthly rate:

☐ Select cell D4, type *=.12/12,* and then press the Enter key.

This formula divides the interest rate (12 percent, or 0.12) by 12 to arrive at the monthly interest rate of 1 percent, or 0.01, as shown. Because this value is an interest rate, let's display it as a percentage:

☐ Choose the Percent command from the Format menu. A dialog box appears and suggests 2 as the number of decimals. Press the Enter key to confirm this selection. Works changes the value 0.01 to 1.00% in cell D4.

For the loan term, we have to enter the number of months in the life of the loan. Whenever you create a formula to calculate a loan payment, you must use the same time interval to refer to the interest rate, the loan term, and the payment. Because we want to know how much the payment will be each month, we must calculate it based on a monthly interest rate and on a loan term specified in months:

□ Select cell D5, and type *36* to specify a three-year loan term.

Now we're ready to calculate the loan payment formula. Works has a number of built-in financial functions that make it a lot easier to analyze investments and debts. (See Appendix B of the *Microsoft Works Reference* manual for a complete listing of all the spreadsheet functions.) For this formula, we'll use the PMT (payment) function.

In Works, the PMT function calculates the periodic payment of a specified loan amount at a specified interest rate for a specified term. This formula·is always structured like this:

PMT(*Principal,Rate,Term*)

In our spreadsheet, the *Principal* is the loan amount, the *Rate* is the monthly interest rate, and the *Term* is the term of the loan in months. So here's the PMT formula we'll enter in cell D6 to calculate this loan's monthly payment:

=PMT(D3,D4,D5)

Enter this formula now:

1. Select cell D6, and type *=PMT(* to begin the formula.

2. Press the Up arrow key to select cell D3.

3. Type a comma (,). The cell selection returns to cell D6.

4. Press the Up arrow key to select cell D4, and type a comma. The cell selection returns to cell D6.

5. Press the Up arrow key to select cell D5.

6. Type) to complete the formula, and then press the Enter key to enter it. The monthly payment amount is calculated and appears in cell D6, like this:

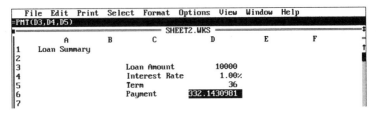

The payment amount is in the spreadsheet's default General format, so it doesn't look much like a dollar amount. Let's change the format of cell D6 to Currency:

1. Press Alt-T-U to change the cell format to Currency. Works displays a dialog box that suggests two decimal places.

2. Press the Enter key to confirm this change. The value in cell D6 is reformatted as dollars and cents.

While you're at it, select cell D3 and change it to the Currency format.

These few cells are all you need to calculate loan payments quickly. The PMT formula in cell D6 refers to the cell locations D3, D4, and D5, rather than to the specific values we entered for the Loan Amount, Interest Rate, and Term. You can simply enter new amounts in these cells, and cell D6 will calculate the new loan payment. Be sure that the loan Interest Rate and Term are always specified as monthly amounts.

Creating the Loan Activity area

The Loan Activity area of this spreadsheet will show exactly how each month's loan payment is divided between reducing the principal and paying the interest. With this area, you can see how much of the principal remains to be paid off on the loan at any given time.

1. Select cell A9 and type *Loan Activity*.

2. Select cell B10 and type *Month*.

3. Select cell C10 and type *Interest*.

4. Select cell D10 and type *Principal*.

5. Select cell E10 and type *Balance*.

6. Select cell A12 and type *Loan Begins*.

7. Select cell B12, and enter the value *0* to indicate that this is the beginning of the loan's term.

In this example, we'll want to create 36 rows of activity data, one for each month in the life of the loan. Because we will eventually have to scroll the spreadsheet screen to view rows farther down in the Loan Activity area, it's a good idea to split the window so that the Loan Summary area is always visible in the upper part of the screen. Let's do this now by following the steps on the next page.

1. Press Alt-W-T to choose the Split command from the Window menu. The split bars are highlighted at the top and at the left side of the screen.

2. Press the Down arrow key to move the horizontal split bar until it's lying across row 7 of the spreadsheet, immediately under the Payment information.

3. Press the Enter key. Works splits the spreadsheet window at row 7, like this:

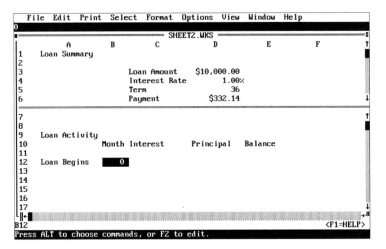

Now we can scroll the lower part of the window to work on the Loan Activity area, and the Loan Summary area will remain in the window pane at the top. (To move the cursor from one window pane to the other, press the F6 key.)

To enter the loan activity information, we'll use formulas that refer to the Loan Amount, Interest Rate, and Payment values that we've already entered or calculated in the summary area above. After we've entered one row of formulas, we'll copy them down into the next 35 rows to show all 36 months of loan activity.

Notice, however, that if we use relative cell references in the Loan Activity area when we refer to specific cells in the summary area, the references will adjust to each new position of the loan activity formulas when we copy them. Consequently, the formulas won't calculate what we want. If, in some formula, we refer to the interest rate value in cell D4, for example, that reference will change to D5 when we copy the formula that contains it down to the next row. (Relative cell references always adjust to the new positions of formulas that contain them.) For this reason, we will use absolute cell references when we refer to the interest rate or to monthly payment values in these formulas. When we specify cell D4 as an absolute reference, then, it will always be D4 no matter where the formula containing it is copied.

First enter the beginning loan balance in cell E12:

1. Select cell E12, and type = to begin a formula.

2. Select cell D3, and press the Enter key. The amount *10000* appears in the cell. (We're not going to copy the =D3 formula anywhere, so you need not use an absolute reference for cell D3.)

This formula tells Works to copy the Loan Amount value from cell D3. Whenever we change the original Loan Amount figure in cell D3, the beginning loan balance here will also change. Now we'll figure the amount of interest, which we can do by multiplying the Interest Rate value in cell D4 by the initial loan amount in E12.

1. Select cell C13, and type = to begin a formula.

2. Type *$D$4* to indicate an absolute reference to cell D4.

3. Type * to indicate multiplication.

4. Select cell E12, and press the Enter key to complete the formula. (We want the reference to E12 to change relative to this formula's position, so we don't make it an absolute reference.) The amount *100* now appears in cell C13.

In the Principal column, we want a formula that determines how much of each month's payment goes toward reducing the loan balance. We already know how much of the month's payment is interest (we just calculated it in cell C12), and we know what the monthly payment is because we calculated it in cell D6. So all we need to do is subtract the amount of monthly interest from the total monthly payment to arrive at the amount of principal:

1. Select cell D13, and type = to begin a formula.

2. Type *$D$6* to enter an absolute reference to cell D6.

3. Type − to indicate subtraction.

4. Select cell C13, and press the Enter key. The amount of principal appears in cell D13.

The last formula will determine the remaining loan balance, which is the previous month's balance minus the current month's principal. Because all the references in this formula must change in each row to calculate the current month's balance accurately, we'll use only relative cell references:

1. Select cell E13, and type = to begin a formula.

2. Select cell E12, and type − to indicate subtraction.

3. Select cell D13, and press the Enter key. The remaining loan balance appears in cell E13, like this:

```
9    Loan Activity
10                    Month Interest       Principal  Balance
11
12   Loan Begins       0                                   10000
13                                    100 232.1430981  9767.856902
14
```

The next step is to copy these three formulas down to the 35 rows below them so that we'll have one row for each month of loan activity:

1. Select cell C13.

2. Press the F8 key.

3. Press the Right arrow key two times to extend the selection through cell E13.

4. Press the Down arrow key until every row through row 48 is selected.

5. Press Alt-E-F to choose the Fill Down command. The three formulas are copied into the selected cells.

At this point, the selected cells in columns C, D, and E are in the default General format, so they're shown to several decimal places of accuracy. While all the cells are still selected, let's change the format to Currency and round the cells to two decimal places:

1. Press Alt-T-U to choose the Currency command. Works displays the Number of Decimals dialog box, and the default entry of 2 shows.

2. Press the Enter key to confirm two decimal places. The numbers are reformatted as dollars and cents. Now select cell E12 and format it for accuracy as well.

The finished amortization spreadsheet is shown in Figure 9-4 in two different ways: The upper window shows the values that result from the formula calculations, and the lower window shows the formulas themselves. The Show Formulas command on the Options menu (Alt-O-F) lets you display spreadsheet formulas rather than their calculated results. This command is useful when you want to show others how you built a spreadsheet.

In this case, we can look at the displayed formulas in Figure 9-4 and see why it was necessary to use both absolute and relative cell references in the Loan Activity area's formulas. As you can see, the absolute references to cells D4 and D6 are the same in each copy of the Interest and Principal formulas, and the relative references change in each row. As a result, the formulas always use the interest and loan payment information from the summary area at the top of the spreadsheet. And, because we used references to the Loan Amount, Payment, and Interest Rate in the Loan Summary area when we calculated the Loan Activity area, we can simply change the Loan Amount, Interest Rate, or Term amounts in the summary area, and the Loan Activity area recalculates to reflect the change.

For finishing touches, we'll add the month number labels in column B and make the column and cell labels boldface. First we want to specify month numbers 1–36 to identify each month of loan activity:

1. Select cell B12.

2. Press the F8 key, and then press the Down arrow key to select cells B12 through B48.

3. Press Alt-E-L to choose the Fill Series command. Works displays the Fill Series dialog box. The Number unit is already selected (which is what we want), and the Step By value is 1 (which we also want).

4. Press the Enter key to confirm the settings. Works fills the range B12:B48 with numbers from 1 through 36.

If you prefer, you can fill the range of cells from B12 to B48 with month names (Jan, Feb, Mar, and so on) or even with specific dates (1/1/90, and so on). Simply use the Fill Series dialog box to insert the range of dates you want. If you know you always pay your mortgage on the 15th, for example, you could enter the 15th of each month as the date in this column.

Finally, we'll add some boldface styles to make the cell and column labels stand out better. We'll do the first label together, and then you can finish on your own:

1. Select cell A1.

2. Press Alt-T-S to display the Style dialog box.

3. Press the B key to specify Bold style, and press the Enter key to confirm the selection.

Now select cells C3, C4, C5, C6, A9, B11, C11, D11, E11, and A12 and make them boldface. Also select cells B11 through E11 and make them right aligned.

Using the amortization table

To make this a practical tool, save it as AMORT so that you can open this spreadsheet whenever you want to project the cost of a loan. You can simply open the file, enter the Loan Amount, Interest Rate, and Term, and then check the Payment amount or the Loan Activity area for payment or amortization information.

This tool is also useful for estimating the remaining balance on any loan you currently have. Simply enter the original Loan Amount, Interest Rate, and Term; determine the number of months since the loan started; count down the rows until you reach the current month; and then check the Balance column. Some processing or payoff fees might be included in addition to the actual loan balance, but the Balance column will give you a good idea of how much you owe.

NOTE: This amortization table might not match your actual loan payment to the penny because of the ways in which different banks determine amortization. It makes a difference in the payment, for example, whether the bank assumes that payments come in at the beginning or at the end of each month.

Modifying the AMORT spreadsheet

You might find it confusing to refer to the interest rate as a monthly rate and to the term in months. Most banks give annual percentage rates. You can easily modify the Loan Summary area by first replacing the formula in cell D6 with this formula:

=PMT(D3,D4/12,D5*12)

Then replace the formula in cell C13 with this formula:

=($D$4/12)*E12

Next, select the range C13 through C48, and choose Fill Down from the Edit menu to update the formulas in the Loan Activity area.

These changes allow you to enter your interest rate and term as annual amounts in cells D4 and D5. The changes also move the rate and term month conversion to the actual payment formula in cell D6. To clarify the data input process in the Loan Summary area, add the label *(in years)* in cell E5. The completed spreadsheet using the example data looks like this:

```
 File  Edit  Print  Select  Format  Options  View  Window  Help

===================================== AMORT.WKS =====================================
        A          B        C           D           E          F
 1   Loan Summary
 2
 3                          Loan Amount   $10,000.00
 4                          Interest Rate    12.00%
 5                          Term                  3 (in years)
 6                          Payment        $332.14

10                Month    Interest   Principal    Balance
11
12   Loan Begins    0                             $10,000.00
13                   1      $100.00    $232.14    $9,767.86
14                   2       $97.68    $234.46    $9,533.39
```

This concludes our practical look at the spreadsheet's features in action. If you need more information about a specific spreadsheet command or function, consult the *Microsoft Works Reference* manual or check the Help Index for on-line instructions. As you gain experience with this powerful number-crunching tool, you'll discover a wide variety of tasks that it can handle with ease.

CHAPTER 10

Basic Database Techniques

The Works Database tool lets you store, sort, organize, calculate, and otherwise manipulate data using some of the same techniques you use in the Works Spreadsheet tool to manipulate numbers. Data can be text—such as names, addresses, and product descriptions—or numbers—such as dates, times, part numbers, or prices—or any combination of the two. With the database, you can store these elements of data and then find them again easily.

Fields, Records, and Files

All database programs let you store and manipulate data, which are items of information about people, places, or things. Normally several related pieces of information are available about each person, place, or thing. In an address database, for example, you might want to store each person's first name, last name, street, city, state, zip code, and telephone number.

In a database file, each type of information (the first name or street address, for example), is contained in its own category, which is called a *field*. Usually, a database file contains many fields. One complete collection of fields is called a *record*. A *file* is composed of a collection of records.

Different database files can contain different fields that store different types of information. In the Works Database, for example, fields can store text, numbers, times, or dates.

233

Before you can begin entering information into a database file, you must decide on its structure. You set up the file's structure to store the types of data it will contain, and their specific categories, by creating and naming fields. After you create and name fields, you can enter information in the fields to create records. And after you have stored some records, you can search for specific information and rearrange that information or create reports from it that you can print.

Creating a Simple Database

To see how the database works, let's create a simple personal database file that contains names and telephone numbers. First, we create a new database file and define the fields that will store the types of information we want. Then we enter some information and see how to sort records and how to select a particular subset of them from the database. Finally, we format the information in a report for printing.

Creating a new database file and defining fields

Let's suppose we want to create a file that stores name, address, and telephone information about business and personal contacts:

1. Press Alt-F-N to create a new file. Works displays the Create New File dialog box in which you can choose the type of new file to create.

2. Press the D key to choose a new database file. Works opens a new database document on the screen, like the one shown in Figure 10-1.

As you can see, a new database screen has some of the standard features of every Works window, including a menu bar, a formula bar, a status line, a message line, scroll bars, and a work area. The work area is the space in which we'll enter field names and where we'll later enter the actual data into the file.

Let's assume we've determined that our file will contain fields with these names: FirstName, LastName, Company, Street, City, ST, Zip, and Phone. The cursor is at the upper-left corner of the work area. To enter the first field name, follow the steps on the next page.

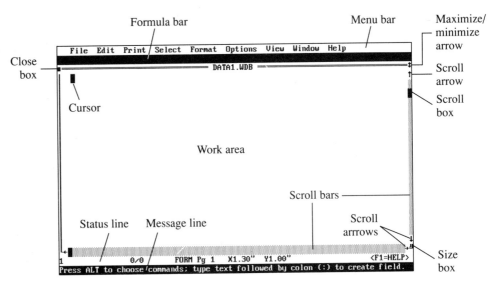

Figure 10-1.

Each Works Database document begins with a blank Form window in which you can enter field names and labels.

1. Type *FirstName:* and press the Enter key. Works displays a dialog box that shows the length and height of the field (the number of characters across and the number of lines high allowed for data entries in that field), like this:

2. Press the Enter key to accept the default field size values. Works enters the field name on the screen and moves the cursor down to the next line.

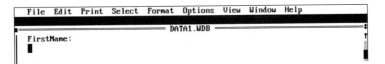

235

NOTE: The database screen examples in this book were made with the screen mode set to Text. (See the Works Settings command on the Options menu.) If your screen mode is set to Graphics instead of Text, the data spaces, after each field you define on the database's Form View screen will contain dotted underlines that show the exact size of each field data space.

Now enter the *LastName:*, *Company:*, *Street:*, and *City:* field names in the same way. Be sure to include the colon at the end of each field name. When you finish, the cursor is in the line below the City field.

So far, we've entered these fields by accepting the default field size values Works has proposed. With the ST field, however, we'll enter only a two-letter state code, so we can save a lot of space by specifying a smaller field size:

1. Type *ST:* and press the Enter key. Works displays the Field Size dialog box.

2. Type *2* to indicate a field length of two characters.

3. Press the Enter key. Works enters the field name and moves the cursor down to the next line.

When we create the Zip and Phone fields, we'll also modify the field lengths so that they are no longer than necessary:

1. Type *Zip:* and press the Enter key.

2. Type *10* to specify 10 characters as the field length (which allows a 9-digit zip code plus one space for a dash after the fifth digit).

3. Press the Enter key to enter the field name.

4. Type *Phone:* and press the Enter key.

5. Type *15* and press the Enter key. (Using 15 characters will allow enough room in this field for area codes, international dialing codes, and the leading 1 or 9 digit for dialing long distance or connecting with an outside line through a company switchboard.)

Now that you have created all the fields for this database document, the screen looks like the example on the next page.

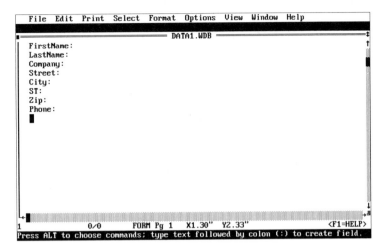

Now we'll use some of the database's formatting features to arrange this screen so that it's more readable.

Changing the form layout

As you'll see in a moment, you can enter information in the document by typing data in any individual field. Because this is the screen we'll ordinarily use for viewing or entering original data in each record, we should reformat it so that it's easier to work with.

First, reposition the fields so that they are formatted more like traditional names and addresses. You can move fields in the database's Form view by using the Move command:

1. Move the cursor to the LastName field by pressing the Up arrow key seven times.

2. Press the F3 key to choose the Move command. Works highlights the field name and the field data space defined for that field. The MOVE indicator appears in the status line.

3. Press the Right arrow key 20 times. As you press the arrow key, the field highlight moves across the screen.

4. Press the Up arrow key one time, and then press the Enter key to move the field. Works displays a warning message.

```
┌─────────────────────────────┐
│  Cannot put item here.      │
├─────────────────────────────┤
│              <  OK  >        │
└─────────────────────────────┘
```

Works won't let you move a field if doing so would infringe upon another field's name or data space. Because we moved the LastName field 20 spaces to the right before moving it up onto the same line as the FirstName field, we have attempted to place it on top of the FirstName field's data space. (Remember, we used the default field length of 20 characters for the FirstName field's data space.)

To ensure that you don't attempt to crowd fields in this fashion, count the number of characters that the field name and its data space occupy, and be sure not to overlap them. In this case, the field name FirstName occupies 11 characters, counting the colon and the space following it, and the field data length is 20 characters. As a result, we have to move the LastName field at least 31 characters from the screen's left edge to avoid overlapping the FirstName field's data space when we move the LastName field up into the same line:

1. Press the Enter key to accept the warning message. The LastName field's highlight remains were it was on the screen.

2. Press the Right arrow key 12 more times to move the LastName field out to the 33rd character from the left edge of the screen.

3. Press the Enter key. The LastName field moves into place to the right of the FirstName field, with one space between the end of the FirstName field's data and the beginning of the LastName field's name.

Now you'll see an empty line on the screen where the LastName field used to be. Let's clean up the screen by rearranging the rest of the field names:

1. Select the Company field name, press the F3 key, and move the field one line up.

2. Select the Street field name, press the F3 key, and move the field one line up.

3. Select the City field name, press the F3 key, and move the field one line up.

4. Select the ST field name, press the F3 key, and move the field 32 characters to the right and two lines up.

5. Select the Zip field name, press the F3 key, and move the field 40 characters to the right and three lines up (so that it's to the right of the ST field).

6. Select the Phone field name, press the F3 key, and move the field name up two lines so that there's a blank line between it and the City,ST,Zip fields. The screen now looks like this:

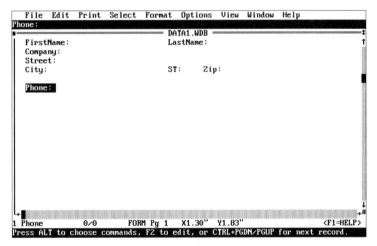

Now let's add a label at the top of this screen. You add labels to the form screen exactly as you add field names, except that you don't type a colon (:) at the end of a label. The colon at the end of a name signals Works that you're creating a field—if you don't put a colon at the end of a word or phrase, Works assumes that it's a label.

1. Press the Page Up key to move the cursor to the top of the screen.

2. Press Alt-E-I (the Insert Line command) two times to insert two blank lines at the top of the form.

3. Press the Right arrow key 20 times. (Unlike the Word Processor tool, the Database tool doesn't let you use the Tab key or centering commands to align text on the screen.)

4. Type *ADDRESS BOOK* and then press the Enter key. Works enters the label.

To finish this form, let's underline the *ADDRESS BOOK* label and make it boldface. The label is still selected.

1. Press Alt-T-S to choose the Style command. Works displays the Style dialog box.

2. Press the B key to select the Bold style option.

3. Press the U key to select the Underline style option.

4. Press the Enter key to confirm these choices. Works changes the label's display intensity (and color, if you have a color monitor) to show that it will print in boldface and with an underline, like this:

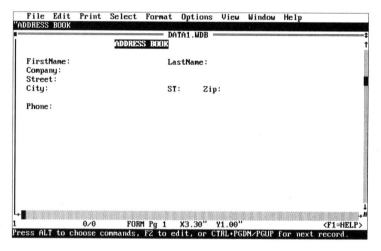

This form is complete for now, but you can add fields, delete fields, or edit field names any time you want:

- To add a field, move the cursor to an unused part of the screen and type the field name. Be sure to end the field name with a colon. Press the Enter key. Change the field size settings, if you like, and then press the Enter key to confirm them.

- To delete an existing field, select the field name and press Alt-E-D to delete it. When you delete a field, note that Works also deletes all the data you've stored in that field.

- To rename an existing field, either select the field name and type a new one or press the F2 key to move the cursor to the formula bar and then change the existing field name there. Press the Enter key when you finish.

Although this form contains only a few fields, you can create forms that occupy more than one screen and contain up to 256 fields. In such a large form, you would use the vertical scroll bar or the Page Up and Page Down keys to move around. Before we do more work on this project, let's save this new file as ADDRESS:

1. Press Alt-F-A. Works displays the Save As dialog box.

2. Type *Address*, and press the Enter key. Works saves the file as ADDRESS.WDB.

So far, we've established and positioned field names and data space on the screen. In the next section, we'll enter data in our document using this same screen.

Entering data in the Form view

For entering or viewing data, Works lets you work in either the Form view or the List view. The Form view is the screen that shows all the fields in a record, one record at a time. The List view is a row-and-column layout that looks like a spreadsheet and shows several records at one time. Let's continue with the Form view for a little longer to see how we use it to enter information and to move from one record to another. Let's enter three records now. The ADDRESS BOOK label should still be selected on the screen. If not, select it, and then do the following:

1. Press the Tab key one time to select the FirstName field. Notice that the field data space, and not the field name, is selected. You can select either field names or fields on this screen. (When you select a field name and begin typing, you edit the field name.)

2. Type *John*. As you type, the characters appear in the formula bar above the work area.

3. Press the Tab key. The name appears in the FirstName field, and the selection moves to the LastName field.

```
  File  Edit  Print  Select  Format  Options  View  Window  Help
═══════════════════════════════ ADDRESS.WDB ═══════════════════════
                        ADDRESS BOOK                                  ↑
  FirstName: John              LastName: ██████████████████████
  Company:
  Street:
  City:                        ST:     Zip:                          ▌
  Phone:
```

If you make a mistake entering field data, either select the field again and retype the data or select the field, press the F2 key, and edit the field's contents in the formula bar.

Pressing the Tab key always enters the data you've typed in the current field and then moves the field selection to the next field in the document. Even if the selection is on a field name when you press Tab, the selection moves to the next field data space and not to the next field name. You can use the Tab key as well as the arrow keys to move to different fields:

- Pressing the Tab key moves the selection to the next field in the record. If the current field is the last field in the record, the selection is moved to the first field in the following record.

- Pressing Shift-Tab moves the field selection to the previous field in the record. If the current field is the first field in the record, the selection is moved to the last field in the previous record.

Let's enter some more data:

1. Type *Jones* and press the Tab key. The name appears in the LastName field's data space, and the selection moves to the Company field.

2. Type *ABC Glass* and press the Tab key.

3. Type *123 3rd St.* in the Street field, *San Jose* in the City field, *CA* in the ST field, and *94111* in the Zip field, pressing the Tab key after each entry.

After you enter the zip code and press the Tab key, you'll notice that the zip code is aligned at the right side of the field data space instead of at the left side as all the text entries were. Works aligns the zip code this way because Works recognizes the zip code as a number and stores it as such. As in the Works Spreadsheet tool, numbers, dates, and times are right-aligned in fields and text is left-aligned.

(If your database will contain any of the many zip codes that begin with zero, you will probably want to designate your Zip field entries as text. To do so, type a quotation mark (") in front of the zip code.)

Finish this record by typing *408-555-1111* in the Phone field and pressing the Enter key. As you can see, pressing the Enter key enters data in the field, but it doesn't advance the selection to the next field. Also notice that because the telephone number contains dashes, Works treats it as a text entry and aligns it at the left edge of the field data space. All text entries are preceded in the formula bar with a quotation mark ("), which designates them as text.

Because the Phone field is the last field in the record, we can move to the next record by pressing the Tab key one more time. When the last field in the Form view is selected and you press the Tab key, Works moves the selection to the first field in the next record, like this:

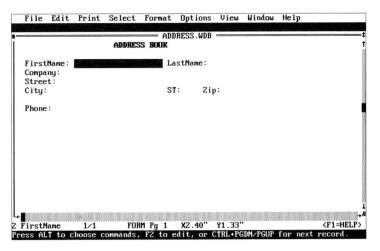

The record-number indicator at the left edge of the status line shows that we're now viewing record number 2 in this file.

You can always press the Tab key or Shift-Tab to move from field to field or from record to record. If you want to browse through records more quickly, you can press Ctrl-Page Down to move to the next record or Ctrl-Page Up to move to the previous record. The *Microsoft Works Quick Reference,* which comes with Works, lists all these shortcuts.

Enter the next two records on your own, using the following data:

Fred Smith
Ace Vending
234 2nd St.
Clearview CA 94122
707-555-1111

Tom Brown
Brown Mailing
3455 Sather Ln.
Barkins CA 94112
408-555-3333

When you finish entering the above data, you'll be ready to explore the List view.

Using the List view

Viewing one record at a time in the Form view is useful if each of your records contains a lot of information and you want to be able to concentrate on that information. But when you want to look at many records at one time, use Works' List view:

☐ Press Alt-V-L to choose the List command from the View menu, and then press Ctrl-Home. (Ctrl-Home is a navigation shortcut that always moves the selection to the first field in the document's first record. See the *Microsoft Works Quick Reference* for a complete list of keyboard shortcuts.) Works changes to List view, like this:

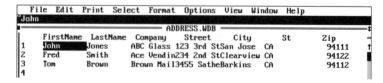

The List view looks like the row-and-column matrix of a spreadsheet. Each record occupies a row, and each column represents a different field, as you can see. You can also see the drawback to the List view: Because the data from each record is arranged in columns, some fields contain more data than can be displayed within the default width of their columns. And anytime you have more than a few fields, you won't be able to see all the fields on the screen at one time. The other fields are off screen to the right, and you need to scroll to the right to see them.

You can, however, make the most of the horizontal space on the screen by changing the field widths to accommodate the amount of data each field contains. For example, the ST field is far wider than it needs to be because it will never contain more than two letters. If we make it narrower, more room will be available to display or widen other fields:

1. Press the Tab key five times to select the data in the first record's ST field.

2. Press Alt-T-W to choose the Field Width command. Works displays the Field Width dialog box, which shows the current width of 10 characters.

3. Type *3* and press the Enter key. Then press the Right arrow key to remove the highlight from the ST field. The field is narrowed, and now the screen has more room for Zip and Phone fields, like this:

```
  File  Edit  Print  Select  Format  Options  View  Window  Help
94111
============================ ADDRESS.WDB ============================
     FirstName  LastName  Company    Street      City     ST   Zip      Phone
1    John       Jones     ABC Glass 123 3rd St San Jose   CA   94111  408-555-111
2    Fred       Smith     Ace Vendin234 2nd St Clearview  CA   94122  707-555-11
3    Tom        Brown     Brown Mail3455 Sathe Barkins    CA   94112  408-555-33
4
```

When the List window is unable to show every field in a document, the other fields are off screen. You can simply keep pressing the Tab key, Shift-Tab, or the Right arrow key to scroll them into view.

Of course, you might not want to look at all of each record's information in this view. Suppose that you want to see only the name and telephone number fields but that you want to be able to see all their data. In that case, you would hide the unwanted fields and make the important ones wide enough to show all their data. Let's hide all but the FirstName, LastName, Company, and Phone fields and then make those fields wider:

1. Press the Left arrow key three times to select an entry in the Street field.

2. Press Alt-T-W to choose the Field Width command. Works displays the Field Width dialog box.

3. Type *0* to indicate a field width of 0 characters.

4. Press the Enter key. The Street field disappears from the screen.

This field is now hidden in the List view, but it's still in the document. To see for yourself, press Alt-V-F to switch back to the Form view, and you'll see the Street field exactly as you left it. Press Alt-V-L to return to the List view.

Now select the City, ST, and Zip fields and set their widths to 0 as well. Finally, set the Company field width to 15 characters, and then press the Right arrow key to remove the selection from the Company field. The List view now shows only the information you want, and you can see all of it there:

In the next section, we'll see how the List view can speed up data entry. But first we'll restore all the hidden fields so that we can see the whole document again.

1. Press Ctrl-Home to select the first record's FirstName field.

2. Press the F8 key to extend the selection.

3. Press the Right arrow key three times to select all the fields in the first record.

4. Press Alt-T-W to choose the Field Width command. The Field Width dialog box shows the default width of 10 characters.

5. Press the Enter key to set all the document's fields to a 10-character width. The previously hidden fields reappear at 10 characters wide.

Copying data in List view

Copying data rather than retyping it can save you time. In List view, you can see the data in the previous records easily. When you're entering a lot of records in a document and you can see that a group of them will contain the same information in certain fields, you can copy that information into a group of new records. Works provides two ways to copy data in List view.

First we'll copy the contents of a field in one record to the record immediately below it. Suppose we know that the next record in this document is for another person who also lives in Barkins, CA, and who has the same zip code. We can copy the City, ST, and Zip data from the record above by using a simple command:

1. In List view, select the City field for record number 4.

2. Press Ctrl-'. Works copies *Barkins* to record number 4's City field, like this:

The Ctrl-' command always copies the data from the field in the record directly above to the currently selected field. Let's go on to select the ST and Zip fields:

1. Press the Tab key to select the ST field in record number 4.

2. Press Ctrl-', and Works copies the CA data from the record above.

3. Press the Tab key to select the Zip field in record number 4.

4. Press Ctrl-', and then press the Tab key to select the Phone field.

Finish entering the data for record number 4 by typing the data in the remaining blank fields, one field at a time:

1. Press the Home key to select the FirstName field in record number 4. (The Home key always moves the selection to the far left of the screen in the database.)

2. Type *Bill* and press the Tab key. Works enters the name and selects the LastName field.

3. Type *Smith* and press the Tab key. Works enters the name and selects the Company field.

4. Type *Able Refrigeration.* You'll notice that the name is longer than the field width can completely display, but the formula bar shows the whole name and the field contains the whole name.

5. Press the Tab key to select the Street field. Notice that although the Street field appears to be overwritten by the company name, the formula bar is empty when the Street field is selected, indicating that the Street field contains no data.

6. Type *400 University* and press the Tab key four times to select the Phone field.

7. Type *408-555-0000* and press the Enter key.

The Ctrl-' command is handy when you want to copy only the data from the field directly above to the current record, but you can also copy entire records or fields. Let's copy the first two records in our document to see how this approach works:

1. Press Ctrl-Home to select the FirstName field of the first record.

2. Press Ctrl-F8 to select the entire record. (Notice that Ctrl-F8 works the same way as selecting an entire row in the Works Spreadsheet tool.)

3. Press the F8 key to extend the selection.

4. Press the Down arrow key one time to select the second record.

5. Press Shift-F3 to choose the Copy command. The COPY indicator appears in the status line.

6. Press the Down arrow key four times to move the selection down to record number 5.

7. Press the Enter key. Works copies the two selected records to records 5 and 6, as shown on the next page.

Just as you can select entire records using Ctrl-F8, you can select entire fields with Shift-F8. This method is handy when you want to copy the same information from a field (say, the same zip code) to a series of new records. In fact, by pressing the F8 key and then the arrow keys (or by dragging the pointer while you hold down the mouse button), you can select any block of field and record data in the same way you select any block of cells in the Works Spreadsheet.

Sorting data

Let's sort these records so that the names are in alphabetic order. The sorting features of the Works Database are much like those in the spreadsheet: You can sort database records on up to three fields of data at a time, in either ascending or descending order. For now, we'll sort the records only on the LastName field:

1. Select an entry in the LastName field.

2. Press Alt-S-O to choose the Sort Records command. Works displays the Sort dialog box, like this:

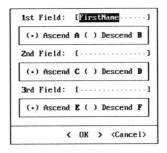

Type *LastName* in the 1st Field box. The Ascend option is already selected, so simply press the Enter key to sort the document in ascending order. Works sorts the records on the LastName field.

```
 File  Edit  Print  Select  Format  Options  View  Window  Help
'Brown
                        ADDRESS.WDB
     FirstName  LastName  Company     Street     City      St      Zip
1    Tom       Brown     Brown Mail3455 SatheBarkins    CA         94112
2    John      Jones     ABC Glass 123 3rd StSan Jose   CA         94111
3    John      Jones     ABC Glass 123 3rd StSan Jose   CA         94111
4    Bill      Smith     Able Refri400 UniverBarkins    CA         94112
5    Fred      Smith     Ace Vendin234 2nd StClearview CA          94122
6    Fred      Smith     Ace Vendin234 2nd StClearview CA          94122
7
```

For more information about sorting data, see the Select Sort Records command in the Help Index on the Help menu.

Because we now have duplicate records in this document, let's delete those records before going on:

1. Select the duplicate John Jones record by selecting a field in record number 3 and then pressing Ctrl-F8.

2. Press Alt-E-D to delete the record.

3. Repeat these two steps with the duplicate Fred Smith record.

You can always find information in a document by scrolling through the List or Form views, but you can also use special commands to find specific data quickly. Next, we'll see how to locate and select information.

Finding data

Works offers two ways to find specific data in a database document. If you're looking for only one occurrence of data, such as one person's last name, you can use the Select menu's Search command. Suppose, for example, that we want to find the record for the person who works for ABC Glass:

1. Press Ctrl-Home to move the selection to the beginning of the document. (Works searches from the selection forward in a database document, so if you want to search the entire document, be sure to press Ctrl-Home first to move the selection to the beginning of the document.)

2. Press Alt-S-S to choose the Search command. Works displays a dialog box in which you can enter the name or number you want to search for.

3. Type *ABC* in the Search For box. The Match options in the dialog box are already set to search for the next record that contains this information, which is what we want.

4. Press the Enter key. Works finds the record that contains ABC and selects the field that contains that string, like this:

If we had wanted to, we could have chosen the Match All records option in the Search dialog box. Then Works would have selected every record that contained ABC in any of its fields, and would have displayed only those records on the screen. In this document, however, selecting the Match All records option would have given us the same results as the Match Next Record option because only one record contains ABC.

The Search command works well if you're looking for only one item of information, but Works has a Query view that lets you search for records using formulas that can match several criteria at once. To query the Works Database, you need to choose the Query command from the View menu and then enter the criteria you want Works to match. You then return to the view you were using previously (Form view or List view), and Works displays only those records that conform to the criteria you specified.

Suppose that we're working with our sample ADDRESS document in List view and that we want to display the records only of people named Smith who live in zip codes numbered higher than 94100:

1. Press Alt-V-Q to display the Query view. Works displays a screen that's similar to the Form view of the document but that shows only field names.

2. Press the Tab key or Shift-Tab to select the LastName field.

3. Type *Smith* and press the Enter key.

4. Press the Tab key five times to select the Zip field.

5. Type *>94100* and press the Enter key.

What you've typed represents your query formula: You've told Works to display the records only in which the LastName field contains the name Smith and the Zip field contains numbers greater than 94100.

6. Press Alt-V-L to display the List view again. Works displays only those records that match the query formula, like this:

The other records in the document aren't gone, they're only hidden from view because they don't match the query formula. The fraction ²⁄₄ in the status line indicates that two of the four records in the database match these criteria.

To show all the records in the document again, press Alt-S-L to choose the Show All Records command—all the records reappear.

After you enter a query on the Query screen, it stays there until you change it. To apply the query again, press Alt-S-Q to choose the Apply Query command. To show all the records that do not match the query instead of those that do, choose the Switch Hidden Records command (Alt-S-W) from the Select menu.

☐ Before you continue with this exercise, be sure the List view is showing all four records in the document. (If it is not, press Alt-S-L.)

Whichever selection of records are displayed will be included in any report you print and will be used to supply data to labels or form letters you create using the Insert Field command in the Works Word Processor tool. If you want to make mailing labels or form letters for only a certain selection of people in an address document, therefore, you must query the database so that it displays only those records at the time you print the labels or form letters.

We used a fairly simple query formula in our example above. But formulas can include other elements, such as wildcard characters or logical conditions like equal to or not equal to, that you can use to specify the records you want Works to display. For more information, see Searching a DB under the Procedures category of the Help Index on the Help menu.

Designing a database report

To print records from the database, you need to create a report format first. (Unless you're merging database data with a form letter or mailing label in the Word Processor—in these cases, see Chapter 5.) Just as you can create and view up to eight chart definitions with the Works Spreadsheet, you can create and view up to eight report formats in the Works Database. To begin a report, do the following:

☐ Press Alt-V-N to choose New Report from the View menu. Works displays the currently selected records in your database document as they will appear in a report, like this:

```
FirstName LastName  Company   Street    City      St

Tom       Brown     Brown Mail3455 SatheBarkins  CA
John      Jones     ABC Glass 123 3rd StSan Jose  CA
Bill      Smith     Able Refri400 UniverBarkins   CA
Fred      Smith     Ace Vendin234 2nd StClearview CA




Page 1                   REPORT                          NL
Press ENTER to continue, ESC to cancel.
```

Any report you create with Works will contain only the currently selected records. Therefore, if you have used the View Query or some of the Select commands to display only certain records from a document, or if you have sorted the records in a particular order, any report you create will contain only those records in that order.

The report format screen shows which fields the report will contain. Notice that the field names are included as column labels above the actual field data. Each report format screen shows several records. When a document contains more records than will fit on one report format screen, you can press the Enter key to view the succeeding pages that contain the rest of the records.

You'll also notice that the Zip and Phone fields in the Address document don't appear in this report format. That's because the current Page Setup & Margins settings do not allow enough room across the page for them. When a report contains too many fields to print in the width of one page, the extra fields are displayed on the following page. Works shows all the records in a report from top to bottom in the first group of fields it can display and then shows all the records from top to bottom in the second group of fields it can display, and so on until all the fields in the report are included.

In this case, you need to press the Enter key to see the Zip and Phone fields in this report. You have to press the Enter key only one time because you can see all the records in this document on two screens. (The first screen shows all the data in the left-hand group of fields, and the second screen shows all the data in the right-hand group of fields.) If this report contained several dozen records, you would have to keep pressing the Enter key until all the data in the left-hand group of fields was displayed before you could see the right-hand group of fields.

After you display a report using the New Report command, Works assigns that report a number and adds the full name to the View menu. The first report you create is Report1, the second is Report2, and so on up to Report8. You can change the name of any report on this menu by choosing the Reports command and typing a new name. (See the View Reports command in the Commands category of the Help Index on the Help menu for more information.)

Every time you view a new report, Works sets default column widths for the fields in that report. You will probably want to make some adjustments to the layout of any report you create. That's where the report definition screen comes in.

You must be viewing a report format screen to display the report definition screen. When you have a report format on the screen, press the Esc key. Works displays the report definition screen, as in Figure 10-2.

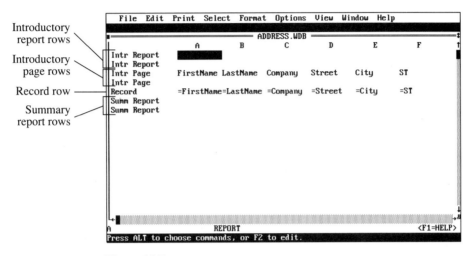

Figure 10-2.
The report definition screen.

This is the screen you use to change a report's format. You can remove fields from the report; make fields wider or narrower; add various titles, headers, or footers to the report page; and produce various calculations from numeric data in the report. As you can see, the report definition screen contains several different types of rows:

- The Intr Report rows can contain text that will be printed as a main report title on the first page of the report.

- The Intr Page rows can contain text that will be printed at the top of each report page. (These rows are usually used to display the field names.)

- The Record row represents the space in the report used for printing actual records.

- The Summ Report rows can contain formulas that calculate totals, averages, or other statistics from data in the report fields. (If a field contains quantities, for example, a Summ Report row could contain a SUM formula to total all the quantities in that field.)

If we were to print the report using the report definition shown in Figure 10-2, no report title would be included because the Intr Report rows are blank. Each page of the report would contain field names because the first Intr Page row contains the field names. (The second Intr Page row is blank, so the report would have a blank line between the field names and the actual data.) Finally, the Summ Report rows contain no entries so the report would include no calculations. Let's make a couple of changes to see how the report definition screen works.

Suppose we want the report to contain only the FirstName, LastName, Company, and Phone data:

1. Press the Down and Right arrow keys until the cell with the formula =Street is selected.

2. Press Shift-F8 to select the entire column.

3. Press Alt-E-D to choose the Delete command. Works deletes the Street column and selects the City column next to it.

4. Press Alt-E-D to delete the City column. Works deletes this column and selects the ST column next to it.

5. Press Alt-E-D to delete the ST column. Works deletes the Zip column and selects the Zip column.

6. Press Alt-E-D to delete this column. Works deletes the Zip column and selects the Phone column. The screen now looks like this:

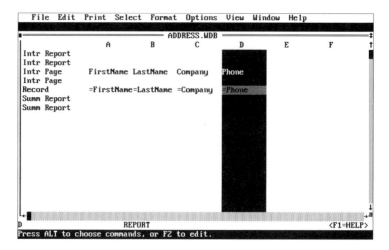

We've deleted the fields from the report definition screen but not from the database document itself. To see for yourself, display the List view of the document:

1. Press Alt-V-L to choose the List view. All the fields are shown.

2. Press Alt-V-1 to view Report1. Works displays the report formatting again. Notice that only the Name, Company, and Phone fields are showing here and that they all fit on one screen.

3. Press the Esc key to return to the report definition screen.

Now let's make the Phone and Company columns a little wider:

1. Press the Right arrow key to select the Phone field (column D).

2. Press Alt-T-W to choose the Column Width command.

3. Type *15* in the dialog box that appears, and press the Enter key. Works widens the Phone field.

4. Press the Left arrow key to select the Company field (column C).

5. Press Alt-T-W to choose the Column Width command.

6. Type *20* in the dialog box, and press the Enter key. Works widens the Company field.

Before leaving the report definition screen, let's add a report title in the Intr Report row at the top of the screen:

1. Press Ctrl-Home to move the selection to the upper-left corner of the screen.

2. Press the Right arrow key one time. The selection moves one field to the right. (Notice that the cursor moves on the report definition screen the same way it does in a spreadsheet.)

3. Type *Phone List* and press the Enter key.

You can apply the same types of format enhancements in database reports that you can in the Works Spreadsheet. Here we'll make the Phone List title stand out by formatting it as boldface and underlined:

1. Press Alt-T-S to choose the Style command.

2. Press the B key to select the Bold option in the dialog box that appears.

3. Press the U key to select the Underline option in the dialog box.

4. Press the Enter key to confirm these settings. Works displays the Phone List title in a different screen intensity.

Now we'll view the report format again by choosing Report1 from the View menu:

1. Press Alt-V-1 to view Report1. Works displays it on the screen, like this:

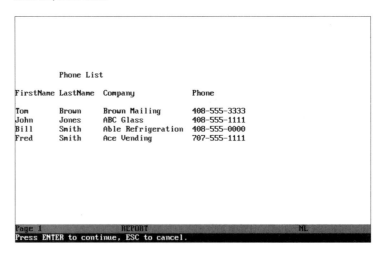

```
          Phone List

FirstName LastName  Company            Phone

Tom       Brown     Brown Mailing      408-555-3333
John      Jones     ABC Glass          408-555-1111
Bill      Smith     Able Refrigeration 408-555-0000
Fred      Smith     Ace Vending        707-555-1111




Page 1                   REPORT                          NL
Press ENTER to continue, ESC to cancel.
```

You can add extra Intr Report, Intr Page, and Summ Report rows to a report definition as needed. In addition, Works provides other special rows that let you insert introductory text for subgroups of data in a report or that let you calculate totals, averages, or other statistics for subgroups of data. Suppose, for example, that an inventory report were sorted so that all the Widgets were in one group and all the Gizmos were in another group. By inserting special Summ or Intr rows in the report, you could add subheadings that identified the Widgets and Gizmos sections of the report, and you could insert formulas to calculate the Widgets and Gizmos subtotals. We'll see some of these features in action in Chapter 12. (For more information about various calculating options in database reports, see the DB Report View topic under Procedures in the Help Index on the Help menu, or see "Customizing A Report" in the *Microsoft Works Reference* manual.)

Printing a report

As with other Works documents, you can choose either to print a report on paper or to preview it on the screen. Let's preview this report to see how it will look when printed. The preview shows all the data in the report, using the font and style selections you have made. To preview the report, follow these steps:

1. Press Alt-P-V to choose the Preview command. Works displays the Preview dialog box, like this:

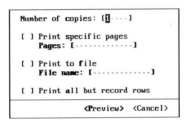

You'll notice that the dialog box contains an option for printing all the information on the report except the record rows. If you choose this option, Works prints the report title, the column labels, and any summations or other calculations you have specified but not the data from individual records. This option is handy when you want to print summaries, such as the subtotals and grand total from an inventory report.

2. Press the Enter key to accept the defaults. Works displays the report on the screen.

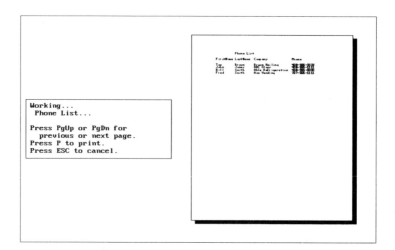

The difference between the preview screen and the report format screen is that the preview screen displays the fonts, font sizes, and correct margins for your report, but the report format screen does not.

Between its query features and its report definition features, the Works Database has a lot of powerful data-management options that let you work with your data the way you want to. In Chapter 12, we'll explore some different practical ways to put the database to use. First, however, we'll cover general database tips in Chapter 11.

Database Tips

The Works Database offers a great amount of flexibility for storing and manipulating various kinds of data. Although it's easy to create a simple address list, as you did in Chapter 10, you'll need to know more about how to use Works' features to their best advantage as your data-handling needs grow. With the right techniques, you can create accounting systems, inventory files, order-entry or reservation systems, and other business and personal data-handling tools. This chapter gives you tips for using the Works Database productively.

Making the Most of the Database

Database management involves four areas of activity: designing the database document, entering and viewing data, manipulating data, and reporting information. We'll look at some ways you can more effectively use the database in each area.

Designing a database

Before you create a field or enter a record, you need to determine how you want your data document to look based on what types of data you want to store and how you want to retrieve or manipulate the data later. You'll find several ways to get the most out of Works' data entry screens as you create the document.

Make a plan

The most common mistake we make when setting up a new database document is neglecting to consider how the data will be used. Often we've already created fields and entered data when we discover that we'd like to divide the data in a different way or that we've arranged the fields in such a way that we can't easily select or report the information we need. Although you can always add new fields, delete fields, change field names, or alter the layout or reports in a Works Database document, it's far easier to design the document properly in the first place.

Start by thinking through the challenge at hand. What types of data will you store, and how will you break up the data into different fields? Make a list of all the types of data you'll want to store, and give each type a suggested field name. Then sit down with your list of names and consider your uses for the database document. Will you use it only to look up information? If so, how do you want to be able to find or select the data? If you're planning to create reports, what data do you want the reports to show? If you're printing on labels or forms, how will the data be broken up on those forms, and will you be able to break up records in your database document in similar ways?

Suppose, for example, that you're creating an address list for sending out form letters. You create a field called Name, in which you plan to store each person's first and last names. Later, when you want to send out a form letter, however, you discover that because you've combined both names in one field, you have to include both names in the greeting line of a form letter. Your letters must begin "Dear Fred Smith," instead of "Dear Mr. Smith." If you know in advance that you'll want to send such letters, you should create three separate fields: one for the appropriate title (Mr., Mrs., Ms., Dr., and so on), one for the first name, and one for the last name. That way, you can use the information in those three fields independently or in any combination.

Another common mistake when setting up a database is failing to create enough fields for a proper address. Many people and businesses have addresses that include floor numbers, mail stops, divisions, or other designations in addition to a street or post office box number. On a typical mailing label, these pieces of information occupy two different lines of the address rather than one. If you have only one street address field in your database document, you'll probably have a hard time creating mailing labels that show full addresses.

By thinking through the various ways in which you'll want to use your data before you begin creating the database file, you're more likely to get the document's design right on the first try.

Use efficient field names to maximize screen space

It's tempting to use long, descriptive names when you create fields, but lengthy names use up a lot of space on the screen and in the printed reports. Keep in mind that the field name needn't do all the work of identifying the information the field contains. As soon as a document or a report contains information, it's fairly obvious what information pertains to which field.

With a little thought, you should be able to come up with a name for each field that is no longer than the longest data entry that the field is likely to contain. In our sample address file in Chapter 10, for example, we used ST as the name for the field of state codes because each state code contains only two characters.

Customize the form window to simplify data entry

As we saw in Chapter 10, it's easy to create a stack of fields in the Form view by typing field names and pressing the Enter key. We also saw that you can easily rearrange fields to suit your needs. The screen-based form for any Works Database can be up to five pages long, and you can arrange fields any way you want over those five pages as long as no two fields overlap.

Knowing how easy it is to create and rearrange fields, you might put fields in a different order to match a printed form you use in your business. Or you might place fields on different pages of the screen form for different uses. For example, suppose you're filling out a database of survey responses, and you're entering data from handwritten forms that the survey population has filled out. If you arrange the fields on the screen the same way they're arranged on the form, you'll find it easier to transfer the data from the forms to your database.

You might use different pages of the screen form when various employees use different groups of fields for a number of purposes. For example, an order-entry clerk might fill in the customer name, number, address, item number, quantity, and price, and a warehouse employee might fill in the date the item was shipped or indicate whether the item is back ordered. By placing these groups of fields on different pages of the screen form, you'll allow each employee to focus on entering only the applicable data.

Finally, you can protect your Form design so that nobody else can change names, sizes, or layouts of the fields. To do so, press Alt-O-F to choose the Protect Form command from the Options menu.

Entering and viewing data

Works offers both Form and List views for entering and viewing data. Each view has features that can make these activities easier. Here are some tips you can use for entering and viewing data in Form view, List view, or both.

Should you use the keyboard or the mouse?

When it comes to entering data, whether in Form view or List view, nothing beats the keyboard. Although you can use the mouse to select individual fields for data entry, it's faster simply to type the entry and then press the Tab key to move to the next field. (Even when you need to skip a field or two before making the next data entry, it's faster to use the Tab key than the mouse.) Here are some other guidelines for deciding whether to use the keyboard or the mouse when you're working with the database:

- **Use the keyboard for commands**. In most cases, it's faster to press Alt-key combination commands from the keyboard than it is to use the mouse to choose commands. Using the mouse makes sense when you know you're selecting a command that will produce a complex dialog box in which you'll want to use the mouse to make several selections. Many of the dialog boxes in the Works Database let you choose options by simply typing a letter key, so it's often faster to use the keyboard with dialog boxes as well. With the Style dialog box, for example, you can select the Bold, Italic, or Underline styles by simply pressing the B, I, or U keys.

- **Use the keyboard to select fields or records**. The Ctrl-F8 and Shift-F8 keyboard shortcuts can quickly select a record or a field, respectively, and it's simple to use the Tab key or arrow keys to select individual field entries. Unlike the Works Spreadsheet, in which you might want to select blocks of cells, you'll probably spend most of your time in the Works Database selecting individual entries, entire fields, or entire records.

- **Use the mouse for scrolling and resizing windows**. The window interface in Works was designed to be controlled with a mouse, and it's much easier to use a mouse than the keyboard for window operations. To move or resize a window using the mouse, for example, you point to the window's title bar or its size box, hold down the left mouse button, and drag to the new location or size. To accomplish the same task using the keyboard, you have to type a Window menu command and then use the arrow keys to move the window around or resize it.

Use the split bars in List view

The row-and-column layout of the List view usually prevents you from viewing all your document's fields on the screen at one time. In Chapter 10, we saw how you can hide or decrease the width of fields to maximize the space on the screen, but you can also use the split bars to divide the window either horizontally or vertically so that you can simultaneously view different parts of the document.

If your document contains two dozen fields, for example, you can use the vertical split bar to divide the screen into two independently scrolling windows or panes. You can then view one set of fields in the left pane and another in the right pane. For example, you might need to view the left-most fields in a document because they contain the name information you use to identify each record, while you simultaneously look up order number information located in fields that would ordinarily be off-screen to the right. In this case, you could use the vertical split bar to view both groups of fields at one time, like this:

```
 File  Edit  Print  Select  Format  Options  View  Window  Help
                                ORDERS.WDB
        Customer      Contact     ShipDate  OrdDate    Amt     Item#
 1   Acme Wheels    Jones          12/1/90   12/1/90   $235.78    357
 2   Frigid Equip.  Hopkins        12/1/90  11/29/90   $547.50    420
 3   Willis Widget  Willis         12/5/90  11/29/90 $1,032.75    101
 4
```

If you want to view two different groups of records in List view, you can use the horizontal split bar to divide the window into upper and lower panes. You could then scroll one group of records into the upper pane and another into the lower pane.

Use formulas to enter standard data

When you have fields that will contain the same data for most of or all the records in your database document, use a formula to have Works enter that data for you. By using text formulas, you can tell Works to create the same entry in a field for every new record. If your customers are all in California, for example, the formula ="CA in a document's ST field will cause Works to enter "CA" in each new record's ST field. If one customer moved to a different state, you could enter the new state code without affecting the formula—Works would continue to enter "CA" in other new records. By using formulas for entering standard data, you also reduce data entry errors.

Manipulating data

Manipulating data means moving data, selecting groups of records, or maintaining the accuracy of data in a database document.

Sort and select to find records quickly

After you have stored dozens or hundreds of records, you might want to rearrange the data. You can choose from several ways to arrange data as well as use Works' selecting commands to make data easier to find.

- If you want to browse through the records, use the List view. The List view will show you 18 records at a time. If you can't see the field you want on the screen, use the split bar to divide the screen into two groups of fields and scroll the right screen to bring the field into view, or rearrange the fields so that only the ones containing the data you want are in view. You can move any field in the List view by selecting the field (Shift-F8), pressing the F3 key to choose the Move command, pressing the Right or Left arrow key to reposition the field, and then pressing the Enter key.

- If you're browsing through records looking for information in a specific field, sort the document on that field so that the record you want will be easier to find. If you want to find a transaction record from a certain date, for example, it will be much easier to find the record quickly if the records are sorted on that field in order of date.

- Use the Search command (Alt-S-S) to jump to specific data in a record. The Search command lets you type a word, phrase, or number and then tell Works to find the first record in which that item occurs. When you use this technique, remember that Works searches only from the current selection forward in the document. If you want to search the entire document, press Ctrl-Home to move the selection to the beginning of the document before you choose the Search command.

■ The Go To command (F5) is useful if you know the number of the record or the name of the field that you want to find. In List view, for example, you could scroll to the field you want instantly by choosing the Go To command and then either entering the field name or selecting it from the list.

Use selection options to validate data

One of the weaknesses in the Works Database tool is that it provides no way to force a certain type of entry in each field. Even though you set a certain field length when you define each field, and even though you can set a numeric, date, time, or text format for each field, these formats and field sizes don't prevent you from entering inaccurate information. A person can enter text in a number field, for example, and Works won't alert the user. Also, Works has no way to check for and warn about the entry of duplicate records. Therefore, you need to validate the data in your file manually by scanning the records and determining that all the entries in the fields are appropriate.

Works offers two ways to use its sorting and selecting features, which are designed to simplify the process of manual data validation. To use the sort method, display the List view of the document and sort the document on an important field, such as the LastName field in an address file. After the sort finishes, any duplicate records are rearranged so that they're next to each other, making them easier to spot as you scroll through the document. Try sorting several different fields in List view, one field at a time. After each sort, scroll through the document and scan for duplicate records, missing data, or incorrect entries.

You can also use Works' query capabilities to search for specific types of mistakes in certain fields. If you have a field called Part# that contains five-digit part numbers between 10,000 and 30,000, for example, you could enter a query formula that searches for records in which the Part# field contains numbers less than 10,000 or greater than 30,000. That way, Works would locate and display any records that have part numbers outside the correct range. A query formula can include record-selection criteria for more than one field, so you can build query formulas that search for common mistakes in as many fields as you want at the same time.

Use wildcards and logical operators to create specific queries

If you've properly designed a database document so that the data is arranged in appropriate fields, you can use Works' Query command to locate any record or group of records. For a simple query, type a name or a number in a field: Works will find all the records that have matching information in that field. For a more complex query, you can use wildcards and logical operators that will allow you to select records based on ranges of numbers, dates, or times or on incomplete strings of text characters.

The wildcards are the question mark (*?*), which you can use to replace any single character in a text string, and the asterisk (*), which you can use to replace any unspecific group of characters in a text string. To find all the addresses for people named Joe or Jon, for example, you could enter *Jo?* in the file's FirstName field. (Note that this causes Works to list addresses for any three-letter name beginning with "Jo.") To find all the addresses for people whose names begin with B, you could type *B** in the FirstName field.

The logical operators you can use in query formulas are

Equal to (=)
Not equal to (<>)
Less than (<)
Greater than (>)
Greater than or equal to (>=)
Less than or equal to (<=)
And (&)
Or (¦)
Not (~)

Use the Equal to, Not equal to, Greater than, and Less than operators to look for information that does or doesn't exactly match your query (*=500* or *<>CA*, for example) and to find ranges of numbers (*<=500*). Use the And, Or, and Not operators to combine query instructions in the same field. If you wanted to find all records that have zip codes between 94110 and 94200, for example, you would select the Zip field in the Query view and enter *=(>=94110&<=94200)*. (You must begin with an equal sign all query formulas that contain more than one logical condition.)

For more information about building queries, see the procedure DB Query View in the Procedures category of the Help Index on the Help menu or the "Query Formulas" section in the Database & Reporting chapter of the *Microsoft Works Reference* manual.

Copy between files to approximate relational features

The Works Database is a "flat file" database as opposed to a "relational" database. In a flat file database, each file is separate from any other file, and no commands are used to merge, compare, or move information between two or more different files. A relational database, on the other hand, is often composed of two or more files, and you can easily combine, extract, or compare information between them.

The ability to work with more than one file at a time and to combine, extract, and compare information between files is often handy. For example, suppose you had a relational personnel database with one file (we'll call it SALARY) that contained current salary information for each employee and another file (we'll call it HISTORY) that contained employment history and educational information for each employee. If you wanted to determine whether a correlation existed between each employee's years of experience and salary level or between each employee's education and salary level, you could extract the education and employment history data from the HISTORY file, the salary information from the SALARY file, and view the information or create a new file that contained both types of data.

You can accomplish similar comparing, extracting, and merging operations in the Works Database by using Works' copying features and flexibile file structure. The following two examples show how you would handle some common data-management requirements in Works.

Suppose, as in the example above, you have two different personnel database documents called SALARY and HISTORY; both have a common field of LastName, and both documents have the same number of records and the same LastName entries. Let's say you want to merge the education and work experience fields from the HISTORY file into the SALARY file. To do so, you can copy the fields from one document to another as long as you're careful to sort both documents in the same way so that the record positions in each document match.

1. Open the SALARY file, display the List view, and sort the file on the LastName field.

2. Open the HISTORY file, display the List view, and sort the file on the LastName field.

   Now, unless your two documents contain different numbers of records or different employees' records, you will have two documents in which the records appear in exactly the same order. (Check the left side of the status line in each document's window to determine the total number of records in each document.)

3. Select the education and work experience fields in the HISTORY document, and choose the Copy command. (If these fields aren't next to each other in List view, use Move to move them together before you select them.)

4. Choose the SALARY file from the Window menu.

5. Press the End key to select the field that's farthest to the right. (You can be sure you've selected the field—rather than the empty column next to it—by checking the status line: The selected field's name will appear there.)

6. Press the Right arrow key to select the next (empty) column in List view.

7. Press the Enter key. Works copies the contents of the education and work experience fields to the SALARY file.

Works initially assigns the next two available field numbers to these two fields. If your salary document contains 10 fields, for example, these new fields will be named *Field11* and *Field12*. You can rename the fields using the Field Name command (Alt-E-N).

Now suppose you have a large mailing list file called ADDRESS, and you want to distribute different portions of it to three salespeople, based on the zip codes in each record. Let's say you want to give the records with zip codes 00001-30000 to Jones, the records with zip codes 30001-60000 to Smith, and the records with zip codes 60001-99999 to Brown:

1. Open the ADDRESS file.

2. Create a new field called Date. (This field will store the date on which each record was last updated.)

3. In List view, enter the current date preceded by an equal sign in the first record's Date field. (Remember, when you use a formula in a field, Works carries the formula through to all the records.) Then select the Date field and assign it a date format. (As you recall, in List view you can use the Ctrl-' shortcut to copy the date from the above

record to the current record, so you can move through the document quickly by pressing Ctrl-' and then pressing the Down arrow key. In fact, you can record a macro that will make the repeated copies for you with only one keystroke. See Chapter 2 for more information about macros.)

Now the document shows that all the records were last updated on the day you split up the document for the salespeople.

4. Sort the document on the zip code field.

5. Save the file to preserve the sort order.

6. Select all the records with zip codes greater than 30000, and delete them from the database.

7. Using the Save As command, save the document with the name JONESADD, and then close it. (Because you've re-named the file, the ADDRESS file remains unchanged on your disk.)

8. Open the ADDRESS file again.

9. Select all the records with zip codes smaller than 30001 and greater than 60000, and delete them from the database.

10. Save the file with the name SMITHADD, and close it.

11. Open the ADDRESS file again.

12. Select all the records with zip codes less than 60001, and delete them from the database.

13. Save the file with the name BROWNADD, and close it.

Now you have three files (JONES, SMITH, and BROWN) that each contain a subset of records, and you still have the original ADDRESS file on disk.

After these files are distributed, Smith, Jones, and Brown will probably add to them or update them. As they do, they'll enter the date that a new record was added or an existing record was changed. At some point, you'll want to merge the records again into a new ADDRESS file that has the latest information, as shown on the following page.

1. Open your old ADDRESS file, and display the List view.

2. Sort the document on the Date field.

3. Select all the records that were entered on or before the date you distributed subsets of the file, and delete them.

4. Open the JONESADD file, and select all its records.

5. Choose the Copy command, and then select the ADDRESS file from the Window menu.

6. Select the first blank record at the bottom of the list, and press the Enter key. Works copies all the Jones records to the ADDRESS file.

7. Repeat steps 4 through 6 for the SMITHADD and BROWNADD files.

8. Save the ADDRESS file. It now contains copies of all updated records for Jones, Smith, and Brown and any new records that were entered or updated in the ADDRESS file itself.

Using the techniques explained above to copy records or fields between files, you can split, merge, and extract information from files.

Enter formulas in fields to calculate within records

Works lets you enter formulas in database fields much as you can in spreadsheet cells. These formulas can calculate a value based on the values in one or more other fields in the record, or they can automatically enter standard data that will usually be found in a field. In an inventory database, for example, you might have one field called Qty that stores the quantity of an item and another field called Price that stores the item's price. You could enter the formula *=Qty*Price* in a third field, called Value, and Works would calculate the value of that item by multiplying the number of items by the price. We'll see more of this technique in Chapter 12.

Use report formats to calculate groups of records

Some of your database documents will contain numeric fields that you would like to calculate, such as total quantities of items of inventory or your total expenses for the month. You can enter values in individual records in a Works Database document, but you have to use formulas in a report format to calculate the values from several records. When you want to see the calculated values without actually printing the report, select the report format from the View menu—any calculations will be shown there. If the document includes a lot of records or the report contains too many fields to be printed across one sheet of paper, you might have to press the Enter key a few times to display the report's bottom row or right-most fields. Nevertheless, this approach is faster for checking the results of calculations in a report than is printing the report on paper.

Save frequently to maintain performance

When you are working with several documents and are close to the limit of your system's memory, Works slows down. You'll notice that Works begins looking on your disk drive for instructions more and more often until—when your computer's memory is nearly full—Works begins checking the disk each time you press a key. To free some memory, save your database document, and then open it again. If you're working with several files, try saving, closing, and reopening each file. You'll find that you have more memory to work with afterward and that Works operates faster.

Reporting

Reporting involves designing report formats, using their features to extract as much information as you can from your data, and then displaying that information in the most useful way. The following are a few tips that you can use when working with database reports.

Use Summ Report rows to produce subtotals and grand totals

Because you can calculate database data in report formats, you can handle many jobs with the database that you might otherwise have tackled with the spreadsheet. Any numeric field in the database can be calculated with the arithmetic operators +, −, *, and /. You can also use the spreadsheet functions AVG, COUNT, MIN, MAX, STD, SUM, and VAR to perform database calculations.

When you enter a formula containing a function in a numeric field's Summ Report row (on the report definition screen), the formula calculates all the values in that field. For example, you might insert a SUM formula in a Quantity field's Summ Report row to determine the total quantity of items in the records the report contains.

If you've sorted a database document into groups of items, you can produce a subtotal for each group by instructing Works to generate a subtotal whenever the contents of another field change. For example, an inventory document might contain a field called Section that stores the name of each storeroom section and a field called Qty that stores the amount of each item in stock. If you sorted the document on the Section field (so that all the items in each section were grouped together in the list), you could create a formula that tells Works to generate a subtotal whenever the entry in the Section field changes. We'll see this technique at work in Chapter 12.

Use macros to speed up repetitive operations

Works' built-in macro feature can help speed up report formatting when you use certain types of rows or calculation formulas in more than one report. You can record strings of commands that insert and format special Intr or Summ rows in reports or that handle repetitive data-entry operations. Any time you have to execute a procedure that requires several commands—whether that procedure involves inserting rows or deleting, inserting, or moving fields—you can automate the procedure with a macro. Be on the lookout for repetitive operations, and try recording a macro to automate those operations.

Remember, you can name and store separate macro files, so you can use the same macro key sequences over and over. You might store a different macro file for one particular database file or group of files, for example, and then load that macro file when you begin working on those files. For more information about creating macros, see Chapter 2.

Use form letter functions for formatting flexibility

The formatting options in database reports are fairly limited because every report must be arranged in rows and columns. Also, you can specify only one font and font size for the entire report. If you merge your database data into a word processor form letter, however, you can format database data any way you want. Works lets you place fields anywhere on a word processor document page and select different fonts, styles, or font sizes for each field using the Word Processor's extensive formatting commands. See this technique at work in Chapter 14.

Select fields, and use Font and Page Setup
options to maximize the printing area

As in a Works Spreadsheet, most of your database documents will contain more fields than you can print across one piece of paper. Also as in the spreadsheet, however, you can narrow fields, narrow the page margins, and use smaller fonts to make the most of the horizontal space on a page. Try deleting unnecessary fields from a report to make room for the fields you do want to print.

The Works Database can handle most personal and small business jobs with ease. By putting some of the tips presented in this chapter to work, you'll soon be handling data like a pro. Turn to the projects in Chapter 12 to see more of these techniques.

CHAPTER 12

Database Projects

Any time you want to store, arrange, select, or calculate collections of information that contain text, numbers, times, or dates, the Works Database is the tool for the job. In this chapter, we put the database through its paces to complete some business and personal data-management projects.

An Appointment Calendar

If you spend a lot of time at your computer, having your appointment calendar in a Works database document can be useful. Works lets you keep up to eight different documents open at a time, so you can easily load your calendar file every day and have it readily available. You can then check your calendar for specific dates, print "to-do" lists, or lay out your schedule for the week or month ahead.

Creating the database file

The calendar file is simple to create. Calendars store information about dates, times, and events, so we'll create three fields to store this information, and then we'll ensure that each field will store the data in the right format.

1. Press Alt-F-N to create a new file, and type *D* to create a database file. Works displays a new database document.

2. Type *Date:* and press the Enter key. Works displays the Field Size dialog box. Press the Enter key again to accept the default size settings. Works creates the field and moves the cursor down one line.

3. Type *Time:* and press the Enter key two times. Works creates the field and moves the cursor down one line.

4. Type *Event:* and press the Enter key two times. Works creates the field and moves the cursor down to the next line, like this:

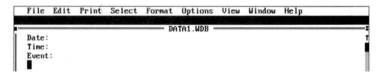

Before we enter the data in this file, we'll set the field formats to match their data types. By setting the Time and Date fields for Time/Date format, we'll be able to sort the file in chronological order later.

1. Press the Up arrow key three times to select the Date field name.

2. Press the Right arrow key one time to select the Date field contents. (You must select field contents and not field names before setting field formats.)

3. Press Alt-T-T to choose the Time/Date format command. Works displays the Time/Date format dialog box, like this:

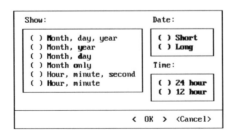

4. Press the M key to select the Month, Day, Year display option, and press the L key to select the Long date format. Using these options, Works displays the date December 1, 1990, for example, as *Dec 1, 1990*. If you selected the Short date format, Works would display the same date as *12/1/90*.

5. Press the Enter key. Works applies this format to the Date field.

6. Press the Tab key to select the Time field contents.

7. Press Alt-T-T to choose the Time/Date format command again.

8. Press the H key to select the Hour, Minute display, and then press the 1 key to choose the 12-hour time format.

9. Press the Enter key to apply this format to the Time field.

Works will now display entries in these fields in the proper format as long as you enter valid data. If you don't use the correct data type in a date-formatted field, Works will treat the entry as text. Here are the accepted data types for date entries:

```
December 1, 1990
Dec 1, 1990
12/1/90
12/1/1990
12/01/1990
```

When you enter data in a time-formatted field, you have to enter hours and minutes—or hours, minutes, and seconds—separated by colons. Works converts most other numeric entries to 12:00 AM. For example, these are the accepted formats for a time entry of 3:00 PM:

```
3:00 PM
3:00:00 PM
15:00
15:00:00
```

You'll notice that 3:00 without the PM designation following it isn't an acceptable format if you want to specify 3:00 PM. Works always assumes that you are specifying AM times, except for times between 12:00 and 1:00. If you enter 12:30 by itself, Works converts that entry to 12:30 PM. But if you enter 3:00 by itself, Works converts the entry to 3:00 AM. To avoid problems, be sure to type *AM* or *PM* after each time entry, unless you're using 24-hour time.

Now we'll enter the date, time, and event data for our first record:

1. Press Shift-Tab to select the Date field.

2. Type *12/1/90* and press the Tab key. Works enters the date and moves the selection to the Time field. Notice that Works displays the date as Dec 1, 1990 because we set the field's format to Month, Day, Year with the Long format.

3. Type *3:00 PM* and press the Tab key. Works enters the time and moves the selection to the Event field.

4. Type *Dentist - Dr. Frobish, 325 Powell St., Suite 240.*

5. Press the Enter key. Works enters the data, and the selection stays on the Event field in this record. (When you press the Enter key, the selection stays where it is; when you `press the Tab key or an arrow key, the selection moves.)

Now, however, we see the consequences of accepting the default field size for the Event field. We accepted the 20-character size, but the field isn't wide enough to display all the data on the screen. The entire event is displayed in the formula bar at the top of the screen, so we know that Works has stored it all. In fact, you can enter up to 255 characters of information in any Works Database field, and Works stores it, whether or not the field is wide enough to display the information.

This field should be fairly large so that we can display a lot of descriptive information about each calendar event. Let's resize the Event field to make it 60 characters wide:

1. Press Alt-T-Z to choose the Field Size command. Works displays the Field Size dialog box.

2. Type *60* and press the Enter key. The field expands, and the entire entry shows.

Let's switch to List view so that we can enter several more appointment records quickly.

1. Press Alt-V-L to display the List view of this file.

Again, we see that the columns aren't the right widths to display our data properly. Works displays a row of pound signs (#) in the Date column because the column width isn't wide enough to display the date completely. Each List view of a database document has a default column width that's set to 10 characters. Even though we set appropriate field sizes in the Form view, the List view arranges fields in columns, and the field widths must be adjusted separately. First, let's adjust the Date column width so that we can see the date properly:

1. Select the row of pound signs in the Date field.

2. Press Alt-T-W to choose the Field Width command.

3. Type *13* and press the Enter key. We have to be careful about how much we widen this field because the screen needs enough room to display all the data in the Event field.

Both the Date and Event columns are also 10 characters wide. The Time field is wide enough to display the time entry. Although the Event field isn't wide enough to display the whole event entry, we can see that entire entry because it flows over into the adjacent columns (like a Works Spreadsheet label does). We could adjust the Event column's width to 60 characters, but if we did, the entire column would move off the screen to the right. Because we won't be adding any other fields to this file, we can let the Event field text simply overflow in the List view.

Now let's enter a few more records so that we'll have some data to manipulate. Enter the records as shown here:

```
 File  Edit  Print  Select  Format  Options  View  Window  Help

 ┌──────────────────────── DATA1.WDB ════════════════════════╗
       Date        Time    Event
 1     Dec 1, 1990    3:00 PM Dentist - Dr. Frobish, 325 Powell St., Suite 240
 2     Dec 19, 1990  12:00 PM Fred's retirement luncheon - El Caballo
 3      Dec 5, 1990  12:00 PM Linda's birthday lunch
 4     Dec 21, 1990   6:00 PM Office party - Antoine's; gift swap
 5     Dec 26, 1990   9:00 AM On vacation until 1/2/91
 6     Jan 15, 1991   9:00 AM Press conference - Alpha introduction
 7      Jan 3, 1991   2:00 PM Product launch mtg - Bud's office
 8      Dec 1, 1990  11:00 AM Project review - Conference rm.
 9     Dec 12, 1990   9:00 AM Q1 Budget due
10      Dec 2, 1990  10:00 AM Racquetball tournament, Apex Athletic Club
11
```

To enter these records, begin by selecting the Date field in the second record:

1. Type *12/19/90* and press the Tab key.

2. Type *12:00 PM* and press the Tab key.

3. Type *Fred's retirement luncheon - El Caballo* and press the Down arrow key. Works selects the Event field in the third record.

4. Press the Home key. Works selects the Date field in the third record.

5. Repeat steps 1 through 4 for the rest of the records shown above.

When you finish entering all the records, save the file as CALENDAR:

1. Press Alt-F-A and type *Calendar.*

2. Press the Enter key to save the file.

Now you can move on to the rest of this project, which involves sorting, finding, and selecting records from the document.

Using the appointment calendar

When you first make appointments and enter them in this database document, they probably won't be in chronological order. Before checking the calendar to determine your availability, you'll want to sort the records in date and time order so that you can see all the appointments on any given day. With the Works Database, you can sort on the contents of up to three fields at one time.

It's easy enough to select only the Date field in the List view and sort the file chronologically by date, but we'll need to sort the file on the Time field as well because for some dates in our calendar more than one appointment has been scheduled. We want the records sorted in ascending order, first by date and then by time.

1. Press Alt-V-L to display the List view, if it isn't already showing.

2. Press Alt-S-O to choose the Sort Records command. Works displays the Sort Records dialog box.

3. Type *Date* in the 1st Field text box. The Ascending option for this sort is already selected because it's the default.

4. Press the Tab key two times to select the 2nd Field text box, and type *Time* to enter the field name. The Ascending option for the sort on this field is already selected.

5. Press the Enter key. Works sorts the records in the List view first by Date and then by Time, so they now look like this:

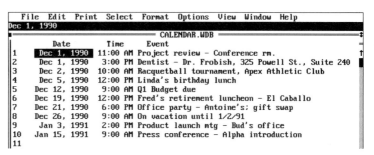

With the records sorted in this order, it will be easy to scan the list and see if you have time available on any day. In fact, if you sort the document in this order one time, you can then jump to the appropriate day and enter new appointments in order, so the document never has to be re-sorted. Suppose, for example, you want to see if you have any time available on January 3:

1. Press Alt-S-S to choose the Search command.

2. Type *Jan* and press the Enter key. Works scrolls the list to the first record that contains *Jan*, which will probably be the first record with a January date. You can then scan the list or scroll manually to check the date in question.

If you make many appointments each day, you can select only one day's records and print those records in a report. Suppose you want to print only the records for December 1. Here's the procedure:

☐ Press Alt-V-N to choose the New Report command from the View menu. Works displays the report format screen, as shown on the next page.

```
Date          Time        Event

 Dec  1, 1990  11:00 AM Project re
 Dec  1, 1990   3:00 PM Dentist -
 Dec  2, 1990  10:00 AM Racquetbal
 Dec  5, 1990  12:00 PM Linda's bi
Dec 12, 1990   9:00 AM Q1 Budget
Dec 19, 1990  12:00 PM Fred's ret
Dec 21, 1990   6:00 PM Office par
Dec 26, 1990   9:00 AM On vacatio
 Jan  3, 1991   2:00 PM Product la
Jan 15, 1991   9:00 AM Press conf




Page 1                    REPORT                              NL
Press ENTER to continue, ESC to cancel.
```

You'll see a couple of problems in this screen. First of all, the report contains all the records rather than only those for December 1. Also, most of the Event information isn't showing because the Event column in this report format isn't wide enough. Let's select the December 1 records with a database query and then straighten out the formatting:

1. Press the Esc key. Works displays the report definition screen.

2. Press Alt-V-Q to display the Query screen.

3. Select the Date field.

4. Type *12/1/90* and press the Enter key. Works will now display only the records for this date.

5. Press Alt-V-1. Works returns to the report definition screen. Let's widen the Event column so that more information shows in the report.

6. Select any row in the Event column and press Alt-T-W to choose the Column Width command.

7. Type *50* and press the Enter key. The Event field widens and moves off the screen to the right.

8. Press Alt-V-1 to choose Report1. Doing so displays the report format screen for this report again so that we can see the effect of widening the event field. The result is shown on the following page.

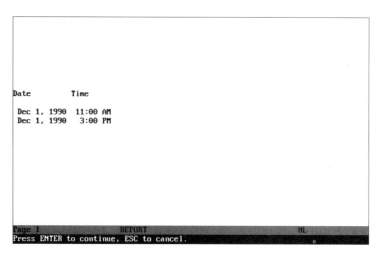

```
Date        Time

Dec 1, 1990  11:00 AM
Dec 1, 1990   3:00 PM
```

Page 1   REPORT   NL
Press ENTER to continue, ESC to cancel.   0

The Event field is no longer visible on the screen because widening the field to 50 characters does not allow enough room to display all three fields across one sheet of paper. (If you press the Enter key to display the second page of this report, you'll see the Event field by itself.) To remedy this problem, we'll narrow the left and right margins so that the page can accommodate more information:

1. Press the Esc key to display the report definition screen.

2. Press Alt-P-M to choose the Page Setup & Margins command. Works displays the Page Setup & Margins dialog box.

3. Press Alt-E to select the Left Margin text box and then type .5.

4. Press the Tab key to select the Right Margin text box and then type .5.

5. Press the Enter key to make these margin changes.

6. Press Alt-V-1 to choose Report1 from the View menu again. Works displays the report format screen, and the event information now appears on the same page of the report as the date and time.

After you set up this report format, you can rename it and then reuse it at any time to print a daily, weekly, or monthly schedule. You simply use the Query command to display all the records for a certain date or date range and then choose this report format and print it. To rename the report:

1. Press the Esc key to display the report definition screen.

2. Press Alt-V-R to choose the Reports command. Works displays the Reports dialog box, which shows a list of the currently defined reports. At this point, the list should contain only Report1. That report name is selected in the list of reports.

3. Press Alt-N to select the Name text box.

4. Type *Daily Sched* and then press Alt-R to rename the report. The new name appears in the Reports list box.

5. Press Alt-D to exit from the dialog box.

This calendar will give you a fast and simple way to store and look up daily appointments.

A Tax Ledger

In this project, you'll use the database to record income and expense information and to create a simple but effective accounting system. Using this ledger, you'll be able to record taxable income and expenses as they occur. This accounting system is useful for projecting future budgets based on current or past expenditures, and it's a lifesaver at tax time, when you'll want a neat, categorized list of deductible expenses and taxable income.

The types of information we need to capture in such a database document are the date of a transaction, the expense or income category, a brief description of the transaction, and the amount. Because we'll want to determine totals or subtotals of only expenses or income, we'll also include a field called Type. All the transactions recorded will be for tax purposes, so we don't need a field to identify them as such. If you wanted to use this system to record all your income and expenses (taxable or otherwise), however, you would need an additional field to indicate whether each transaction was tax related. The List view of the completed tax ledger document looks like the one shown in Figure 12-1.

```
 File  Edit  Print  Select  Format  Options  View  Window  Help
```

```
═════════════════════════════ LEDGER.WDB ═════════════════════════
         Date      Type      Account        Description        Amount
1     10/27/90 Expense   Donation    Jones for Mayor         $10.00
2      11/8/90 Expense   Donation    Goodwill Indust.        $15.00
3     11/26/90 Expense   Donation    Church                  $10.00
4     10/12/90 Expense   Interest    VISA bill               $22.65
5     10/26/90 Income    Interest    Central Bank Acct.       $6.30
6     11/16/90 Expense   Interest    VISA bill               $10.13
7     11/22/90 Income    Interest    Central Bank Acct.       $5.24
8     10/27/90 Income    Paycheck    Paycheck             $2,465.00
9     11/22/90 Income    Paycheck    Paycheck             $2,465.00
10    11/28/90 Expense   Prop. taxes 2nd Installment 1990    $320.00
11
```

Figure 12-1.
A simple ledger of taxable income and expenses.

As with the calendar document, creating the fields for this document is the simple part. The real secret is in knowing how to select records and create reports to produce useful information.

Creating the ledger file

To begin, you'll need to create a document like the one shown in Figure 12-1. First, create the fields:

1. Press Alt-F-N to create a new file, and then press the D key to choose database. Press the Enter key to create a new database file.

2. Type *Date:* and press the Enter key; then type *15* (to specify the field size), and press the Enter key again.

3. Type *Type:* and press the Enter key; then type *10,* and press the Enter key again.

4. Type *Account:* and press the Enter key two times.

5. Type *Description:* and press the Enter key; then type *30,* and press the Enter key again.

6. Type *Amount:* and press the Enter key; then type *10,* and press the Enter key again.

Next, we'll set the field formats to match the data they'll contain:

1. Select the Date field contents and press Alt-T-T to choose the Time/Date format.

2. Press the M key to select the Month, Day, Year date display, and press the Enter key. Works selects the Short date format as the default.

3. Select the Amount field and press Alt-T-U to choose the Currency format, and then press the Enter key to accept the default of two decimal places.

Our last task is to enter some sample expense records, which we can do more quickly in List view because many of the records contain identical Type entries. Before entering the records, we'll widen the Account and Description columns in the List view so that we can see most or all of the information in them:

1. Press Alt-V-L to display List view. Works shows the default column widths of 10 characters.

2. Select the Account column, and press Alt-T-W to choose the Field Width command.

3. Type *15* and press the Enter key.

4. Select the Description column, and press Alt-T-W.

5. Type *25* and press the Enter key.

Now enter the records shown in Figure 12-1. In some cases, you can use the keyboard shortcut Ctrl-' to copy the entry from the field above when it's the same as in the currently selected field. In record numbers 2 and 3, for example, the Type (Expense) and Account (Donation) is the same as it is in record number 1. So, when the Type field in record number 2 is selected, you can Press Ctrl-' to copy the entry from the field above.

If you have a lot of recurring entries, such as a monthly paycheck, a quarterly dividend, quarterly taxes, or a regular donation, you can insert all the records for the year by copying the first record and then pasting it several more times to blank records in the list. In Figure 12-1, for example, we could select the first Paycheck entry and then paste it to 11 other blank records using the Repeat Copy command (Shift-F7). After all the records were copied, we could go back and manually change the date entry in each record to match the correct month.

Before moving on in this project, let's save the file as LEDGER:

1. Press Alt-F-A.

2. Type *Ledger* and press the Enter key to save the file.

Viewing selected records

Suppose you want to determine how much money you gave in donations during a year. You can use Works' Search command with the Match All Records option to show all the records that contain donations:

1. Press Alt-S-S to choose the Search command.

2. Type *Donation* and press Alt-A to choose the Match All Records option.

3. Press the Enter key. Works displays only the records that contain the word *Donation*, like this:

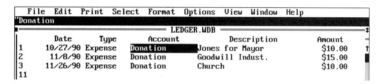

Note that with such a search request, Works displays all records that contain the word *Donation*, regardless of where the word appears. If for some reason this word appeared in a record that wasn't a donation, then that record would also appear on the screen.

Using Works' Query feature, you can display an even more specific group of records. Suppose, for example, that you wanted to view only the records that contain expenses for the month of November:

1. Press Alt-V-Q to display the Query screen.

2. Select the Date field.

3. Type *=(month()=11)* to indicate that the Date field must contain a month entry with the number "11."

4. Press the tab key one time to select the Type field.

5. Type *Expense* to indicate that the Type field must contain the word "Expense," and then press the Enter key.

6. Press Alt-V-L to return to List view. Works displays only the expense records with dates in November, as shown on the following page.

```
 File  Edit  Print  Select  Format  Options  View  Window  Help
──────────────────────────── LEDGER.WDB ════════════════════════
       Date      Type      Account        Description       Amount
   2   11/8/90  Expense   Donation    Goodwill Indust.      $15.00
   3   11/26/90 Expense   Donation    Church                $10.00
   6   11/16/90 Expense   Interest    VISA bill             $10.13
  10   11/28/90 Expense   Prop. taxes 2nd Installment 1990 $320.00
  11
```

Using these query formulas and some of the calculating features of
Works reports, you can spot check your ledger throughout the year to
see how much you've spent in specific expense categories during certain
periods. For more information about entering query formulas, see the
DB Query View procedure in the Help Index on the Help Menu, or turn
to the "Query" section in the Database & Reporting chapter of the
Microsoft Works Reference manual.

Creating a monthly expense report

At this point, our Database document shows only the expense records
for the month of November. Let's leave this selection of records displayed and see how we can make a report that will show a total of the
expenses—either on the screen or on paper:

1. Press Alt-V-N to display a new report. The report format
   screen appears, like this:

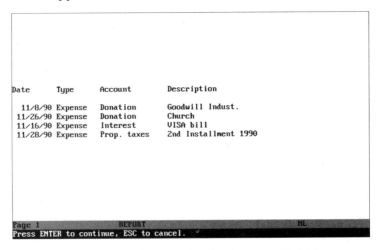

```
Date       Type      Account     Description

  11/8/90  Expense   Donation    Goodwill Indust.
 11/26/90  Expense   Donation    Church
 11/16/90  Expense   Interest    VISA bill
 11/28/90  Expense   Prop. taxes 2nd Installment 1990




Page 1                  REPORT                            NL
Press ENTER to continue, ESC to cancel.
```

Notice that this report doesn't contain the Amount field because not
enough space is available to print all the fields across one page. We don't

need to display the Type field in this report because we know that this report will contain only Expense records. Let's delete the Type column to make room for the Amount field:

1. Press the Esc key to display the report definition screen.

2. Select a cell in any row of the Type column.

3. Press Shift-F8 to select the Type column.

4. Press Alt-E-D to delete this column.

Now the report format contains the Amount field. You can see for yourself:

1. Press Alt-V-1 to view the report format again. The Amount field is shown at the right.

2. Press the Esc key to return to the report definition screen.

Next, we'll add a formula in the Summ Report row to calculate the total of the expense amounts:

1. Select the cell in the Amount column in the upper of the two Summ Report rows.

2. Press Alt-E-S to insert a field summary. Works displays the Field Summary dialog box, like this:

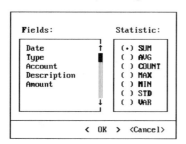

3. Press the Down arrow key five times to select the Amount field.

Works has already selected the SUM calculation as the default, so press the Enter key to choose this Summary formula. Works inserts a formula in the first Summ Report row of the Amount column, as shown on the following page.

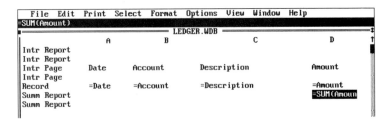

With this formula inserted in the Summ Report row, Works will display the total of the Amount entries in the bottom row of the report. You can view this total on the report format screen, on the Print Preview screen, or on a printed page. Let's view it on the report format screen:

□ Press Alt-V-1 to view Report1. Works shows the report format screen, complete with the total in the Amount column.

As before, let's rename this report so that we know what it's going to be used for:

1. Press the Esc key to display the report definition screen.

2. Press Alt-V-R to display the Reports dialog box. Report1 is the only report listed, so it's selected.

3. Press Alt-N to select the Name text box, and type *Mo Expenses*.

4. Press Alt-R to rename the report.

5. Press Alt-D to hide the dialog box.

Now we can use this report to determine a month's total expenses at any time. To see and calculate the expenses for a different month quickly, simply press Alt-V-Q to display the Query view, and change the formula in the Date field so that it tells Works to find and display the records for the month you want to view. To see records for April instead of November, for example, change the formula in the Date field to *=(MONTH()=4)*. Then select *Mo Expenses* from the View menu.

Creating an annual expense report

Using the query and reporting features of the database, we can produce a year-end report that shows expenses by category, subtotals after each category, and a grand total of all expenses for the whole year. The finished report is shown in Figure 12-2.

```
               Year-End Expenses

 Date          Description              Amount

               Donation

 10/27/90      Jones for Mayor            $10.00
 11/8/90       Goodwill Indust.           $15.00
 11/26/90      Church                     $10.00

                                          $35.00
               Interest

 10/12/90      VISA bill                  $22.65
 11/16/90      VISA bill                  $10.13

                                          $32.78
               Prop. taxes

 11/28/90      2nd Installment 1990      $320.00

                                         $320.00

               Grand Total              $387.78
```

Figure 12-2.
This annual expense report contains category labels and subtotals as well as a grand total for all its expense amounts.

The first task in creating this report is to select only the expense records. Remember, a Works report always includes the current selection of records in the file, as specified by the Search or Query command. For this report, we'll query the database to select only expense records:

1. Press Alt-V-L to display the List screen if it is not already showing.

2 Press Alt-V-Q to display the Query screen. It still shows the query formulas for the November expenses report that we created before.

3. Select the Date field and press Alt-E-E to clear the formula from this field. Now the only formula left is the Expense entry in the Type field, which tells Works to show only Expense records. This is the selection of records we want.

4. Press Alt-V-L to return to List view. Only expense records are showing.

Next, let's be sure the report will show the fields we want by displaying the report format and then adjusting the report layout on the report definition screen:

1. Press Alt-V-N to create a new report. Works displays the new report format on the screen. As in the monthly expense report, the Amount field does not appear on the screen because not enough room is available. We'll remedy this space problem as we did before by deleting the Type field column.

2. Press the Esc key to display the report definition screen.

3. Select a cell in any row of the Type column.

4. Press Shift-F8 to select the Type column.

5. Press Alt-E-D to delete this column.

Now enough room is available across one page for all the other fields in the report. Let's move on to sorting.

We want the finished report to be sorted by Account so that all the expenses for each category will be together. Within each Account category, we want the records to appear in chronological order. In Chapter 10 and in the Calendar project earlier in this chapter, we saw how you can sort a database document from List view. You can also sort a database document, however, from the report definition screen. Whether you perform the sort from the List or Form view or from the report definition screen, you always change the order of the records that are displayed in the document. When you sort from the report definition screen, though, Works adds the extra rows that you will need to create category labels and subtotals. Let's see how this works:

1. Press Alt-S-O to choose the Sort command. Works displays the Sort dialog box, as shown on the next page.

As you can see, the Sort dialog box contains two extra options for each sort level when you display the dialog box from the report definition screen. We'll see how these options work after we specify the sort order for the records.

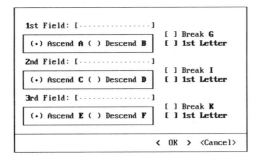

2. Type *Account* to enter this name in the 1st Field text box, and then press the Tab key two times to select the 1st Field Break option.

3. Press the spacebar, and then press the Tab key two times to select the 2nd Field text box.

4. Type *Date* and press the Enter key. With these sort fields specified, the document (and the report) will be sorted by account name and then by date within each account name.

Works uses the Break and 1st Letter options in this dialog box to create groups of records in a report. If neither of these options is checked, Works prints all the records in a report in one group, with no breaks between them. When all the records are printed in one group, you cannot create category labels or category subtotals. We want Works to divide the records in our expense report by account category so that all the records for each account will be in a distinct group and will be followed by a subtotal.

Works does not assume that you want breaks between sort categories in every report, so you must check the Break option in the Sort dialog box for each sort level. The Break option tells Works to break up the report into groups based on the contents of the field specified at that sort level. In our case, we want the report's records grouped by account, but we don't want them grouped by date (or else a break would be included after each different date). Therefore, we only want to check the Break option on the Account sort level.

With the Break option checked, Works will break up a new group whenever the contents of the Account field change. Because we're sorting the document on the Account field, Donation expenses will become one group of records, Interest expenses will become another group of records, and so on. (At the end of this chapter, we'll see how the 1st Letter option works in the Inventory project.)

Now we'll see how sorting the report from the report definition screen gives us new capabilities. The report definition screen now looks like this:

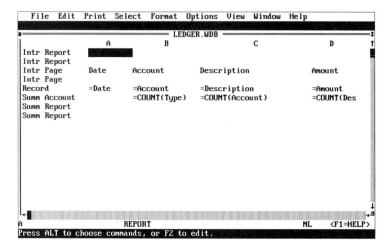

Because we sorted the report and specified a break on the Account field, Works has inserted a Summ Account row below the Record row on this screen. In fact, Works has inserted COUNT formulas in the Summ Account row's Account, Description, and Amount columns. The COUNT formulas will calculate the number of records in each group. We don't need that information in this report, so we'll delete these formulas from the Summ Account row:

1. Select the COUNT formula in the Account field, and press the F8 key to extend the selection.

2. Press the Right arrow key two times to select all occurrences of the formula.

3. Press Alt-E-E to clear these formulas from the screen.

The formula we do want to include in this report is a SUM formula that will add up all the amounts in each category. This formula goes in the Summ Account row because that row will produce subtotals for each category of account records in the report.

1. Select the Amount column in the Summ Account row.

2. Press Alt-E-S to choose the Insert Field Summary command. Works displays the Field Summary dialog box.

3. Press the Down arrow key five times to select the Amount field.

Works has already selected the SUM calculation as the default, so press the Enter key to choose this Summary formula. Works inserts it in the Summ Account row.

Next, we'll enter a formula in the Summ Report row to calculate a total of all the expenses in the report:

1. Select the Amount column in the last Summ Report row at the bottom of the report.

2. Press Alt-E-S to choose the Insert Field Summary command. Works displays the Field Summary dialog box.

3. Press the Down arrow key five times to select the Amount field.

4. Press the Enter key to place a SUM formula in the field.

While we're at it, let's enter the title "Grand Total" in the Summ Report row:

1. Press the Left arrow key one time to select the Description column in the last Summ Report row at the bottom of the report.

2. Type *Grand Total* and press the Enter key. This text will now appear to the left of the grand total at the end of the report.

The report definition screen now looks like the screen at the top of the following page.

Let's rename this report and then check the report format screen to see the totals these formulas will produce:

1. Press Alt-V-R to choose the Report command. Works displays the Report dialog box, which now lists our monthly expenses report along with Report2, which is the current year-end expense report. Report2 is selected because it's the report we're currently working with.

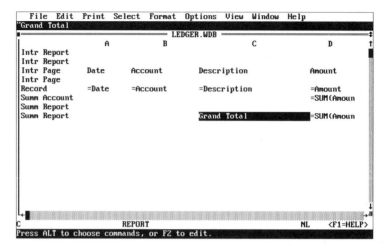

```
   File  Edit  Print  Select  Format  Options  View  Window  Help
"Grand Total
├────────────────────── LEDGER.WDB ──────────────────────
                    A           B                C                D
Intr Report
Intr Report
Intr Page     Date        Account      Description        Amount
Intr Page
Record        =Date       =Account     =Description       =Amount
Summ Account                                              =SUM(Amoun
Summ Report
Summ Report                            Grand Total        =SUM(Amoun




C                         REPORT                         NL    <F1=HELP>
Press ALT to choose commands, or F2 to edit.
```

2. Press Alt-N to select the Name text box, and type *Year Expenses*.

3. Press Alt-R to rename the report, and then press Alt-D to return to the report definition screen.

Let's see how this report looks now:

☐ Press Alt-V-2 to view the Year Expenses report. The report format screen is displayed, as in Figure 12-3.

You can see that the expenses are grouped into categories by account name and within each account category by date, and that each category's expenses contains subtotals. Let's clean up the formatting of

```
Date       Account       Description          Amount

10/27/90 Donation     Jones for Mayor          $10.00
 11/8/90 Donation     Goodwill Indust.         $15.00
11/26/90 Donation     Church                   $10.00
                                                   35
10/12/90 Interest     VISA bill                $22.65
11/16/90 Interest     VISA bill                $10.13
                                                32.78
11/28/90 Prop. taxes  2nd Installment 1990    $320.00
                                                  320

                      Grand Total              387.78
```

Figure 12-3.
With a formula entered in the Summ Account row of its report definition screen, this report now contains account category subtotals.

this report so that it's easier to read. In the first place, the subtotal amounts aren't formatted as currency like the rest of the amounts. You must set the formatting for formulas in the report definition screen, just as you format cells in the Works Spreadsheet:

1. Press the Esc key to return to the report definition screen.

2. Select the SUM formula in the Amount column for the Summ Account row.

3. Press Alt-T-U to select the Currency format for this formula, and press the Enter key to accept the default setting of two decimal places.

4. Select the SUM formula in the Summ Report row at the bottom of the report, and then repeat step 3.

You'll also notice in Figure 12-3 that no space appears between the rows that contain records in each category and the subtotals rows. The report would look better with some extra spacing. We can add spacing rows by inserting an empty row between the Record row and the Summ Account row:

1. Select an entry in the Summ Account row.

2. Press Alt-E-I to choose the Insert Row/Column command.

3. Press the Enter key to accept the option to insert a row. Works displays a list of the different row types that you can insert. The Summ Account row type is selected, like this:

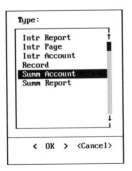

Works proposes the Summ Account row as the type to insert because we've selected that type of row on the report definition screen.

4. Press the Enter key to insert a new Summ Account row. Works inserts a new Summ Account row between the existing Summ Account row and the Record row.

With this row as a spacer, a blank line will now appear between the last record in each category and the subtotal for that category. Next, let's insert an Intr Account row that will let us print the name of each account category at the beginning of that category. By doing so, we'll be able to eliminate the Account field from the report because the name of each account category will appear above it.

1. Press Alt-E-I to choose the Insert Row/Column command.

2. Press the Enter key to insert a row. Works displays the list of row types you can insert. The Summ Account row is still selected because the row below the Record row is still selected.

3. Press the Up arrow key two times to select the Intr Account row, and then press the Enter key to insert this row. Because this is a row that will contain text to introduce each category of expenses, Works inserts it above the Record row, like this:

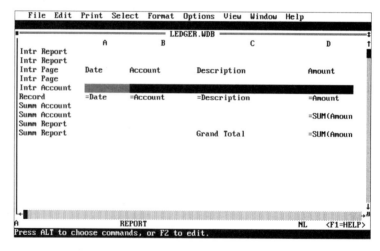

Now we need to insert a formula that will tell Works to insert the name of the Account category at the beginning of each category.

1. Select the Description field in the Intr Account row.

2. Press Alt-E-O to choose the Insert Field Contents command. Works displays a dialog box that shows the field names.

3. Select the Account field from the list, and then press the Enter key. Works inserts the formula *=Account*, which inserts the Account category name at the beginning of each group of expenses.

Now we can delete the Account field from the report. Because we'll be inserting the category name at the beginning of each category, it isn't necessary to have the name from the Account field repeated in each of the group's records.

1. Select a cell in any row of the Account column.

2. Press Shift-F8 to select the whole column.

3. Press Alt-E-D to delete the column.

Let's add another spacing row, this time between the Intr Account row and the record row, so that a blank line will be included between the name of each category and the records in that category.

1. Select any field in the Record row.

2. Press Alt-E-I and then press the Enter key to insert a row.

3. Select the Intr Account row type from the list in the dialog box, and then press the Enter key. Works inserts a second Intr Account row between the existing Intr Account row and the record row.

Now we'll see how all this looks on the report format screen:

1. Press Alt-V-2 to view the report format screen. Works displays the report format, as shown on the next page.

The report is almost done. For the finishing touches, we'll widen the Date and Description fields and left-align the Date field to improve readability, add a report title at the top of the page, create a header to print the page number on each page, and apply some boldface and underline formatting to several items in the report. As before, we'll handle all these operations from the report definition screen.

```
Date       Description              Amount

           Donation

10/27/90  Jones for Mayor          $10.00
 11/8/90  Goodwill Indust.         $15.00
11/26/90  Church                   $10.00

                                   $35.00
           Interest

10/12/90  VISA bill                $22.65
11/16/90  VISA bill                $10.13

                                   $32.78
Page 1                   REPORT                      NL
Press ENTER to continue, ESC to cancel.
```

1. Press the Esc key to return to the report definition screen.

2. Press Ctrl-Home to select the first field in the Intr Report row.

3. Press the Right arrow key one time to select the Description field in this row.

4. Type *Year-End Expenses* and press the Enter key.

5. Press Alt-T-S to choose the Style command.

6. Press the B key and then press the U key to choose the Bold and Underline styles for this title; then press the Enter key to apply the styles.

7. Press the Down arrow key two times to select the Intr Page row.

8. Press Ctrl-F8 to select the entire row.

9. Press Alt-T-S to choose the Style command, press the U key to select the Underline style, and then press the Enter key to apply this style.

Next, we'll widen the Date and Description fields:

1. Select any entry in the Date field.

2. Press Alt-T-W to choose the Column Width command.

3. Type *15* and press the Enter key to widen the column.

4. Press Alt-T-S to choose the Style command.

5. Type the *L* key to choose the Left alignment option, and then press the Enter key to return to the report definition screen.

6. Press the Right arrow key to select an entry in the Description field.

7. Press Alt-T-W.

8. Type *30* and press the Enter key to widen the column.

Next we'll apply boldface formatting to the account headings to separate the groups more effectively:

1. Press the Down arrow key two times to select the *=Account* cell in the Intr Account Row.

2. Press Alt-T-S to choose the Style command.

3. Press the B key to choose the Bold style for this heading, and then press the Enter key to apply this style.

Finally, we'll insert a header for this report:

1. Press Alt-P-H to choose the Headers & Footers command. Works displays the Headers & Footers dialog box, and the cursor is in the Header text box.

2. Type *&RYear-End Expenses - Page &P*. Works inserts this text in the Header text box.

3. Press Alt-N to choose the No Header On 1st Page option.

4. Press the Enter key to enter this header.

The *&R* command tells Works to right-align the header on the page, and the *&P* command tells Works to insert the page number. Because you selected the No Header On 1st Page option, the header is only printed on the second and subsequent pages of the report. For more information about headers in the database, choose the Print Headers & Footers command from the Commands category of the Help Index on the Help menu.

The report is done. If you print it or preview it on the screen, it should now look like the one shown in Figure 12-2.

Using the ledger

You can use the ledger document you just created to record and print financial transactions for a small business or for your personal finances. The challenge is to divide your expenses and income into meaningful categories (for example, categories that match your tax return so that you can simply transfer them at the end of the year). Then you must be consistent about how you enter the account names you set up. (If you call a donation "Donations" one time and "Donation" the next, for example, you won't be able to include both records in the same category with a database sort.)

At the end of the year, you can validate your data and check to see that you entered account names the same way every time by sorting the file on the Account field and checking for correct spellings of account names. You can also create similar reports for your income, sorting the report on the account categories.

With monthly or quarterly reports, you can see how well you're sticking to a budget or whether your income is meeting your projections. This ledger document has many uses and has served as the basic accounting system for many small businesses.

An Inventory File

The Works Database is a good tool for creating an inventory file because it allows you to sort, select, and organize items in an inventory. You can use a database formula to calculate the total value of each item in stock, and you can use subtotal and grand total formulas in a report to calculate total quantities and the value of items in various categories.

To begin this inventory project, create the database file shown in Figure 12-4.

| | File | Edit | Print | Select | Format | Options | View | Window | Help |

INVENT.WDB

	Item#	Name	Qty	Price
1	G0001	Small Gizmo	246	$0.30
2	G0002	Medium Gizmo	527	$0.35
3	G0003	Large Gizmo	89	$0.45
4	W0001	Small Widget	340	$0.05
5	W0004	Widget Washer	700	$0.11
6	W002	Medium Widget	125	$0.10
7	W003	Large Widget	189	$0.20
8				

Figure 12-4.
A sample inventory document in the database.

This document isn't yet complete, but it will give us the data we need to begin this project.

Creating the inventory document

To create this document, open a new database file, create the four fields shown, and then enter the records, like this:

1. Press Alt-F-N to choose the Create New File command, and then press the D key to choose a new database file.

2. Type *Item#:* and press the Enter key two times.

3. Type *Name:* and press the Enter key two times.

4. Type *Qty:* and press the Enter key two times.

5. Type *Price:* and press the Enter key two times.

6. Press Alt-V-L to switch to List view. Each field is 10 characters wide.

7. Press the Home key, then press the Right arrow key one time to select the Name field in the first record, and press Alt-T-W to choose the Field Width command.

8. Type *20* and press the Enter key.

9. Press the Right arrow key two times to select the Price field in the first record.

10. Press Alt-T-U to choose the Currency format for this field, and then press the Enter key to confirm it.

Now you can enter the records shown in Figure 12-4. When you finish, press Alt-F-A and save the file with the name INVENT.

This document contains information about the name, item number, quantity, and unit cost of each item in inventory, but it won't show us the total value of each item. We'll solve that problem next.

Entering a database formula

To determine the total value of each item in stock, we'll add a new field and then enter a database formula that multiplies the quantity of each item by its price. First, we'll add the new field using List view:

1. Press Ctrl-Home to select the Item# field in the first record.

2. Press the End key to select the Price field in the first record.

3. Press the Right arrow key one time to select the empty field directly to the right of the Price field.

4. Press Alt-E-N to choose the Field Name command. Works displays the Field Name dialog box.

5. Type *Value* and press the Enter key. The new name appears at the top of the column.

To calculate the value of each inventory item, we'll enter a formula in this field. As in the spreadsheet, you can enter database formulas either by typing their contents or by pointing to and clicking on the fields you want referenced in the formula. We'll use the pointing method here.

1. Type = to let Works know you're beginning a formula. The equal sign appears in the formula bar.

2. Press the Left arrow key two times to select the Qty field. The Qty name appears in the formula bar.

3. Type * to indicate that you want to multiply. The asterisk is entered after Qty in the formula bar, and the selection moves back to the Value field.

4. Press the Left arrow key one time to select the Price field. This field name appears in the formula bar, so the formula now reads: *=Qty*Price*.

5. Press the Enter key to enter the formula. Works calculates the value for each inventory item, like this:

```
   File  Edit  Print  Select  Format  Options  View  Window  Help
=Qty*Price
                             INVENT.WDB
        Item#         Name        Qty      Price    Value
 1    G0001   Small Gizmo          246     $0.30     73.8
 2    G0002   Medium Gizmo         527     $0.35    184.45
 3    G0003   Large Gizmo           89     $0.45     40.05
 4    W0001   Small Widget         340     $0.05     17
 5    W0004   Widget Washer        700     $0.11     77
 6    W002    Medium Widget        125     $0.10     12.5
 7    W003    Large Widget         189     $0.20     37.8
 8
```

The values are displayed in the default General format. Let's change the format to Currency.

▫ Press Alt-T-U to choose the Currency format, and press the Enter key to accept the default of two decimal places. Works reformats all the values in this field. Notice that when you change the format of a field in any record, you change the format of the field in every record. So, the contents of that field in every record will be formatted the same way.

Calculating subtotals in a report

Now let's create a report that calculates subtotals of each category of items by part number.

1. Press Alt-V-N to choose a new report. The report format screen appears.

2. Press the Esc key to display the report definition screen.

   As it is, the report definition screen doesn't contain a Summ Item# row in which we would want to enter SUM formulas to produce category subtotals. To add such a row, we must first sort the file on the Item# category.

3. Press Alt-S-O to choose the Sort command.

4. Type *Item#* in the 1st Field box.

5. Press the Tab key two times, and then press the spacebar.

By selecting the Break option, you tell Works to divide each group of items into different categories. With only the Break option selected, however, Works will create a new group of Item records each time the contents of the Item field change. Because the item number changes with each record, Works will place each record in a separate category.

Looking at Figure 12-4, you can see that the logical categories for this inventory would be Widget-type items, which have item numbers that begin with the letter W, and Gizmo-type items, which have item numbers that begin with the letter G. In this case, we want Works to create a new category of items only when the first character in the field changes. So we need to select the 1st Letter option in the Sort dialog box to tell Works to create new categories only when the first letter of the Item# field's contents change:

▫ Press Alt-H to select the 1st Letter option, and press Enter. Works returns to the report definition screen and adds a new Summ Item# row, as shown on the next page.

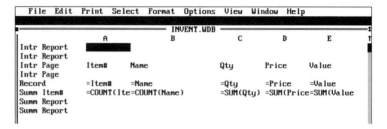

Works has already entered some formulas in the new Summ row. The SUM(Qty) and SUM(Value) formulas will create subtotals for the number of items and for the total value of those items in each category. This subtotal information is what we want to calculate. The SUM(Price), COUNT(Item#), and COUNT(Name) formulas, however, are useless, so we'll delete them:

1. Select the COUNT formula in the Item# column of the Summ Item# row.

2. Press F8, and press the Right arrow key one time to select the formula in the Name field.

3. Press Alt-E-E to clear these fields.

4. Select the SUM formula in the Price column of the Summ Item# row.

5. Press Alt-E-E to clear this formula.

Now the remaining formulas will calculate category subtotals of the number of items in and the value of each group. As yet, however, neither of the Summ Report rows contain formulas, so no grand totals of items or value for the entire inventory will be created. Let's enter these formulas now. We could enter them by typing or choosing the Insert Field Summary command, as before, but because these same SUM formulas already exist in the Summ Item# row, let's copy them into the Summ Report row:

1. Select the SUM(Qty) formula in the Summ Item# row.

2. Press Shift-F3 to choose the Copy command.

3. Select the Qty cell in the lower of the two Summ Report rows.

4. Press the Enter key to enter the formula there.

5. Repeat steps 1–4 for the SUM(Value) formula in the Summ Item# row.

You've now entered all the formulas. Let's display the report format screen again to see how the calculations look:

☐ Press Alt-V-1 to choose the report from the View menu. Works displays the report with the category subtotals and grand totals, as in Figure 12-5.

```
Item#      Name             Qty        Price       Value

G0001      Small Gizmo       246       $0.30       $73.80
G0002      Medium Gizmo      527       $0.35      $184.45
G0003      Large Gizmo        89       $0.45       $40.05
                             862                  $298.30
W0001      Small Widget      340       $0.05       $17.00
W0004      Widget Washer     700       $0.11       $77.00
W002       Medium Widget     125       $0.10       $12.50
W003       Large Widget      189       $0.20       $37.80
                            1354                  $144.30

                            2216                  $442.60
```

Figure 12-5.
After you enter subtotal and total formulas in the report definition screen, those totals appear in the report format screen.

The only remaining tasks are formatting adjustments that will make the report look better. Let's add a report title, a spacing row between categories, and some titles to identify the totals:

1. Press the Esc key and select any cell in the upper of the two Summ Report rows.

2. Press Alt-E-I to choose the Insert Row/Column command, and press the Enter key to select a row. Works displays a dialog box that lists the different row types you can insert in the report.

3. Select the Summ Item# row type, and press the Enter key. Works inserts a new Summ Item# row below the existing one. We'll leave this row blank so that it will appear in the report as a blank line.

4. Select the Name column in the last Summ Report row at the bottom of the report.

5. Type *Grand Totals* and press the Enter key.

6. Select the Name field in the upper Summ Item# row.

7. Type *Subtotal* and press the Enter key.

8. Select the Name column in the top Intr Report row.

9. Type *Inventory Report* and press the Enter key.

Figure 12-5 has only one other formatting problem: The numeric entries in the Qty, Price, and Value fields aren't centered below their titles. Let's change the alignment of the column titles:

1. Select the Qty label in the upper of the two Intr Page rows.

2. Press F8, and press the Right arrow key two times to select the Price and Value labels.

3. Press Alt-T-S to choose the Style command, and then press the R key to choose the Right alignment option in the Style dialog box.

4. Press the Enter key. You can't see the alignment change on the report definition screen, but when you press Alt-V-1 to view the report format again, you'll see that the field labels are now aligned directly above the amounts.

If you like, you can add other formatting enhancements to this report, such as boldface or underlined field labels.

Using the inventory database

This project used a simple inventory database that was created for a small business. You could use it as it is to complete quarterly or year-end inventories. As you add to your existing stock or acquire new items, you can update or add records to track them. An inventory document like this one is handy for calculating inventory taxes or for filing insurance claims in the event of theft or other losses.

With a little modification, this document can also serve as a home inventory in which you can store the names, serial numbers, initial purchase prices, dates of purchase, and warranty information for your household goods. You can use it to look up serial numbers and purchase dates for warranty claims or to be specific about serial numbers, item descriptions, and original purchase prices in case of emergency.

The projects included in this chapter have covered all the major features of the Works Database tool. By now, you should know enough to put the database to work on data-handling tasks of your own.

13

Basic Communications Techniques

The Communications tool in Microsoft Works lets you communicate with other computers either over standard telephone lines or through a cable directly linking your computer with another. Works lets you connect your computer to other computers so that you can receive or transmit data or files with them. In this chapter, we'll look at how the Communications tool works and at some different ways in which you might want to use it. First, though, we'll look at personal computer communications in general.

How Computers Communicate

For computers to exchange information, they must first have a physical means of transmission, and they must also be running software that enables them to communicate. Although it's possible for computers to exchange data using radio waves, other means are more common, such as a simple cable that links two nearby computers to each other, a local area network that links several computers in a single office or building, or the wiring and microwave channels of the telephone system that links computers at great distances from one another. The telephone system of computer linkage is popular and easily used because the wires are already installed almost everyplace you'd want to put a computer.

Although any of these physical means can establish a data path between two computers, you must have a communications program in order to establish the specific method of communication and to select and send data or receive data and store it on your disk. The Works Communication tool lets you exchange data with other computers either over telephone lines or by means of a simple cable directly linking your computer with another. (You need a special type of software called a "network operating system" to communicate with other computers over a network.)

How modems work

Most telephone systems are designed to carry continuously varying voice-frequency signals rather than discrete bits of computer data. To exchange data over telephone lines, computers must transmit and receive their bit streams through a modem. This device allows them to communicate by impressing (or modulating) computer data onto a voice-frequency carrier signal, in much the same way that a radio transmitter impresses voice signals onto the station's carrier frequency. The modem at the receiving end, like your radio, reverses this process and restores the computer data to its original form. (The name "modem" is short for MOdulator/DEModulator.) You connect a modem to a serial communications port on the back of your computer.

You can buy a modem from any computer dealer or through any of dozens of mail-order firms. Modems for the IBM PC and PC-compatible personal computers range in price from less than $100 to over $1000. All modems perform the same basic modulation/demodulation function, but modems differ in how fast they can transmit data, which sets of software commands they understand, whether they reside inside or outside the computer, and what extra features they have.

Modem transmission speeds are measured in bits per second (bps). Expensive modems can transmit data at much greater rates, but most common modems operate at 1200 or 2400 bps. The faster the modem, the faster you can transmit your data. Any modem that transmits at 1200 or 2400 bps can also transmit at slower speeds, so if you have a 300 bps modem and you call another computer that's using a 1200 bps modem, the faster modem will automatically lower its transmission rate to match yours. Modem prices have dropped dramatically in the last few years, and 2400 bps modems are now available for around $150.

Modems are internally programmed to accept certain commands from the communications software you use on your computer. These commands prompt the modem to adjust its transmission speed, dial a number, hang up, answer the phone when it rings, or perform other tasks. The most common set of modem commands is the Hayes command set. (Hayes Microcomputer Products was the first well-known personal computer modem manufacturer, so its command set was adopted by other makers as the standard.) The Works Communication tool uses the Hayes command set, so you should shop for a modem that is Hayes-compatible.

If you want to save space and a little money, you can buy an internal modem that plugs into one of your computer's internal expansion slots. Internal modems are usually less expensive than external modems because they are sold on a circuit board rather than in a cabinet.

Beyond the basic consideration of speed, it's the extra features that set one modem apart from another. Some of these features might include extra error-checking circuitry that allows a modem to transmit or receive data more reliably, or a built-in memory buffer that can store data for later transmission or receive data and store it while the computer itself is turned off.

A modem is usually sold with a data cable that connects the modem to a serial communications port on your computer. If not, you'll have to buy a data cable separately.

How communications software works

After you choose a physical method of linking your computer with others, you still need software to control the computer and modem so that they can properly transmit and receive data. A communications tool like the one in Works translates your commands into instructions that your computer, your modem, and the remote computer and remote modem can understand. These instructions relate to:

- The speed at which data is transferred through your modem.

- The data format, which controls such matters as the number of bits that make up each character of information in the data you send and the number of bits used to identify the end of one character and the beginning of the next character.

- The data type. Communications data in Works is of two basic types, ASCII and binary. ASCII (Text) files contain only characters—letters, numbers, or symbols—without any formatting. Binary files can contain text as well as formatting codes, formulas, graphics, or program instructions. Binary files that you might create and send with Works include spreadsheet or database files.

- Whether to use special error-correction methods that can help to maintain the accuracy of data transmissions.

The communications settings established for your communications program must match those in use by the remote computer's communications program or you'll experience a variety of problems, from garbled data to an inability to connect.

Because several levels of interaction are possible, it can be difficult to determine exactly what's wrong if you're having trouble connecting with or transferring data to another computer. If you can't make the connection, for example, the problem could be your software settings; your modem; the physical connections linking your computer, modem, and telephone line; the telephone line itself; or the remote computer, modem, or software. (See the "Communications Tips" section at the end of this chapter for advice about how to prevent communications problems.)

Even if your telephone line is working, the quality of the telephone line also affects communications. For example, you might get a telephone connection that is noisy. Such background noise makes it harder for computers to interpret the precise signals their modems use to transmit data.

To get a better idea of how this process actually works, let's go through it now.

Setting Up a Modem

Because you need both hardware and software to communicate, let's set up the hardware first. Presumably, you'll be using a modem to communicate over telephone lines.

Your modem hardware will include the modem itself, a telephone cord with modular connectors at both ends, and a power cable. You connect your modem to your computer by following the steps listed on the next page.

1. If you have an external modem, connect one end of the data cable to the modem and the other end to the computer's serial port. (Consult your computer's manual if you can't identify the serial port.) If you have an internal modem, install it in one of your computer's available internal expansion slots.

2. Connect one end of the telephone cable to the modular telephone jack on the modem and the other end to the modular telephone jack in your wall. (If you don't have a modular wall jack, you can buy an adapter from an electronics store.) If your modem has two telephone jacks, be sure to connect the telephone cable to the jack marked "Line." (The second jack, marked "Phone," is for connecting a regular telephone to the modem so that you can have both the modem and the phone connected to the same modular phone jack in the wall.) If the two jacks on your modem aren't marked "Line" and "Phone," you can plug the telephone cable into either jack.

3. If you are using an external modem, connect the modem's power-supply cord to the modem, and plug it into a standard electrical outlet.

4. Check your modem's manual to see if you need to set any switches on the modem.

5. Turn the modem on.

After the modem is set up, you must set up a Works Communications document to control it properly.

Setting Up a Works Communications Document

Each time you want to call another computer, you must use a communications document. You must choose from several communications settings to specify how your data will be transmitted, and these are set with the communications tool's commands. The settings are stored with the document when you save it, so you can set up and save different documents with different groups of settings. Works, however, will allow you to have only one communications file open at a time.

You have many communications settings to choose from. For two computers to communicate properly, though, the settings on both computers must be the same. So, before you try communicating with another computer, try to find out what communications settings you should use by contacting the system operator of the other computer.

When you know the remote computer's settings, you can select the same settings for your Works communications document. After you choose the proper settings, you specify the telephone number you want to call and then issue a command to make the call (or you can set Works to answer a phone call when it comes). After the connection is established, you can transmit or receive information using various Works options.

Let's run through a typical Works communications session from the beginning:

1. Press Alt-F-N to select a new Works file.

2. Press the C key to choose a communications file. Works displays a blank communications document, like this:

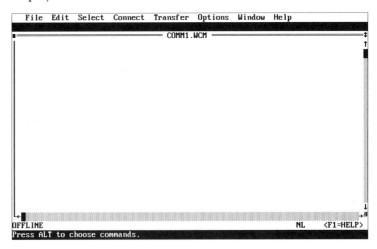

You'll notice the communications menus at the top of the screen and the message OFFLINE in the status bar. (OFFLINE means you're not currently connected to another computer.)

☐ Press Alt-O-M to choose the Communication command. Works displays a dialog box like the one at the top of the following page.

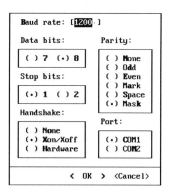

The cursor is in the Baud Rate box, which contains a default value of 1200. You enter the baud rate to indicate the speed at which you want to communicate, and then you type the Alt-key commands or click with the mouse to select the other options you want. These are the options:

■ The Baud Rate that you specify determines the maximum speed at which your modem will transmit and receive data. This speed should match that of the modem on the computer you're calling and should not exceed your modem's limitations.

■ The Data Bits option is the number of bits used to represent each character of data. The default here is 8 data bits.

■ The Stop Bits option is the number of bits used to represent the end of each character of data. The default here is 1 stop bit.

■ The Parity setting option checks for transmission errors. Normally, both computers must be using the same parity setting, but the Mask option in this dialog box (which is the default option) tells Works to communicate with the other computer no matter how its parity is set. If you know the other computer's parity setting, however, it's better to choose that specific option here. The default parity setting is None.

■ The Handshake setting option controls how data flows from one computer to another. Use the Hardware setting only when you're communicating over a direct cable connection. The standard handshake method is Xon/Xoff, which is the default choice here. If you don't know the handshake, or if Xon/Xoff doesn't work for some reason, choose None.

■ The Port setting option tells Works which serial port your modem is connected to if your computer has more than one. If you only have one serial port, it is already selected. Unless you are already using the Com1 port for another communications task (such as printing or linking to a local area network), you don't need to change the Port setting.

For now, let's assume the default settings are the ones we want.

☐ Press the Enter key to accept all the default settings.

Now we'll enter a telephone number to dial:

☐ Press Alt-O-P to choose the Phone command. Works displays the Phone dialog box like this:

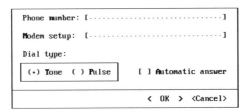

These are the options in this dialog box:

■ The Phone Number text box stores the phone number you want Works to dial. Notice that you can store only one phone number for each Works communications document, so you must create and store a different communications document for each telephone number you call regularly. You can enter phone numbers with or without dashes between prefixes, or with or without parentheses around area codes; your modem ignores such punctuation. Also, you can enter commas (which your modem recognizes) to make your modem pause briefly and wait for secondary dial tones. If you have to dial 9 to reach an outside line, for example, you might enter a comma between the 9 and the rest of the phone number so that the modem will pause for a moment to allow for an outside dial tone before continuing to dial. Your modem manual will tell you exactly how many seconds your modem will pause when it receives a comma as part of a phone number.

■ The Modem Setup text box lets you enter commands to set other options on your modem, such as turning off the modem's speaker or enabling its built-in storage buffer. Check your modem manual for a list of these commands.

■ The Dial Type setting lets you choose the type of telephone line dialing your phone system requires. Most telephone equipment in the United States and Canada uses the newer, faster Tone dial type, but if you are in an area that still has older equipment, you might need to choose Pulse dialing. If you have a push-button (as opposed to a rotary-dial) telephone, your system probably supports Tone dialing.

■ The Automatic Answer option sets the modem to answer incoming calls. Check this option if you're waiting for another computer operator to call you.

Normally, you'll simply enter a telephone number and then press the Enter key. Let's do that now:

☐ Type *5551222*, and press the Enter key. Works stores the telephone number and the dialog box disappears.

With the settings and telephone number stored, you're ready to make contact.

Making a Connection

To establish a connection with another computer, you use the Connect command on the Works Connect menu:

1. Make sure your modem is properly connected and turned on.

2. Press Alt-C-C to choose the Connect command.

Works dials the phone number. If your modem's speaker is turned on, you hear the dial tone as the phone is taken "off the hook," and then you hear it dialing. As soon as the number has been dialed, Works activates a timer in the status bar, indicating the duration of the call. When the other computer's modem answers the call, you hear the two modems exchanging high-pitched acknowledgment signals, and then your screen displays the word CONNECT. (If you are following this exercise, and you dialed the number in this book, you won't reach another computer and your modem will automatically disconnect.)

Once you are connected to another computer, you can type messages on your keyboard, and they are sent to the other computer. If the other computer's operator types a message, you see it on your screen. You can also choose commands to send files from your disk or to receive files from the other computer and store them on your disk.

Managing text on the screen

Whenever you're connected to another computer, anything you type, anything typed at the other computer's keyboard, and any text transmitted by the other computer will appear on your screen. (If you can't see text you type on the screen, choose the Local Echo option in the Options Terminal command's dialog box. See the Options Terminal command in the Help Index on the Help menu for further information.)

As the screen fills, the text scrolls up out of sight. Any text displayed this way is stored in a memory buffer maintained by the communications document. The default buffer size is 100 lines, but you can reset it to 300 or 750 lines by choosing the Medium or Large buffer option in the Terminal command's dialog box. As a result, normally the first 100 lines of text that you type or receive from the other computer are kept in your computer's memory, and you can scroll up in the communications document to view them. When your buffer's limit is reached, new text you receive or type is added to the buffer, and the oldest text in the buffer is discarded.

You can scroll around the communications document a line or a character at a time by using the arrow keys. If you are still connected, however, choose the Connect Pause command (Alt-C-P) before using these keys. You can use the following keys:

Keys	Movement
Arrow keys	Over one character
Page Up	Up one screen
Page Down	Down one screen
Home	To the beginning of the line
End	To the end of the line
Ctrl-Home	To the first character in the buffer
Ctrl-End	To the last character in the buffer

After you finish viewing the data in the buffer, choose Connect Pause again to continue communicating with the other computer. The text you receive stays in the communication document's buffer after you disconnect from the remote computer. As soon as you close or save the communications file, however, Works empties the buffer.

You can select all the text in the buffer by using the Select All command (Alt-S-A). You can select a particular part of the text by choosing the Select Text command (Alt-S-E) or by choosing Connect Pause, pressing the F8 key, and then highlighting the text you want to select by pressing any of the cursor movement keys shown in the preceding table. After text is selected, however, the only thing you can do with it is copy it. You can't delete selected text by using the Delete key, and you can't move text elsewhere in the communications buffer with the Move option.

To save the contents of the buffer after you receive text, copy its contents to a Works Word Processor document and then save the word processor file. These are the steps you would use to copy all of the text in the buffer to a word processor document while you're still connected to another computer:

1. Press Alt-S-A to choose the Select All command. Works selects all the text in the buffer and pauses the communications session. You're still connected, but the display of incoming text is temporarily stopped.

2. Press Shift-F3 to choose the Copy command.

3. Press Alt-F-N to choose the New File command, and then press the Enter key to open a new word processor file.

4. Press the Enter key. The text from the communications document will be copied to the word processor document.

5. Press Alt-F-S to choose the Save command.

6. Type a name for the new word processor file, and then press the Enter key.

7. Select the communications document from the Window menu to return to it.

8. Press Alt-C-P to resume the display of incoming text.

When you finish your communications session with the remote computer, you can disconnect your call before selecting and copying text in the buffer. Note that you can copy text from the communications document to Works Database or Spreadsheet documents as well. This feature is useful if your captured text contains columns of numbers or other data.

Capturing incoming text

As an alternative to capturing incoming text in the buffer, you can set Works to store incoming text directly on your disk as you receive it by choosing the Capture Text command from the Transfer menu. Here's how the procedure works:

1. Press Alt-T-C to choose the Capture Text command. Works displays a dialog box like this:

2. Type the name of the captured text file, and then press the Enter key.

Works will now save all incoming text to that file. After you open a captured text file, the word CAPTURE is displayed in the status line and the Capture Text command on the Transfer menu changes to End Text Capture. You can stop capturing text to the file at any time by choosing the End Capture Text command (Alt-T-E). Or, if you close the communications file, the captured text file will be automatically closed.

Notice, however, that Works starts saving captured text in a file only after you open a captured text file using the Capture Text command. When you choose Capture Text, any text that is already in the buffer (or on the screen) will not be saved. To save such text, you must select it and copy it to another Works document.

Any text you capture in a file is stored as a text file. When you open such a file in Works, you'll have to decide which type of file you want to open (word processor, spreadsheet, or database).

Receiving Files

Along with capturing text as it appears on your screen, you can also receive text or other data as a complete file. To receive a file:

1. Press Alt-T-R to choose the Receive File command from the Transfer menu. When you do, Works presents a dialog box like this:

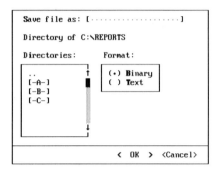

As you can see, you must specify the name of the file you want Works to create in the Save File As text box when it receives the file from the remote computer. Type a file-name, and then press the Tab key two times.

3. You must also indicate whether the file being received is a text or a binary file. Select a file format option, and press the Enter key. Works displays a status box on the screen like this:

This box shows you the progress of the receive operation. The remote computer begins transmitting the file and displays messages in the status box about the status of the file transfer. When the whole file has been received, the status box indicates that the transfer is complete and the file is safely stored on your disk. Now press the Enter key to resume the communications session. The files you receive in this way can be text files, or they can be binary files that contain program code, graphics, or other information that can't be stored in text format.

The Receive File option sends special signals to the remote computer, telling it when to begin transmitting the file. Because a whole file is being received, the Works program knows when the transmission is complete. This is the advantage of receiving text files with the Receive File option: You don't have to watch the screen to know when the whole file has been received.

Sending Text

To send text from a Works communications document, you have three alternatives: typing at the keyboard, sending a text file, and copying text from another Works document.

Sending text from the keyboard

Anything you type will be sent to the remote computer. This alternative is the one to use when you first establish a connection and you want to determine whether the other computer is properly receiving your data. When you connect your computer with a friend's computer, for example, you might type *Hello* after you see the CONNECT message. If everything is all right, your friend will see your "Hello" message and respond. After you know that you can read your friend's message and that he or she can read yours, you can proceed to transfer larger amounts of text from files.

Using the Send Text command

The second alternative is to send a file in Works' Text format using the Send Text command on the Transfer menu. Here's how the process works:

1. Establish a connection with the remote computer.

2. Type a message telling the other user that you are about to send a text file so that he or she will know to set up a capture text file.

3. Press Alt-T-T to choose the Send Text command. Works displays a dialog box, as shown on the next page.

   This dialog box shows you all the files in your current directory. When you use this command, however, Works will send only text-formatted files properly. If you select a word processor, spreadsheet, database, or other

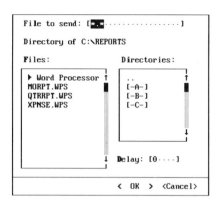

```
File to send: [*.* ...............]

Directory of C:\REPORTS

Files:                    Directories:

  ▶ Word Processor ↑       ..            ↑
    MORPT.WPS              [-A-]
    QTRRPT.WPS             [-B-]
    XPNSE.WPS              [-C-]

                                         ↓
                      ↓   Delay: [0····]

            <  OK  >  <Cancel>
```

normally formatted file and try to send it with this option, Works will include a lot of meaningless characters as it tries to interpret formatting commands, formulas, and other information as text. To send a Works Word Processor file, Database file, or Spreadsheet file with the Send Text command, you should first save the file in Text format using the Save As command. The Delay option in this dialog box causes Works to pause after sending each line of text for the number of seconds you enter here. This option is sometimes necessary when the remote computer can't receive and process your data as quickly as you can send it.

4. Select a file to send from the list.

5. Press the Enter key. The dialog box disappears, and Works displays the contents of the text file on the screen as it sends them to the remote computer.

To cancel the Send Text operation before the whole file has been sent, press the Esc key.

Copying text from another Works document

As long as you are connected to another computer, anything you copy to the communications document is sent, exactly as if you had typed it from the keyboard. For example, if you began a communications session and then decided to send a paragraph from a word processor document, you'd follow the steps on the next page.

1. Press Alt-F-O, and then select the word processor file you want to open.

2. Press the Enter key to open the word processor file.

3. Select the paragraph of text you want to send.

4. Press Shift-F3 to choose the Copy command.

5. Select the communications document from the Window menu. Works displays the communications document.

6. Press the Enter key. The text you selected in the word processor document will be entered into the communications buffer and transmitted to the remote computer.

You can also select data or numbers in database or spreadsheet documents and then copy them to a communications document. See Chapter 14 for more information.

Sending Files

If you want to send entire formatted word processor, spreadsheet, or database files to another computer, or if you want to send other programs or graphic files, you can use the Send File command (Alt-T-S). Here's the procedure:

1. Establish a connection with the remote computer.

2. Press Alt-T-S to choose the Send Files command. Works displays a dialog box like this:

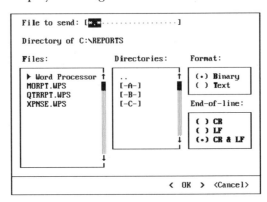

Like the Send Text dialog box, this dialog box also offers a list of files that you can choose to send. Because you can send binary as well as text-formatted files, however, you must choose the type of file that you want to send. These are the other options in this dialog box:

- The Format options let you specify whether the file is text or binary. You must choose the Binary option to send spreadsheet, database, graphics, or program files.

- The End-of-Line options tell Works whether to add a line feed and carriage return at the end of each line in the file. Usually, you'll want to select the default CR & LF option as this is the normal format for files.

After you choose a file and press the Enter key, Works displays a progress dialog box like the one you see when you use the Receive Files command. After the entire file has been sent, the progress dialog box disappears.

Ending a Communications Session

Hanging up the phone and finishing your computer call is simple. If the remote computer terminates the call, the timer in the status line on your screen will stop and be replaced by the OFFLINE message.

When you want to disconnect a call from within Works:

1. Press Alt-C-C to choose the Connect command from the Connect menu. Works displays a dialog box asking if you want to disconnect.

2. Press the Enter key. Works disconnects the phone line. The timer in the status line stops and is replaced by the OFFLINE message.

Because telephone calls using a computer cost money just as voice calls do, you'll want to be sure to disconnect from the computer as soon as you're finished. Works' integration allows you to open and work with other documents while you're still connected to a remote computer, so it's important to disconnect when you finish to avoid inadvertently maintaining the connection while you work with another document.

Calling an Information Service

One of the uses for the communications tool is to connect your computer to an information service. Services like CompuServe, Dow Jones News/Retrieval, and MCI Mail maintain huge mainframe computers that store thousands of computer files and programs such as magazine articles, stock quotations, and electronic shopping catalogs. You can interact with these mainframe computers to play games, send messages to electronic mailboxes for others to read, or even order merchandise.

To call a commercial information service, you need a subscriber ID number and a password. You get these by contacting the information service in advance and signing up as a member.

Soon after you sign up for a commercial information service, you'll receive your subscriber ID and password. You'll also get an information kit that explains how to use the service. You'll find out which communications settings to use, how to dial in, and what commands are available for looking up information, for sending messages, and for performing other activities on that particular service. After you browse through the information, you're ready to log on.

Works has a built-in feature that remembers and stores the subscriber ID and password information that you use to log on to an information service so that you don't have to type it each time you call. We'll use this feature in this exercise:

1. Open a new Works communications document.

2. Press Alt-O-C, and set the communications settings so that they match those specified in the service's information kit. Press the Enter key when you finish.

3. Press Alt-O-P, and enter the information service's telephone number. Be sure the number you enter is the computer phone number and not the voice phone number. Press the Enter key when you finish.

4. Press Alt-C-R to choose the Record Sign-On command.

5. Press Alt-C-C to connect with the information service. Works dials the telephone number, the information service's modem answers, and you see the CONNECT message followed by the information service's prompt. The prompt looks something like this:

User Name:

6. Type the user name you received from the information service, and press the Enter key. The information service presents a second prompt that looks like this:

Password:

7. Type the password you received from the information service, and press the Enter key. Usually, you can't see the password as you type it on the screen. This prevents anyone from reading the password as you type. (If you can see the password, choose the Local Echo option from the Terminal command dialog box.)

A few seconds after you enter your password, you'll see a greeting message like this:

Welcome To MCI Mail

☐ Press Alt-C-R again to stop recording the sign-on. Works stores the sign-on information so that, like a macro, you can automatically play it back the next time you call. (For more information about macros, see "Use macros to speed up complex operations" later in this chapter.)

You are now connected to the remote system, and you can proceed to use its commands to access information, create electronic mail messages, play games, or conduct other activities.

To call an information service after you record a sign-on, choose the Sign-On command (Alt-C-S) after you open the communications document. Works dials the number, waits for the prompts sent by the remote system, and then responds to the prompts with your subscriber name and password.

Communications Tips

Although the communications tool has fewer commands and is simpler to use than the other Works tools, it presents its own challenges because of the various levels of interaction between you and the remote computer. The following sections provide some tips for trouble-free communications using Works.

Check your setup

If you have trouble initiating a communications session, be sure your modem is properly connected and turned on. Improper hardware setup is the cause of many communications problems. Here are some steps that will minimize your chances of trouble:

- If you have an external modem, it should have an indicator light that tells you the modem is on and ready to go. If the light isn't on, the modem isn't turned on, its switches (if any) aren't set properly, it isn't plugged in, or the electrical outlet is dead.

- If the modem is turned on but it doesn't respond to the Connect command, check the data cable or slot connection to be sure it's secure. Also be sure you've chosen the right COM port for connecting the modem, both in the Works Settings dialog box (Alt-O-W) and in the Communication dialog box (Alt-O-M).

- If your modem's speaker is turned up, you can hear the dial tone and the actual dialing of numbers when you choose the Connect command. If you can't hear a dial tone, check your telephone line connection. If it seems all right, check the line itself by temporarily plugging a regular telephone into it, lifting the receiver, and listening for a dial tone.

- If you can hear a dial tone but you can't hear the modem dialing, be sure you've entered a telephone number in your communications document.

Get the other computer's settings

Your data format, parity, speed, and other communications settings must match those of the remote computer you're calling. Be sure to get the settings before you try communicating with another computer, and be sure to choose the same settings in the Communication dialog box (Alt-O-M).

If you can make contact with the remote computer but the data you receive on your screen is garbled, you might have the wrong parity setting. Try changing the Parity, Stop Bits, Data Bits, and Handshake settings in the Communication dialog box. Works automatically transfers data with Xon/Xoff handshaking, for example, but the remote computer might not support it. If so, changing the Handshake setting to None should solve the problem.

If you can't make contact with the remote computer, you'll usually hear the two modems trying to establish the connection, and then you'll be disconnected. This problem is usually the result of different Parity, Stop Bits, or Data Bits settings, or possibly incompatible Baud Rate settings between yours and the other computer.

Try redialing

If the problem is a noisy telephone line, you might get a clearer line by redialing. You can check the line condition by lifting the handset of a phone connected to the same line—if the line is noisy, you'll hear the static. Modems themselves normally make a roaring noise, but the noise is distinctive, and you can learn to distinguish between the modem's noise and a noisy line.

Usually, a noisy line will occasionally cause garbled characters to appear on your screen. You'll see most of a line or screen, but then you'll see some symbols instead of characters in certain words or sentences. If the line is particularly noisy, it can cause a disconnection.

Check the Local Echo setting

Most computers transmit in what's called Full Duplex mode, which means that, as you send text to the other computer, the text is echoed to your screen so that you can see it. If you find that you can't see your own outgoing text when you type, send text, or copy text in a communications document, choose the Local Echo option in the Options Terminal command's dialog box to display the text on the screen.

If, on the other hand, you see double characters on your screen (two occurrences of each character for each one you type or transmit), you need to turn off the local echo by choosing the Local Echo option.

When you call an information service, it's normal for the password you type not to appear on your screen. This is a security feature. If you can see the password, you will probably see double characters for anything else you type. Again, the answer is to turn off the local echo feature.

Reformat data in the word processor

When you receive data in the communications buffer or when you capture a text file, no formatting is included. To reformat the text easily, copy the buffer to a word processor document (or open the captured text file as a word processor file), and then use the formatting commands to format the text.

You can have trouble with transmitted files when extra carriage returns are inserted in the file, causing lines to break in odd places. Use the word processor's Search command to search for paragraph markers, which you can delete to eliminate extra carriage returns:

1. Press Ctrl-Home to move the cursor to the beginning of the word processor file.

2. Press Alt-O-L to show all the hidden characters in the document. The paragraph markers (carriage returns) are displayed.

3. Press Alt-S-R to choose the Replace command.

4. Type ^p in the Search For text box.

5. Press the Enter key. Works searches for paragraph markers, stopping at each one and giving you a chance to replace it. Because you didn't enter anything in the Replace With box in the Replace command's dialog box, Works replaces the paragraph marker with nothing, and the extra carriage return is deleted.

You can also search for extra tab stops and spaces in the word processor. See the Edit Search command in the Help Index on the Help menu for more information.

Use the Template feature to store common settings

If you normally use the same group of communications settings to call other computers, and they're not the default settings that you get when you open a new Works communications document, you can create a template file that will allow you to open new documents with your custom settings. To set up a Template:

1. Open a new communications document.

2. Select the terminal, communications, and phone settings you want.

3. Press Alt-F-A to choose the Save As command.

4. Press Alt-A to choose the Save As Template option. (You don't need to type a filename.)

5. Press the Enter key. Works saves the file as a template, and the next time you open a new communications document, the custom settings will be selected.

You can store only one template file for each Works tool in the same disk directory, so if you change the template's settings and then save the file as a template, it will replace the original template file.

Save a different document for each remote computer

If you regularly communicate with several different computers, create a different communications document for each one and save it. If you use MCI Mail and Compuserve, for example, create a document for each service. Each document will contain one service's telephone number, communications settings, and log-on procedure, so you'll be able to connect to the computer simply by opening the file and pressing Alt-C-S to choose the Sign-On command. Although the communications document's screen fills with lines of text while you exchange data with a remote computer, the buffer clears when you close the file. So, each time you open a stored communications document, its screen will be blank and its buffer will be empty, ready for the current session.

Use macros to speed up complex operations

Works' macro feature lets you store sequences of keystrokes so that you can link a series of commands and store them under one keyboard macro command. Here are three ideas for macros in the communications tool:

■ Copying the buffer to a new word processor document. As described earlier in this section, the process of selecting data in the buffer and copying it to a new word processor document involves several steps. You can record those steps as a macro and automatically execute them all. Turn on the Record Macro feature, select the buffer data, choose the Copy command, create a new word processor file, copy the buffer data there, return to the communications document, and then turn off macro recording.

Then, the next time you play that macro, you'll be able to copy data to a new word processor document and return to the communications document with only one macro command.

■ Toggling the Local Echo function. As explained earlier, you'll want to choose the Local Echo function when you can't see your outgoing text on the screen. To do so, choose the Terminal command from the Options menu and choose the Local Echo option in the dialog box. You can record this operation as a macro and then perform it with only one keyboard command.

■ Recording complex sign-on information. The built-in Record Sign-On feature in the communications tool is designed to respond to the same prompts from the remote computer each time. Sometimes, the prompts you get from a remote system aren't the same each time you log on. In this case, the recorded sign-on command in Works won't work properly. Using the macro feature, however, you can record a macro for each sequence of sign-on responses that you need to make, assign each macro to a different key, and then play them back as needed. For a commercial information service like MCI Mail, for example, you can record your user name as one macro and your password as a second macro. Then, when you are prompted to enter your user name or password, type the macro command to enter it. Storing sign-on information or any text that you repeatedly type when communicating with a remote computer also lets you use Works to enter the correct text every time, with no chance of a typing error.

For more information about using Works' macro feature, see Chapter 2 or the Macros procedure in the Help Index on the Help menu.

Use special software when appropriate

The Works Communications tool is a good basic terminal program, but sometimes it pays to use another software package for communications. If you need to connect your computer to a mainframe computer at your company, for example, special mainframe communications programs offer menus of mainframe-specific commands. Some information services, such as Lexis or Dow Jones News/Retrieval, also offer special software that makes it easier to navigate through their systems. If you have a specialized communications need, check on the availability of specialized software that can make your communications job easier.

By allowing you to connect with other computers and exchange data with them, the Works Communications tool offers extra power that you can use to your advantage. By capturing or receiving data from other computers, you can include data from other sources in your Works Word Processor, Spreadsheet, or Database files. Receiving the data and copying it to another Works document is much faster than typing it. In Chapter 14, we'll see how the communications tool can help you to capture and use data created on other computers.

Integrating the Works Tools

Works is an excellent software value because it combines in one program word processor, spreadsheet, database, and communications tools. So far, we've focused on using these tools individually, but this chapter shows you how you can use the Works tools together.

You can easily move data between the tools—or between Works and other programs—to work with your data in the format and with the specific features you need at a given time. Using the communications tool, for example, you can access numbers on another computer and save them as a text file in a word processor document on your computer. If you need to calculate the numbers, you can open that text file as a spreadsheet; but if your primary need is formatting, you can open the text file as a word processor file. In this chapter, we'll look at the basics of moving data to and from Works and among its four tools. Then we'll tackle some projects that take advantage of these data-interchange capabilities.

Manipulating Data with Works

Works gives you several ways in which to manipulate data:

- You can copy data from tool to tool.

- You can merge database data into a word processor document.

- You can open text files from other programs.

- You can save Works files in Text format.

- You can open or save spreadsheet files in Lotus 1-2-3 format.

- You can convert word processor files to specific file formats used by other programs.

You'll want to use different data-interchange capabilities in different situations. Let's look at these options one at a time.

Copying Data with Works

Just as you can select and copy data from one place to another in the same document, you can select and copy data from any Works document to any other Works document. The procedure is simple:

1. Select the data you want to copy.

2. Choose the Copy command.

3. Open the destination file or select a destination document from the Window menu.

4. Move the cursor to the place where you want the copied data to appear.

5. Press the Enter key. Works copies the data to the specified location in the destination document.

What makes this procedure tricky is how the target document treats the incoming data. The following sections include some guidelines for determining what will happen when you copy data to each of the four types of Works documents.

Copying data to word processor documents

Word processor documents are the most logical destination for copied data because they're usually the place where you integrate various types of data for presentation in a report, article, or other printed document. Here's what happens when you copy data into a word processor document:

- Copied data is inserted at the current cursor position. If there is existing text in the document after the cursor position when you perform a copy operation, the copied data is inserted in front of that existing text. So if the cursor is located between paragraph 1 and paragraph 2 when you press the Enter key to complete a copy operation, the copied data will be placed between paragraph 1 and paragraph 2.

■ The margin and indent settings in a word processor document always determine the length of its lines. If your word processor document is set for 6-inch text lines and you copy 8-inch lines into it, the incoming lines will wrap around to fit the shorter line length. This is an issue particularly when you select and copy records from a database document or rows from a spreadsheet because database documents and spreadsheets are often wider than 6 inches.

■ Works inserts tab stops to separate columnar data. When you copy columnar data (such as database records or spreadsheet rows) to a word processor document, Works inserts tab stops to maintain the column formatting in the word processor.

Here's an example of what you can expect when copying data to the word processor:

```
  File  Edit  Print  Select  Format  Options  Window  Help
 ======================== WORD1.WPS ========================
 [L········1·········2···R···3····R···4····R···5···R···]···R···7·····
 » The following table shows our advertising responses for the
 last four months of this year:
   Magazine              Sep       Oct       Nov       Dec
   Totals

   Young Modeler          11         8         9        24
   52
   Kit Craft              17        14        14        18
   63
   Model Maven            13        28        19        18
   78
   Car Modeling           25        35        45        40
   145

 As you   File  Edit  Print  Select  Format  Options  View  Window  Help
 perform
 October ========================== ADVANAL.WKS ==========================
 Modeler        A          B          C          D          E          F
    ◆    1    Magazine      Sep        Oct        Nov        Dec      Totals
         2
Pg 1/1   3    Young Modeler  11         8          9         24         52
Press ALT 4   Kit Craft      17        14         14         18         63
         5    Model Maven    13        28         19         18         78
         6    Car Modeling   25        35         45         40        145
         7
         8    Totals         66        85         87        100        338
         9
```

339

The data from the ADVANAL.WKS spreadsheet was copied to the word processor document. Because the cursor was located between the two text paragraphs, the data was inserted there when the copy operation was completed. Also, the rows of spreadsheet data were too wide to fit within the word processor document's margins, so the rows wrapped around. (The Totals column and the numbers in it in the original spreadsheet wrapped around to new lines in the word processor document.) Finally, Works inserted tab stops to maintain the data in columns.

Copying data to spreadsheet documents

The spreadsheet is a number-handling tool, so the data you copy to a spreadsheet document will usually be data or text in columns. Here are the considerations for copying data to the spreadsheet:

- Works copies data to a spreadsheet beginning at the selected cell and moving down and to the right. For example, if you copy three records (each containing five fields) from a database and then select cell A1 as the destination in the spreadsheet, Works fills the range A1:E3 with the data, as in Figure 14-1.

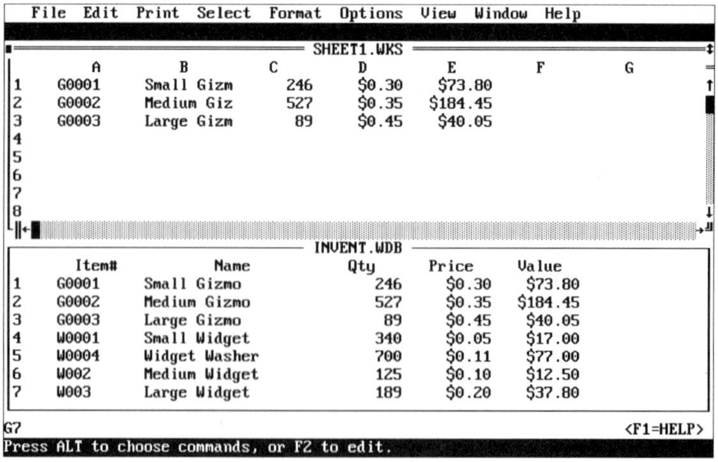

Figure 14-1.
When you copy data to a spreadsheet, Works fills the spreadsheet cells down and to the right of the cell you select.

This illustration also shows that database fields and records (shown in the file at the bottom of the screen) are converted to spreadsheet columns and rows (shown in the file at the top of the screen). Each field's contents in the database are copied to one cell in the spreadsheet, and each record becomes one row in the spreadsheet.

- Database formulas won't copy to the spreadsheet, but the values of those formulas will. If you've inserted formulas in a database file to calculate results, the database displays those results on the screen. When you select database data from such a screen, you select the displayed results (and not the formulas), and Works copies the displayed results (but not the formulas) to spreadsheet cells. In Figure 14-1, for example, the entries in the Value field of the database at the bottom of the screen are calculated with the formula *=Qty*Price*. In the spreadsheet, however, only the results of those calculations appear. This example also shows that database formatting is copied intact to the spreadsheet. The Value field here has been formatted as Currency, for example, and it remains in the Currency format after it is copied to the spreadsheet.

- Unlike the word processor, the spreadsheet won't move existing data out of the way to make room for data you copy in. If you select a cell in the middle of a block of filled cells as the copy destination, Works replaces the existing data with the copied data. As a result, you must be careful to select an empty area of the spreadsheet as the destination for copied data if you want to avoid destroying existing data.

- Text separated by tab stops is placed in separate columns. When you copy data from the word processor, any text separated by tab stops in the original document will be placed in separate cells in the spreadsheet. So, if you copied three columns of names or numbers (separated by tab stops) from a word processor document, the columns would be placed in three separate spreadsheet columns, as shown on the next page.

```
 File  Edit  Print  Select  Format  Options  View  Window  Help

═══════════════════════ SHEET2.WKS ═══════════════════════
        A         B        C          D        E       F       G
1    Employee  Territory Sales
2
3    Jones     Southwest  $10,248
4    Smith     East       $11,300
5    Brown     Midwest     $9,495
6
7
══════════════════════ WORD2.WPS ══════════════════════
  [ · · · · · · ·1· · · · ·L· · · · · · · ·3· · ·L· · · ·4· · · · · · · ·5· · · · · · · ] · · · · · · ·7· · · · ·
» Employee              Territory      Sales

  Jones                 Southwest      $10,248
  Smith                 East           $11,300
  Brown                 Midwest        $9,495
  ◆


D5                                                          <F1=HELP>
Press ALT to choose commands, or F2 to edit.
```

In this case, the word processor document at the bottom of the screen had custom tab stops set so that there would be only one tab stop between each column in every line of the document. This illustration also shows that text lines separated by carriage returns are placed in separate rows of a spreadsheet (which is why there's a blank row between the column labels and the data in the spreadsheet) and that dollar-formatted numbers in the word processor copy to the spreadsheet in Currency format.

■ Spreadsheet cells won't hold more than 256 characters. When you copy text to a spreadsheet, all the text between tab stops and carriage returns is placed in one cell. Works copies only the first 256 characters of text in the selection to the spreadsheet cell. Any text after the 256th character is lost.

Copying data to communications documents

The reason you copy data to communications documents is to transmit that data. Here are the considerations for copying to a communications document:

■ You can't complete a Copy operation in a communications document unless your computer is currently connected to a remote computer. If you try to press the Enter key to complete a Copy operation when the OFFLINE message is showing in a communications document's status line, Works displays a warning saying that you must first be connected.

- Text or data copied to a communications document is immediately transmitted to the remote computer.

- Columnar data is copied and transmitted in columns. If you copy data in text columns or from spreadsheet columns or database fields, it is transferred to the communications document in columns as well. Because such data is transmitted as text, tab stops that would normally separate columnar data are replaced with space characters.

- Any data that is too wide to fit within the communications document's window wraps around to the next line and is still transmitted. In this respect, the communications tool treats text as the word processor does, wrapping it down to the next line when it's too wide.

Merging Database Data into a Word Processor Document

As explained in Chapters 3, 5, 10, and 11, you can merge data from a database file into a word processor document. Such merges take place when a document is being printed or written to a file—you can't see them on the screen—and you must use either the Print Form Letters or the Print Labels command to effect the merge. If you use the regular Print command, Works will print one copy of the document, showing the field merge markers rather than the actual merged data.

This merging capability is useful for creating form letters, labels, or other documents in which you want to format database data in a way that database reports themselves don't allow. As you might recall from Chapters 10 and 11, you can arrange database reports only in row-and-column format.

The following steps list the basic procedure for merging database data with a word processor document.

1. Open the database file from which you want to merge data.

2. Open or create a new word processor file.

3. Move the cursor to the place where you want merged data to appear.

4. Press Alt-E-F to choose the Insert Field command. Works presents a dialog box that lists all the database files you currently have open.

5. From the list, select the database file you want. Works displays a list of the fields in that database file.

6. Select the field whose data you want to merge, and press the Enter key. Works places a field marker in the word processor document.

7. Specify other database fields to merge in different places in the document, and finish entering and formatting the other text in the document.

8. Press Alt-P-F (if you're printing data in a letter format) or Alt-P-L (if you're printing mailing labels) to print the document. If you specify one copy in the Print dialog box, Works will print one copy of the word processor document for each record currently displayed in the database document, merging the data in the merged fields from one record into each copy of the printed document.

For more information about how to merge data from the database into the word processor, see Chapters 3, 5, 10, and 11, or choose the Form Letters procedure from the Help Index on the Help menu.

Opening Text Files from Other Programs

Whenever you choose the Open command from the File menu, Works displays a list of files in the current disk directory. It shows the files in categories by the name of the Works tool that was used to create the files. The category called Other, however, shows all the other files in that directory. You can select and open any of these Other type files with Works, but unless the files are text format files, you won't be able to make much sense of what you see. If you open one of the Works program files as a word processor document, for example, you'll see a screen of meaningless graphics symbols and other characters.

Text files are files that contain only characters, without any formatting, formulas, macros, or other information. Most word processing, spreadsheet, database, and communications programs that run on any personal computer can create text files, so this format allows you to import data that was created with a different DOS program or with another personal computer, such as the Macintosh.

When you select an Other type file to open in Works, you'll see a dialog box in which to choose the type of Works file to create when the text file is opened. You can open a text file as a new word processor, spreadsheet, or database document. Each of the Works tools, however, treats text-format data differently.

Text files in the word processor

- When you open a text file with the word processor, Works shows you all of the file's text. Most other word processing programs create text files that are one continuous stream of data, so your Works screen will show the text without any carriage returns after the lines or breaks between the paragraphs.

- If you're opening a text file that was created by a spreadsheet or database program, the text will probably be arranged in columns or with tab stops or commas between the entries that are in different columns or fields.

- Communications programs sometimes end each line in a text file with a carriage return. If such a text file's line is wider than the 6-inch default format of a new word processor document, Works displays the first 6 inches on one line and then displays the rest of the text on the following line.

Text files in the spreadsheet and database

As explained earlier in this chapter, the Works Spreadsheet and Database tools recognize incoming text separated by tab stops as different cells or fields. They treat each carriage return in a file as the signal to begin filling a new spreadsheet row or database record.

Most text files that you'll want to import into the spreadsheet or database will have been created by other spreadsheet or database programs, and the data in them will be properly separated by tabs (or commas) and carriage returns. If the text isn't separated by commas or tabs, Works will place up to 256 characters of text in the first cell or field, delete the remaining text from that point to the first carriage return, and then fill the first cell or field in the second row or record with up to 256 characters, and so on.

Saving Works Files in Text Format

Just as you can open text files from other programs, you can save Works Word Processor, Spreadsheet, and Database files as text so that they can be opened by other programs. The basic procedure is the same with each tool:

1. Press Alt-F-A to choose the Save As command. Works displays the Save As dialog box.

2. Type the name of the text file.

3. Choose the desired text format for the file in the Format box.

4. Press the Enter key.

The text-file format options in the word processor are different from those in the spreadsheet and database. In the word processor, you can choose either Text format or Printed Text format. The Text format saves the file as a stream of characters with carriage returns separating paragraphs. The Printed Text format inserts a carriage return and a line feed at the end of each line. Some word processing programs can use files in this format more effectively than in plain Text files.

In the spreadsheet and database, you can choose to separate the columns or fields in the file with either commas or tabs. Some programs recognize only commas or only tabs as the means of separating data, so Works gives you a choice.

Opening or Saving Spreadsheets in Lotus 1-2-3 Format

Another data access option for the Works Spreadsheet is Lotus 1-2-3 format. Works Spreadsheet files are directly compatible with Lotus 1-2-3 (version 1A or 2) files. You can open a Works Spreadsheet file with Lotus 1-2-3, and you can open a Lotus 1-2-3 file in the Works Spreadsheet. Some of the functions and features of Works aren't supported by 1-2-3, and some of 1-2-3's functions and features aren't supported by Works. (See Appendix C in the *Microsoft Works Reference* manual for more information.)

Converting Word Processor File Formats

Because word processor files from different programs have distinctly different formats, you can order a conversion utility from Microsoft that translates files from or into a few popular word processor formats. You can convert a Works file to Microsoft Word, RTF (Rich Text Format), or DCA (IBM's Document Content Architecture). You can also convert files in any of these formats to Works files. Here's the procedure for converting files, assuming you've installed the conversion utility (WPTOWP.EXE) to the WORKS directory on your hard disk:

1. Press Alt-F-V to choose the Convert command from the File menu. Works displays a file-selection dialog box.

2. Select the file you want to convert, and press the Enter key. Works displays another file-selection dialog box:

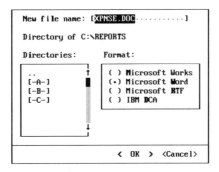

3. Type the new name for the converted file. (If you don't type a name, Works uses the existing filename, but it adds a different extension to the filename, depending on its format: WPS for a Works file, DOC for a Microsoft Word file, RTF for Rich Text Format, and DCA for Document Content Architecture files.)

4. Select the format to which you want to convert the file.

5. Press the Enter key. Works converts the file's format and saves the file to the designated disk and directory.

These are all the ways in which you can transfer, convert, and copy data in Works from one place to another or from one format to another. Now let's try a few projects that show these capabilities at work. The instructions for each of these projects aren't quite as detailed as those in the earlier chapters that cover each Works tool. Here we assume you already have experience with each Works tool and that you don't need keystroke-by-keystroke instructions. If you run across an instruction you don't understand, refer to Chapters 2, 3, 6, 12, and 13 for help.

Importing Remote Data as a Database

For this project, let's suppose a colleague in another office has compiled a mailing list file using a different DOS program, and you need to print some mailing labels from that data immediately. Your colleague could send a disk that contains the file via overnight courier, but let's assume that you both have modems on your computers and that you can't wait a day to get the data. So you'll use the communications tool to receive the file as text, open the text file as a database file, and then create a word processor document to produce labels from the data.

To begin this project, you'll need to create a text file that will simulate the one you would receive from your colleague. If you completed the exercise in Chapter 10, you can use the ADDRESS.WDB file you created there. If you did not complete that exercise, create the ADDRESS.WDB file now. (It isn't necessary to do the reporting and sorting exercises in Chapter 10; simply create the new file, create the fields, and save the file as ADDRESS.WDB.)

1. Open the ADDRESS.WDB file.

2. Choose the Save As command, type *TEXT* as the filename, and choose the Text & Tabs format option.

3. Press the Enter key to save the file in text format.

4. Close the ADDRESS.WDB file.

Now we'll simulate connecting with the remote computer.

Receiving the text file

Before you performed this step, you would want to call your colleague on the telephone and agree on the communications settings you'd use, the time you'd make the call, and which of you would call the other. Also, you would ensure that your colleague saved his or her mailing list file in text format before you attempt to transmit it via computer. The steps on the following page show how communication might actually proceed.

1. Open a new communications file.

2. Press Alt-O-M and, in the Communications dialog box, enter the communications settings you've agreed on; then press the Enter key.

3. Press Alt-O-P, and type the telephone number for your colleague's computer. (We'll assume that you're the one making the call and that your colleague has set up his or her software to answer the call.)

4. Turn on your modem, and ascertain that it's properly connected.

5. Press Alt-C-C to connect. Works dials the remote computer's number, and when the other computer answers, you see the word *CONNECT* on your screen.

6. Type *Hello,* and press the Enter key. Your colleague sees the message on the screen and types *How are you?* You see that response on your screen.

7. Type *Ready to receive in ten seconds,* and press the Enter key. Your colleague types *Okay,* and you see it on your screen. (This response gives you time to open a captured text file before your colleague begins sending.)

8. Press Alt-T-C (the Capture Text command), type *DATA* as the name for the captured text file, and press the Enter key to begin saving incoming text on your disk. Your colleague begins sending the data file, and you see it as it comes in on your screen. Works saves it on disk.

9. Press Alt-T-E (the End Text Capture command) to close the captured text file when you receive the last of the data. (You'll know when the last of the data has arrived because no more new text appears on your screen.)

10. Type *Thanks* to acknowledge your receipt of the data.

11. Press Alt-C-C, and then press the Enter key to disconnect from the remote computer.

At this point, the database file from your colleague would be stored as text on your disk. Because we haven't actually communicated with a remote computer, however, we'll use the dummy text file we created from the ADDRESS.WDB file.

Creating a new database file

The next step is to open the text file as a database file and name the data fields properly.

1. Press Alt-F-O, select the file named TEXT that you created and stored on your disk, and press the Enter key.

2. Press the D key to choose the Database file option, and then press the Enter key. Works opens the file and displays it, like this:

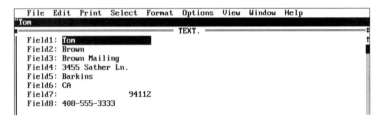

Notice that Works opens the file in the Form view and that the field names are generic. We'll rename the fields in this document and then save the document as a standard database file with the name LIST.WDB.

1. Press the Left arrow key to select the Field1 field name.

2. Type *FirstName:* and press the Down arrow key to enter the new field name and select the field name below it.

3. Repeat this process to name the rest of the fields as shown:

Old Field Name	New Field Name
Field1:	FirstName:
Field2:	LastName:
Field3:	Company:
Field4:	Street:
Field5:	City:
Field6:	ST:
Field7:	Zip:
Field8:	Phone:

After you rename the fields, you can save the file with the name LIST.WDB. Works proposes the default name TEXT for this file (because that was the name of the file you opened it from), so you'll have to use the Save As command and type the new name, LIST, before saving the file. After Works saves the file, leave the file open—we'll need it in a moment.

Making the labels

The last part of this project is to create a word processor document that contains the merged data for mailing labels. We'll assume that the labels will be printed on 1-by-2.5-inch label stock, three labels across a page.

1. Open a new word processor document.

2. Press Alt-E-F to insert a field. Works displays the Insert Field dialog box.

3. Select the LIST.WDB database file in the dialog box. Works displays the list of field names in the LIST.WDB file.

4. Select the FirstName field, and press the Enter key. Works places a field marker in the word processor document.

5. Press the spacebar to leave a space between the first and last names, and then merge the LastName field.

6. Press the Enter key to move the cursor to a new line, and merge the Company field.

7. Press the Enter key, and merge the Street field.

8. Press the Enter key, and merge the City field.

9. Type a comma, press the spacebar, and merge the ST field.

10. Press the spacebar, and merge the Zip field.

The data fields are now merged into this document, which looks like this:

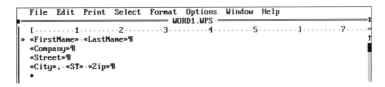

Let's save the document and print it:

1. Press Alt-F-A, type *LABEL*, and press the Enter key to save the file.

2. Press Alt-P-L to print the document as labels. Works displays a dialog box with the label setup data.

3. Choose the LIST database in the databases list.

4. Press Alt-H to select the Horizontal Label Spacing text box, and type *2.5*.

5. Press Alt-A to select the Number Of Labels Across Page text box, and type *3*.

6. Press the Enter key to confirm the options and to activate the Margins dialog box. If you want to test print the labels, press Alt-T instead of Enter to print only two rows of labels.

7. Adjust the left-margin and right-margin settings in the Margins dialog box to accommodate the width of the labels, and then press Enter to activate the Print dialog box.

8. Press Enter to begin printing the labels.

This project shows how you can capture data from another computer and manipulate it in Works. The communications tool gives you access to data on virtually every computer everywhere, and the Works Database and Word Processor let you convert the data to a useful format.

A Complex Report

In this project, we'll combine data from various sources into one word processor document for final formatting. We'll include in the finished report some spreadsheet data, a spreadsheet chart, and a selection of database records. The spreadsheet file we'll use is called FINANCES and is shown in Figure 14-2. The database file is the CALENDAR.WDB file created in the exercise at the beginning of Chapter 12. If you haven't yet created that file, you can do so by creating the fields and entering the data shown in Figure 14-3.

Here's how to create these two files:

1. Open a new spreadsheet file, and type the labels and numbers in the cells as shown in Figure 14-2.

2. Save the spreadsheet as FINANCES, and leave the file open.

```
          A        B       C        D
1    Apex Widget Sales - 4th Quarter Finances
2
3    Income      Oct      Nov      Dec
4
5    Sales       3500     4500     5000
6    Services    1000     1200     1100
7    Interest      50       45       52
8
9    Total Inc.  4550     5745     6152
10
11   Expenses    Oct      Nov      Dec
12
13   Parts        500      700      900
14   Utilities    150      175      180
15   Leases       750      900      900
16   Salaries    2000     2000     3000
17   Benefits     400      400      400
18   Insurance     60       60       60
19
20   Total Exp.  3860     4235     5440
21
22   Cash Flow    690     2200     2912
```

Figure 14-2.
The FINANCES spreadsheet shows the last quarter's expenses and income for a small business.

```
 File   Edit   Print   Select   Format   Options   View   Window   Help
┌──────────────────────────────────────────────────────────────────────┐
│                        CALENDAR.WDB                                    │
│       Date         Time       Event
│1    Dec 1, 1990   11:00 AM  Project review - Conference rm.
│2    Dec 1, 1990    3:00 PM  Dentist - Dr. Frobish, 325 Powell St., Suite 240
│3    Dec 2, 1990   10:00 AM  Racquetball tournament, Apex Athletic Club
│4    Dec 5, 1990   12:00 PM  Linda's birthday lunch
│5    Dec 12, 1990   9:00 AM  Q1 Budget due
│6    Dec 19, 1990  12:00 PM  Fred's retirement luncheon - El Caballo
│7    Dec 21, 1990   6:00 PM  Office party - Antoine's; gift swap
│8    Dec 26, 1990   9:00 AM  On vacation until 1/2/91
│9     Jan 3, 1991   2:00 PM  Product launch mtg - Bud's office
│10   Jan 15, 1991   9:00 AM  Press conference - Alpha introduction
│11
```

Figure 14-3.
*The CALENDAR file shows appointments, some of which we'll want to
include in our report.*

3. Open a new database file, create the fields shown in Figure 14-3, and enter the records shown.

4. Save the database file as CALENDAR, and leave the file open.

This report is only two pages long, but the data-copying techniques used here will serve you well for reports of any size. To begin, open a new word processor file and enter the title and introductory text shown below:

Quarterly Report

The last quarter of 1990 was a good one for Apex Widget Sales. We experienced rising income, relatively steady expenses, and calm waters on the competitive front. All in all, we're in a good position to move into 1991 with a new product launch early in the year.

Financial Highlights

Our fourth quarter balance sheet shows increasing cash flow during the period, with rising sales and generally flat expenses. Here are the numbers for total income, expenses, and cash flow:

After you enter the above text, save the document as QTRREPT. That document name will appear on the Window menu, which will make it easier to select this document again as we copy data from the other two files.

At the end of the second paragraph in the QTRREPT document, we want to copy in some rows of data from the FINANCES spreadsheet:

1. Press the Enter key to move the cursor two lines below the last sentence in the second paragraph.

2. Select the FINANCES.WKS spreadsheet from the Window menu. Works displays the spreadsheet.

3. Select the Total Inc. label and the three values to the right of it in row 9 of the spreadsheet, and press Shift-F3 to copy them.

4. Select QTRREPT from the Window menu. Works displays the document.

5. Press the Enter key. Works copies the spreadsheet data to the document, as shown on the following page.

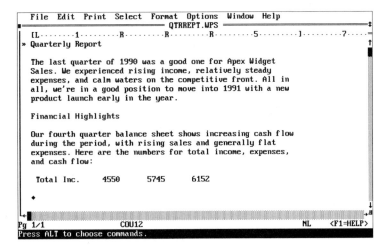

```
   File  Edit  Print  Select  Format  Options  Window  Help
   ═══════════════════════ QTRREPT.WPS ═══════════════════════
   [L·········1·········R·········R·········R·······5·········]·········7·····
 » Quarterly Report

   The last quarter of 1990 was a good one for Apex Widget
   Sales. We experienced rising income, relatively steady
   expenses, and calm waters on the competitive front. All in
   all, we're in a good position to move into 1991 with a new
   product launch early in the year.

   Financial Highlights

   Our fourth quarter balance sheet shows increasing cash flow
   during the period, with rising sales and generally flat
   expenses. Here are the numbers for total income, expenses,
   and cash flow:

     Total Inc.    4550      5745      6152

     ◆

Pg 1/1                   COU12                    NL   <F1=HELP>
Press ALT to choose commands.
```

Each column of spreadsheet data is separated by a tab stop, and the cursor is at the beginning of the copied line of numbers. Now let's copy more data:

1. Press the Down arrow key to move the cursor to the next line of the word processor document.

2. Select the FINANCES spreadsheet from the Window menu.

3. Select the Total Exp. label and the three values to the right of it in row 20, and press Shift-F3.

4. Select the QTRREPT document, and press the Enter key.

5. Press the Down arrow key again to move the cursor down a line.

6. Select the FINANCES spreadsheet from the Window menu.

7. Select the Cash Flow label and the three values to the right of it in row 22, and press Shift-F3.

8. Select the QTRREPT document, and press the Enter key.

Now we have the data in our report document, but the document contains no column labels to indicate to which months the numbers refer. We'll copy these labels from the spreadsheet:

1. Move the cursor up to the blank line between the last line of the text paragraph and the Total Inc. row of numbers.

2. Press the Enter key two times, and then press the Up arrow key one time.

3. Select the FINANCES spreadsheet from the Window menu.

4. Select the three month labels from row 3 of the spreadsheet, and press Shift-F3.

5. Select the QTRREPT document from the Window menu, and press the Enter key. Now all the data and labels we need are in the word processor document, like this:

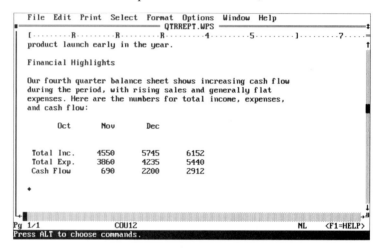

You'll notice that the column labels don't line up above the columns. That's because the first three lines we copied contained four columns of data, but there are only three columns of data formatted here. To move the labels over, press the Tab key. Works has also added an extra line between the column labels and the data rows. Delete this extra line.

Now let's continue with the text. Enter the following paragraph:

While income rose 27% from October to December, expenses increased at a slightly faster rate (30%) during the same period. However, as the following chart shows, the discrepancy in the rate of increase is attributable mostly to salaries in December, which of course included our holiday bonuses.

When you reach the end of the paragraph, press the Enter key two times to move the cursor down. At this point, we want to insert a chart that shows how each expense contributes to the total monthly expenses for each of the three months so that we can see how the salary expense for December accounts for a larger share of the expenses than in the other months. We'll have to create a stacked bar chart from the appropriate data in the spreadsheet, and then we'll insert the chart in this document:

1. Select the FINANCES spreadsheet from the Window menu.

2. Select the block of data from the Expenses label (cell A11) through the Insurance expense for December (cell D18).

3. Press Alt-V-N to display a chart of this data. Works displays a color bar chart.

We have a black-and-white printer, so we'll change Works' options to display the chart segments with patterns instead of with colors. Also, we'll reformat the chart as a stacked bar chart:

1. Press the Esc key to display the Chart mode screen.

2. Press Alt-O-F to select the Format For B&W command.

3. Press Alt-T-S to select the Stacked Bar format.

This chart is now ready to go. We'll see it in a moment on the Print Preview screen. For now, let's insert this chart in the report document:

1. Select the QTRREPT document from the Window menu.

2. Press Alt-E-I to choose the Insert Chart command. Works displays the Insert Chart dialog box.

3. Select the FINANCES spreadsheet from the spreadsheets list.

4. Select the Chart1 chart from the Charts list, and press the Enter key. Works places a chart marker in the document.

You can't see charts in the word processor, so Works inserts a marker to show you where they will be inserted. The page break is also adjusted to accommodate the chart at its current size. Here, for example, you'll notice that the page break marker is directly opposite the chart marker. Let's find out how the chart will look in the document at this point:

1. Press Alt-P-V to preview the document. Works displays the Preview dialog box.

2. Press the Enter key. Works displays the second page of the document, which contains the bar chart we just inserted. Let's examine the first page of the report.

3. Press the Page Up key. Works displays the first page of the document, like this:

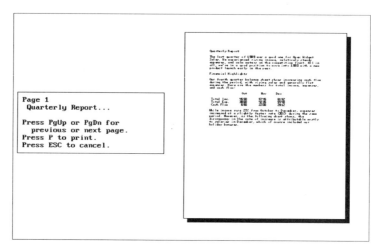

The first page has a big gap at the bottom because the chart is too tall to fit in the space left on this page. You can change the chart size, making it a little shorter so that it will fit on page 1 of our report.

NOTE: If Works displays a message telling you that the current printer can't print a chart, it won't show you the chart in the Preview screen. To remedy this situation, select a different printer with the Printer Setup command (Alt-P-S). If necessary, install the printer driver you need from the Printer 1 and Conversion Utility or Printer disk. See Chapter 2 for more information.

1. Press the Esc key to return to the document.

2. Move the cursor to the asterisk at the beginning of the chart marker in the document.

3. Press Alt-T-A. Works displays the Indents & Spacing dialog box, which includes options for chart height and orientation. The current chart height is 4 inches.

4. Press Alt-C to select the Chart Height box.

5. Type *3.5* to change the chart height to 3.5 inches, and press the Enter key.

Now, if you preview the document, you'll see that the chart fits nicely on the first page. Continue the report by entering the following two paragraphs and section title:

The sales-and-expenses trend during the quarter was a healthy one. I hope we can continue to keep expenses in line with income during the coming year.

Alpha Update

The Alpha product introduction is proceeding on schedule. The product launch meeting is scheduled for early next year, with the actual introduction coming a couple of weeks later. For those of you involved, here's a reminder of the key dates:

When you finish entering this text, press the Enter key two times to move the cursor down two lines. Now we want to copy a couple of records from the CALENDAR database file:

1. Select the CALENDAR document from the Window menu.

2. Select the List view (if the document isn't already displayed in this view).

3. Sort the records in chronological order (if they aren't already in that order).

4. Select the last two records in the list.

5. Press Shift-F3.

6. Select the QTRREPT document from the Window menu.

7. Press the Enter key. The two records are inserted in the document, like this:

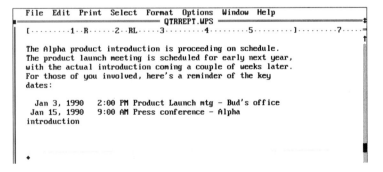

Notice that some of the appointment information in the second record has wrapped around to the next line because it's too wide to fit within the document's margins. Let's edit to fix this format problem:

1. Delete the extra spaces between the beginning of each appointment date and the left margin.

2. Delete the dash and the words *Alpha introduction* from the second record.

Now the records each fit on one line. The data in the appointment records, however, is still crowded. Let's reset the tabs that separate the columns of information so that the spacing is better:

1. Select the lines that contain the two appointments.

2. Press Alt-T-T to display the Tabs dialog box.

3. Delete the existing tabs in the ruler.

4. Set new left-aligned tabs at 1.5 inches and 2.6 inches.

Now the data is easier to read. To finish the project, enter the data in the following paragraph:

Because the product launch comes in mid-January, I'd like everyone to avoid scheduling vacation time during the latter half of January or the month of February, as we expect to be busier than usual filling orders for the new Alpha widget. That's about it for this report. If anyone has any more new product or productivity-boosting suggestions, please get them to me. My door is always open.

Now that you've entered all the data, you can spice up the format by using boldface section titles, selecting a larger font size for the report title, and adding a cover page and a table of contents. See the Monthly Report project in Chapter 5 for tips about such topics as creating a title page and a table of contents and adding footnotes.

An Invoice

In this final project, we'll see how you can use the word processor to create custom-formatted database documents. The database itself lets you print data only in row and column reports, but by merging the data from records into word processor documents, you gain considerably more formatting flexibility.

To handle this project, you'll need the ORDERS database file shown below:

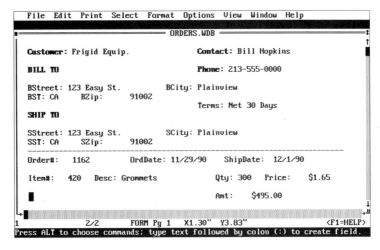

This type of layout shows you some of the flexibility you have in formatting data-entry forms in the database. The purpose of this project is to transfer some of that layout flexibility to a printed document by merging this data with the word processor.

You'll notice that Street, City, ST, and Zip each have two fields to accommodate different billing and shipping addresses. Here are some quick tips to help you create this file.

- The BST, SST, Order#, OrdDate, ShipDate, Item, Qty, and Price fields were all created with smaller field sizes than the default of 20 characters so that they would fit in the space allowed.

- It isn't necessary to put the fields in this exact arrangement, but if you want to do so, use the Move command. Select the name of the field you want to move, press the F3 key, and then move the field using the arrow keys.

- The Price and Amt fields were formatted as Currency with two decimal places.

- The Customer, Contact, Bill To, Ship To, and Phone field names and labels were formatted as Bold.

- The Bill To and Ship To labels are only labels and not field names. The dashed line was also entered as text.

After you create the fields in this form, enter the data shown in the example and save the file with the name ORDERS. Then leave the file open. Now you're ready to create a word processor document that will contain some text and some merged data. The finished document looks like the one in Figure 14-4.

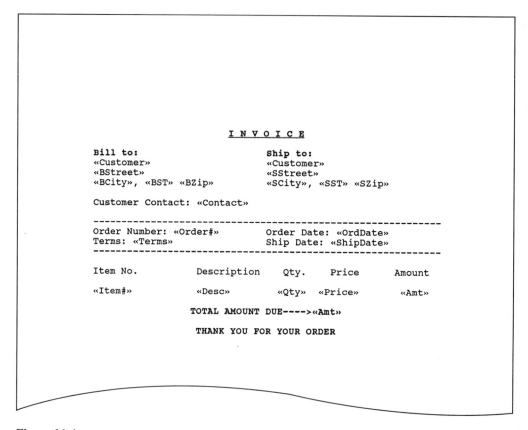

Figure 14-4.
Using the word processor's data-merging feature, you can design custom formats for printing database data, like this invoice.

To create this form, follow these steps:

1. Open a new word processor document.

2. Type *INVOICE,* leaving a space between each letter.

3. Press the Enter key two times.

4. Set a left-aligned tab stop at 3 inches.

5. Type *Bill to:* and press the Tab key.

6. Type *Ship to:* and press the Enter key.

7. Press Alt-E-F, select the Customer field to merge, and then press the Tab key.

8. Press Alt-E-F and merge the Customer field again, and then press the Enter key.

9. Merge the BStreet field, press the Tab key, and then merge the SStreet field.

10. Merge the rest of the fields in the Bill To: and Ship To: areas, as shown. Remember to type a comma and a space after the BCity and SCity merge markers and to leave a space after the BST and SST merge markers.

11. Press the Enter key two times at the end of the SZip field.

12. Type *Customer Contact:* and a space, and then merge the Contact field.

13. Press the Enter key two times, and then hold down the hyphen key (-) to create a single line of hyphens across the screen.

14. Press the Enter key, and type *Order Number:* followed by a space.

15. Merge the Order# field, and press the Tab key.

16. Type *Order Date:* followed a space, and merge the OrdDate field.

17. Press the Enter key, and type *Terms:* followed by a space.

18. Merge the Terms field, press the Tab key, and type *Ship Date:* followed by a space.

19. Merge the ShipDate field, press the Enter key, and type another line of hyphens.

20. At the end of the line of hyphens, press the Enter key two times.

21. Delete all the tabs, and then set a left-aligned tab stop at 1.8 inches. Set right-aligned tab stops at 3.7, 4.6, and 5.8 inches. These tabs will separate the categories of information in the invoice detail area.

22. Type *Item No.*, press the Tab key, and type *Description*.

23. Type the *Qty.*, *Price*, and *Amount* labels, pressing the Tab key before you type each label.

24. Press the Enter key two times at the end of the Amt label, and then merge the corresponding fields into the tab positions that match, as shown in Figure 14-3.

25. Press the Enter key two times, type *TOTAL AMOUNT DUE* followed by four hyphens and the greater-than sign (>).

26. Merge the Amt field after the greater-than sign.

27. Press the Enter key two times, and type *THANK YOU FOR YOUR ORDER*.

Now we can go back and add the formatting enhancements to make this document look like the one in Figure 14-4.

1. Select the INVOICE text at the top of the screen, and make it centered, boldface, and underlined.

2. Select the line that contains the Bill to: and Ship to: text, and make it boldface.

3. Select the lines that contain TOTAL AMOUNT DUE and THANK YOU FOR YOUR ORDER, center them, and make them boldface.

Finally, save this form as INVOICE so that you can use it again when you need it.

This invoice form is now complete. To use it, open the ORDERS database, use the database's Query feature to display the selection of records that represent the invoices you want to print, open the INVOICE document, and choose the Print Form Letters command from the Print menu. Works prints a separate invoice for each order record currently displayed in the ORDERS database.

If you were preparing invoices for orders shipped during November, 1990, for example, you could query the ORDERS database so that only records with ship dates in November were displayed. (To do this, you would enter the formula *=(month()=11)* in the ShipDate field on the Query view screen.) Then you could use the Print Form Letter command in the INVOICE document to print invoices for only those records. (See "Query Formulas" in the Database & Reporting chapter of the *Microsoft Works Reference* manual for further information.)

Doing It Yourself

The examples in this chapter have shown you how you can move data among Works tools to apply the unique strengths of each tool to the problem at hand. Armed with these techniques, you can use Works to capture, convert, format, calculate, sort, select, and otherwise manipulate data to suit nearly any business or personal computing need. As you explore the possibilities for using Works to tackle your own projects, you'll find that you're only at the beginning of a long and productive relationship with Works.

APPENDIX

Works
Specifications

A program's *specifications* define its physical limitations. This appendix lists the specifications of both the Works program as a whole and its tools. You might want to refer to this list as you approach various data-handling problems. For example, if you know that a database field can contain no more than 256 characters, you might choose to create two or three separate fields to store lengthy notes in database records. Specifications are of six types: general (pertaining to the Works program as a whole); word processor; database; spreadsheet; chart; and communications.

General Specifications

Type of Extended Memory Supported: EMS
Maximum Extended Memory Supported: 8 MB
Maximum number of files open at one time: 8
Maximum number of screen windows per open file: 1
Maximum paper height: 22 inches
Maximum paper width: 22 inches
Minimum paper height: 1 inch
Minimum paper width: 1 inch
Range of page numbers: 1–32,767
Default paper size: 8.5 by 11 inches
Default top and bottom margins: 1 inch

Default left margin: 1.3 inches

Default right margin: 1.2 inches

Maximum length of one-line headers or footers in word processor, spreadsheet, and database: up to 250 characters, limited by page size and margin settings

Word Processor Specifications

Maximum file size: limited by available disk space

Default line length: 6 inches

Default tab settings: every 0.5 inch

Maximum length of search-and-replace strings: 63 characters

Maximum length of header or footer paragraph lines: limited by page size and margin settings

Maximum height of header or footer paragraphs: one page, limited by top and bottom margin settings and other text on the page

Range of numbered pages in a document: 1–32,767

Maximum number of merged database fields in a document: up to 128 fields or 1920 bytes, whichever comes first

Maximum length of bookmark names: 15 characters

Database Specifications

Maximum file size: up to 8 MB, depending on available memory

Maximum number of fields per file: 256

Maximum size of Form view screen: 256 characters by 256 lines

Maximum number of records per file: 4096, depending on record size and amount of available memory

Maximum length of field names: 256 characters

Maximum number of characters in a field: 255

Maximum length of database formulas: 255 characters

Maximum number of database formulas: 256

Maximum number of database reports per file: 8

Maximum length of search-and-replace strings: 63 characters

Spreadsheet Specifications

Maximum file size: up to 8 MB, depending on available memory

Maximum spreadsheet size: 4096 rows by 256 columns

Maximum number of displayed decimal places in a value: 7

Maximum viewable column width: 79 characters
Maximum length of text of a cell value: 256 characters
Maximum length of a formula: 255 characters
Maximum length of search-and-replace strings: 63 characters

Chart Specifications

Number of chart types: 8
Maximum number of chart definitions per spreadsheet: 8
Maximum number of Y-series: 6
Maximum length of legends: 19 characters
Maximum length of chart titles: 37 characters

Communications Specifications

Buffer sizes: Small (100 lines); Medium (300 lines); Large (750 lines)
Default buffer size: Small (100 lines)
Maximum size of a captured text file: limited by disk space
Data formats supported: text and binary
Default handshake mode: Xon/Xoff
Default data bit setting: 8
Default stop bit setting: 1
Default parity setting: mask
Default terminal type: VT-52
Default COM port: COM1
File send/receive error-checking protocol: XMODEM

Index

Note: Italicized page numbers refer to figures and illustrations.

Numbers

1st Letter option (Sort command) 295, 307
1st Page Number text box 93
100% Bar chart *188*

Special Characters

" (text entry) 172, 243
(in database columns) 281
$ (absolute references) 153–54
&C (format command) 117
&D (format command) 213
&L (format command) 82
&P (format command) 82, 117, 213, 303
&R (format command) 213, 303
* (multiplication operator) 52, 143
* (wildcard searching) 167, 268
+ (addition operator) 52, 143
– (subtraction operator) 52, 143
… (following commands) 32
/ (division operator) 52, 143
: (field creation) 239
= (formula) 146, 150, 165, 306
>> (page break) 117
? (wildcard searching) 167, 268
\ (directories) 10
[] (OK option) 33
[] (word processor margin indicators) 62–63

A

Absolute references 153–54, 227
Accessories 51–54. *See also* Alarm Clock accessory; Calculator accessory; Dial This Number accessory
Accounting system. *See* Tax ledger

Address directory, printing 121
Address fields, inserting, into form letters 107–10
ADDRESS.WDB file 106, 118, 348
creating 234–41
ADVANAL.WKS file 340
Advertising analysis charting project 214–21
creating charts 217–21
creating tracking spreadsheet 215–17
Alarm Clock accessory 52–54
Alt key 87
AMORT file 230
Amortization table spreadsheet project 221–31
creating Loan Activity area 225–30
creating Loan Summary area 221–25
modifying 230–31
using 230
Annual expense report, creating 292–303
Apply Query command 252
Appointment calendar 277–86
creating database file 277–82
entering data in List view 280–81
entering data in time-formatted fields 279–80
saving 282
setting time and date fields 278–79
integrating data from, into complex report 352–60
using 282–86
report printing 283–86
searching 283
sorting field contents 282–83
Area line chart *189*–90
Arithmetic operators 52. *See also* Formula(s), spreadsheet
Arrange command 31

Charles Rubin grew up in Los Angeles, California. He attended Antioch College, the University of Southern California, and San Francisco State University. He holds both a bachelor's and a master's degree in English. He has been writing about microcomputers since 1981, and his work has appeared in magazines such as *PC Week, InfoWorld,* and *Personal Computing.* His previous books include **Microsoft Works for the Apple Macintosh** and **AppleWorks**, both published by Microsoft Press. Rubin is currently a freelance writer and lives in Oakland, California.

The manuscript for this book was prepared and submitted to Microsoft Press in electronic form. Text files were processed and formatted using Microsoft Word.

Cover design by Becker Design Associates
Interior text design by Darcie S. Furlan
Illustrations by Rebecca Geisler-Johnson
Principal typography by Ruth Pettis
Color separations by Wescan Color Corp.

Text composition by Microsoft Press in Baskerville with display in Baskerville Bold, using the Magna composition system and the Linotronic 300 laser imagesetter.

Printed on recycled paper stock.